# Fifty Key Concepts in
# Gender Studies

*Recent volumes include:*

**Key Concepts in Social Research**
Geoff Payne and Judy Payne

**Key Concepts in Medical Sociology**
Jonathan Gabe, Mike Bury and Mary Ann Elston

*Forthcoming titles include:*

**Key Concepts in Leisure Studies**
David Harris

**Key Concepts in Critical Social Theory**
Nick Crossley

**Key Concepts in Urban Studies**
Mark Gottdiener

The SAGE Key Concepts series provide students with accessible and authoritative knowledge of the essential topics in a variety of disciplines. Cross-referenced throughout, the format encourages critical evaluation through understanding. Written by experienced and respected academics, the books are indispensable study aids and guides to comprehension.

# JANE PILCHER AND IMELDA WHELEHAN

# Fifty Key Concepts in
# Gender Studies

**SAGE Publications**
London • Thousand Oaks • New Delhi

© Jane Pilcher and Imelda Whelehan 2004

SAGE Publications Ltd
1 Oliver's Yard
55 City Road
London EC1Y 1SP

SAGE Publications Inc
2455 Teller Road
Thousand Oaks, California 91320

SAGE Publications India Pvt Ltd
B-42 Panchsheel Enclave
Post Box 4109
New Delhi 100 017

**British Library Cataloguing in Publication data**

A catalogue record for this book is available from the British Library

ISBN 0 7619 7035 5
ISBN 0 7619 7036 3

**Library of Congress control number available**

Typeset by M Rules
Printed in Great Britain by
The Cromwell Press Ltd, Trowbridge, Wiltshire

# contents

V

# acknowledgements

Jane wishes to thanks past and present colleagues at the University of Leicester for their help in the preparation of this book, especially Julia O'Connell Davidson, Laura Brace and Nirmal Puwar. Imelda wishes to thank David Sadler for his support during the preparation of this book. Eddie May helpfully provided IT technical support and advice. Both Chris Rojek and Kay Bridger at SAGE have been patient and supportive during the writing process, and we thank them for that.

JP:  To my daughter, Ana, this one is for you!
IW:  For Miriam and Laurence, with love.

viii

# introduction

## everywhere and somewhere: gender studies, women's studies, feminist perspectives and interdisciplinarity

### Imelda Whelehan and Jane Pilcher

What is gender studies and from where has it originated? We begin our introduction to this book by providing a brief account of the development of gender studies, before going on to make some general remarks about the key concepts themselves and how readers might make best use of them.

The academic study of gender has a relatively short history. Its emergence can be dated as recently as the late 1960s, and its development triggered by second wave feminism. Along with developing a critique of gender inequalities, in both personal relationships and in social positioning (especially economically and politically), second wave feminism began to draw attention to the ways in which academic disciplines and sets of knowledge acted to exclude the experiences, interests and identities of women. For example, prior to the 1970s, the social sciences in general, and sociology in particular, largely ignored gender. The 'people' it studied were mainly men and the topics it focused on were aspects of the social world especially significant for men, such as paid work and politics. Women were almost invisible in pre-1970s' gender-blind sociology, only featuring in their traditional roles as wives and mothers within families. Differences and inequalities between women and men at this time were not recognised as an issue of sociological concern and were not seen as problems to be addressed. In the context of second wave feminist critiques, however, a number of disciplines across the social sciences, the arts and humanities began to pay increasing attention to gender. Thus, in sociology during the 1970s, differences and inequalities between women and men came to be regarded, especially by women sociologists, as problems to be examined and explained. Initially, studies were focused on 'filling in the gaps' in knowledge about women, gaps left by the prior male

ix

bias. Attention gradually moved to those aspects of experiences especially significant to women, including paid work, housework, motherhood and male violence.

In disciplines such as English Literature, women had begun to contest the hegemony of a 'canon' of great works of literature, which practically excluded women writers altogether and had nothing to say about the material and social conditions that prohibited the emergence of 'great' women in this arena. Once such questions were asked, the momentum was extraordinary and the search for answers took scholars beyond the normal boundaries of their 'home' disciplines. Kate Millett's pathfinding *Sexual Politics* (1971) moved effortlessly from literary criticism to a critique of Freud and Marx (perspectives that were later to become very much the 'business' of literary studies). At this time in the 1960s and early 1970s, the sheer number of women concentrated in the humanities in comparison to other academic fields made it an area ripe for feminist critique, since women's existence in such numbers here was itself the result of the gendered logic of the workplace. It is at this stage, during the late 1960s in the US and from the mid- to late 1970s in the UK, that women's studies as a specialised area of academic interest began to develop, as well as rapidly spreading elsewhere around the globe (the first British women's studies programmes were all taught MAs, emerging first in Kent (1980) and then York and Warwick). Thus women's studies as a discrete area of study was born, even though the early days were characterised by a huge rush of energy, where 'such courses began to be taught, quite spontaneously and without substantial prior organisation, at many US colleges and universities beginning in 1969' (Tobias 1978: 86). It was a similar story in the UK and it was only retrospectively that teachers in the field communicated nationally and internationally and debated what women's studies was and could be (the first national women's studies conference in the UK took place in 1976). Early on the link to feminist politics was tangible – these scholars were often found beyond the academy, in women's liberation newsletters, at conferences and generally networking with like-minded thinkers. They saw women's studies as not only challenging the boundaries of existing knowledges and developing new areas of study, but also as legitimising the differing social and cultural experiences of women. Many women's studies courses contained a consciousness raising (CR) component where the experiences and identities of the students themselves determined the dynamics of the classroom. Formal characteristics of academic study, particularly the teacher–student relationship and assessment, were kept under scrutiny and other means of teaching and assessment than the formal lecture or seminar, the essay or examination were experimented with. One thing is certain: the creation of this area announced with confidence that women were worthy of study in their own right, and suggested a clear success for feminist political analysis.

Firmly interdisciplinary in perspective, women's studies initially resided mainly (if uneasily) within the disciplines of English, history and sociology, and was dependent upon the energies of sometimes isolated individuals working within a generally male-oriented curriculum. Once women's studies programmes emerged, often gathering together the work of scholars across the disciplines into one centre or as the core team of a master's or undergraduate degree, the area developed a clearer identity. Rather than seeing its major role as casting a critical eye over the traditional disciplines, women's studies could become more broadly a contestation of knowledges under patriarchy and allow a revaluation of knowledge, art and experience that had formed the basis of women's lives. Broadly speaking it is still centred around the social sciences, arts and humanities rather than the physical sciences and related disciplines such as engineering and medicine, but the presence of women's studies in the academy has had wider ramifications as the core practices and prejudices of the latter come under scrutiny.

Even though the 'women's studies' identity suggests a degree of empowerment for feminist knowledge, it is always pulled in two directions – as a critique that transforms existing disciplines and as a specialist, even separatist, area of academic concern. Within the disciplines, this critique sometimes amounted to 'adding women in' rather than recognising that men too are gendered beings. Gradually, though, and arising out of men's pro-feminist politics, there began to develop in the 1980s a body of knowledge and theorising around men *as* 'men'. Consequently, books (both popular and academic) on men and masculinity proliferated in the 1990s, to the extent that 'men's studies' is now recognised as a specialist area of academic focus. 'Gender studies' is seen by many to further open up the field of women's studies, beyond its beginnings in the politics of the Women's Liberation Movement.

At the same time that women's studies and, later, men's studies became established as specialised areas of academic inquiry, broader theoretical developments began to undermine their very rationale. In postmodernist and post-structuralist approaches, the very idea of 'women' and 'men' as discrete and unitary categories is challenged. The individual status and position of those we group together and call 'women' and of those we call 'men' are argued to vary so greatly over time, space and culture that there is little justification for the use of these collective nouns. Similarly, in post-structuralist analysis, 'women' and 'men' are regarded as constructions or representations, achieved through discourse, performance and repetition rather than being 'real' entities. Together, these theoretical approaches have had a great impact on feminism, women's studies and men's studies, and have been a key driver of the increased recognition of diversity and difference. Inequalities and differences, not just between genders but within genders, based on class, sexuality, ethnicity, age, dis/ability, nationality, religion, and citizenship status, for example, are now attended to. In this context, 'women's studies' and 'men's studies' have become increasingly contested terms. As understandings of gender have developed as a complex, multi-faceted and multi-disciplinary area, involving the study of relationships within as well as between genders, the term 'gender studies' has gained currency, albeit not uncontested.

For some women's studies proponents, 'the rise of gender studies can take the form of making women *per se* invisible in the study of masculinity or male/female relations' (de Groot and Maynard 1993: 6). Concurrent with this is the sense that the fact of women's continued social inequality becomes obliterated, resulting in the depoliticisation of a subject that grew out of controversy and political radicalism. Some feel that women's studies has lost its confidence and sense of direction and that 'gender studies' is a dilution – a sign that feminist knowledge has been tamed and reconstituted by the academy. There are elements of truth in these positions, in that 'gender studies' does fit more easily within the institution and feminist politics are not the key motivating force behind its maintenance: gender studies also better incorporates not only men and masculinity studies, but also those who take the post-Judith Butler view that gender assignation only takes meaning through performance and iteration. Women's studies has had to accept that a monolithical model of 'woman' can exclude and affirm inequality, and gender studies is one way of addressing this concern.

Whatever label given to the academic study of gender relations in the twenty-first century, there are a number of features that have endured. First, the study of gender remains resolutely multi- and inter-disciplinary and that is its key strength, and has had the most profound impact on contemporary theory and attitudes to the production of knowledge. Second, alongside the more focused, if varied, constellation of texts, knowledge and theorising on and about gender that constitutes gender studies, gender issues continue to penetrate mainstream disciplines more widely (though not always with ease) and are enthusiastically embraced by students. Third, feminism remains a central perspective for the study of gender relations, reminding us that this discipline emerged from the identification that women as a group were misrepresented – in both the public sphere and in the conception of their 'real' natures. As gender relations continue to change and mean different things, so feminism as a political ideology will change and find new avenues to explore. Academic institutions themselves have changed markedly in the last 30 years and, in Britain, the shift from the university/polytechnic divide to the old/new university one (from 1992) has had an impact on the development of women's studies, not least because of a certain broadening of access and a higher proportion of mature or non-standard applicants coming into university, many of them women. Furthermore, many women's/gender studies academics now in the academy constitute the first generation to be educated in gender as students themselves and are correspondingly distant from the heady politics and campus activism of the 1960s and 1970s. While challenges can be made from within the institution from a gendered perspective, these are performed with an awareness that gender/women's studies remains itself dependent upon the academy (and the means by which it receives funds) for survival and for the support of feminist and gender-related research.

*50 Key Concepts in Gender Studies* reflects the shift in thinking about gender as a complex, multi-faceted topic but within which feminist perspectives remain central. The 50 concepts focused on here are not random, and value-free selections, but instead represent an account of gender studies, both as an academic specialism and as a broader perspective across a range of disciplines and knowledge boundaries. Our selection of 50 key concepts was by no means straightforward, or fixed. It evolved during the period of writing, and reflects our understanding of those issues of enduring presence along with issues of more recent and current concern. Our selection of concepts reflects too our own political and disciplinary selves, and so we write as white, middle-class feminists, working within the disciplines of sociology (JP), and English and women's studies (IW). Our view of gender studies, reflected in this book, also reveals to some extent our positioning within Western industrial societies, and more specifically, Britain.

xiii

The shifts in approaches to gender over the last few decades themselves make a compelling reason for a book focusing on the key concepts that have shaped, and continue to shape, gender studies as a discipline. Conveying the complexity of gender as a topic of study to students, working within a wide range of academic disciplines, is a challenging task. Ideas, debates and theories are presented in this book with such diversity in mind. We have tried to provide clear definitions and explorations of each concept in a way that is easy to understand, but which does not sacrifice the level of detail and critical evaluation essential to grasp the complexity of the subject matter. Each key concept begins with a concise definition, followed by illustrations of how the concept has been applied within the field. Examples of use are further developed into a critical revaluation of the concept under focus. Cross-references to related key concepts are included, along with suggestions for further reading. Unlike dictionaries of gender concepts or glossaries of terms found in some textbooks, the intention is to offer a full and informed discussion of each concept and demonstrate how they are utilised in a gender studies context. Each entry is long enough to do justice to the, on the face of it, more complex concepts (such as psychoanalytical feminism, postmodernism, queer theory and cyborg) while drawing attention to the hidden complexities of other oft-used terms (such as identity politics, backlash and equality). To get the fullest benefit of this book, you will find it useful to read all the entries cross-referred to the concept you are interested in. In many ways, the attempt to separate out and explain these concepts in all their distinctness has drawn more interconnections and links than we had first imagined. In this way, as is often the case in feminist research, the process of explication has resulted in new insights for us. As suggested above, no such volume could pretend to neutrality, but we have tried to afford the reader a variety of stances in relation to many of the concepts, as well as trying to aid an understanding of why some issues, such as pornography, became so controversial at certain points in modern feminism's history and why a concept such as consciousness raising should explain both the success and failures of feminism's second wave.

Our book is not intended as a substitute for reading the original works from which the key concepts are drawn, but rather as an aid to reaching an informed understanding of them. Our selection of 50 key concepts inevitably means that the important contributions to the study of gender made by a wide range of authors are not included, despite the originality and significance of their writing. We hope, however, that through the representation of gender studies made within this book, students are encouraged to read more widely. Hopefully the extensive bibliography also operates as a source for books that have been landmarks in the study of gender over the past 30 years and more, including as it does useful student-friendly volumes alongside long out-of-print feminist classics. This book gives testimony to the health of gender studies and the study of gender issues within a wide range of disciplines and looks forward to an ever-shifting dynamic of debates and ideas. As academics who teach at undergraduate and postgraduate levels, we are only too aware of how popular gender-related topics remain, and how much satisfaction many students gain from working in this area – many finding fundamental echoes with their lived social and political experiences. Not only does this remind us of one of the key aims of early women's studies courses (the focus on the authenticity of experience as a valuable tool of research and knowledge), but it is also testimony to the fact that gender and women's studies remain a vibrant and productive area of academic activity, whose full integration continues to have significant implications for the larger body of academic knowledge as a whole. Moreover, it is an area that has clear applications in the world beyond the academy, and its effects continue to change the way people think about themselves.

XV

# androcentrism

Deriving from the Greek word for male, androcentrism literally means a doctrine of male-centredness. Androcentric practices are those whereby the experiences of men are assumed to be generalisable, and are seen to provide the objective criteria through which women's experiences can be organised and evaluated. Some writers, particularly those influenced by psychoanalytical theory, prefer the terms phallocentrism or phallocentric, in order to draw attention to the way the penis (or phallus) acts as the symbolic representation of male-centredness. A related concept is that of phallogocentrism. Deriving from the work of Derrida and Lacan, this term describes those ideas centred around language or words (*logos*) that are masculine in style. Postmodern feminist writers such as Cixous argue that phallogocentric language is that which rationalises, organises and compartmentalises experience and it is on this basis that terms ending in 'ism' (e.g. feminism) may be rejected (Brennan 1989; Tong 1998).

An early use of the term 'androcentric' was made by Charlotte Perkins Gillman who subtitled her 1911 book, 'Our Androcentric Culture'. In feminist analyses, most societies, historically and in the present, exhibit androcentric tendencies whereby their culture, knowledge, organisations and institutions reflect and reproduce the dominance and power of men. As Smith writes with reference to the modern Western context, 'The problem is not a special, unfortunate and accidental omission of this or that field, but a general, organisational feature of our kind of society' (1988: 22). One simple illustration is provided by the androcentric use of language. In Britain up until at least the 1980s, 'mankind' and 'men' were widely used in a generic way, instead of the more gender-neutral 'humankind' or 'people'. Similarly, the pronoun 'he' was routinely used in preference to 'she', or even to 'he or she'. Feminist analyses have problematised the generic use of masculine nouns and pronouns, arguing that such linguistic practices both reflect and contribute to the marginalisation of women and are symbolic of their status in general.

Several writers have addressed the issue of the ways in which the 'male standpoint' (Smith 1988) or the 'male espistomological stance' (Mackinnon 1982) is evident in academic theories and research. In general terms, the consequences of the 'male standpoint' are that findings from men-only research studies have been generalised to women, and that areas of enquiry have focused on issues important to men's interests and

1

experiences, while those important to women have been overlooked. As Maynard (Maynard and Purvis 1996) explains, the perception that what counts as knowledge derives from masculine interests and perspectives has been the impetus for the development of women's studies. In its critique of androcentric knowledge, women's studies has shifted from an early concern with 'adding women in' to pre-existing fields of enquiry (leading to studies of women and paid work, or women artists, for example), to focusing on previously ignored topics of importance to women (such as motherhood, or sexual violence), to devising new concepts and theories with which to analyse women's experiences.

A classic example of feminist work in response to the androcentricity of academic theories and research is provided by Carol Gilligan (1982). Gilligan's work engages with psychological theories of development, in relation to morality and the self–other relationship. She criticises the repeated exclusion of women from theory-building psychological studies and their tendency to adopt the male life as the norm. Gilligan argues that the androcentrism embedded in psychological research has led to a disparity between academic theories of 'human' development and the experiences of women, a disparity seen to be caused by women's development rather than the faulty research and theory itself. In her own research, Gilligan includes the group previously left out in the construction of theory (that is, women) and aims to show the limitations of androcentric psychological research for an adequate understanding of the development of men, as well as of women. Arising from studies of men's moral development, morality has been constructed as being concerned with justice and fairness, and moral development has been seen as the understanding of rights and rules. In this moral code, the individual self is paramount and personal achievement, autonomy and separatism are orienting values. On the basis of her research, Gilligan argues that women's morality and self–other relationships may differ. In women's constructions, morality tends to be centred around an ethic of care, of responsibility for others, so that moral conflicts or problems must be resolved with a view to maintaining relationships with others. In this moral code, self and other are seen as interdependent and relationships with these others are seen as central to life. For Gilligan, her findings reveal the need for development theories in psychology to be revised, so that their analysis of the characteristics of moral conceptions in both women and men is more expansive.

Initial criticisms of androcentrism, in all its many forms and guises, have been supplemented by an increased critical awareness of the partiality of some feminist-produced knowledge itself. In the 1980s and

1990s, feminist critics argued that feminism displayed a tendency to centre white, middle-class and heterosexual femininities at the expense of other femininities (for example, Ramazanoglu 1989b; Maynard and Purvis 1996). Developments in masculinity studies have also pointed to the diversity of men's status and position in society, a diversity which belies the notion of a unitary androcentric culture whereby all men have a privileged standpoint over all women (see Connell 1987, 1995). Morgan (1992) has shown that androcentrism in sociology meant that, not only were the experiences and interests of women overlooked, but that the research and theorising on men lacked a critical awareness of them as gendered beings.

**See also:** *(the) Other, standpoint*

### FURTHER READING

A collection of classic statements on the rationale for women's studies as a counter to androcentric culture and knowledge can be found in Bowles and Duelli Klein (1983). Marshall (1994) examines the debates around modernity and postmodernity and finds a common tendency to neglect the role of women and the significance of gender in the making of contemporary societies. Hekman (1995) critically evaluates the work of Gilligan in relation to feminist moral theory.

## backlash

3

Backlash literally means the jarring of a wheel, or other part of machinery, which is not properly in alignment. Figuratively, it is a term that has come to mean a strong reaction against a system or state of affairs that had been changed. In the 1950s and 1960s the word was used in the US to describe a political reaction against black integration and generally connotes a forceful swing back to a previous status quo (see also *OED* online, 2002).

In feminist parlance it has become used to describe a fierce rejection of an ideology by forcefully reiterated counter-arguments. In the case of second-wave feminism, backlash commentators often used the language of feminism itself to turn against its own principles. These tendencies were brought into wider debate by the American journalist Susan Faludi

4

in her book *Backlash* where she coined the term and characterised it as 'at once sophisticated and banal, deceptively "progressive" and proudly backward. It deploys both the "new" findings of "scientific research" and the sentimental moralizing of yesteryear; it turns into media sound bites both the glib pronouncements of pop-psych trend-watchers and the frenzied rhetoric of New Right preachers' (Faludi 1992: 12). As can be gleaned from this, her identification of the sources of the backlash are numerous, but also diverse and not necessarily connected in any way. Faludi is not claiming that the backlash against feminism is part of a united attack on feminism, but she seems to be arguing that its effects can be felt in all aspects of political, social and cultural life. She asserts that the 'backlash is not a conspiracy, with a council dispatching agents from some central control room, nor are the people who serve its ends often aware of their role; some even consider themselves feminists' (Faludi 1992: 16). Regardless of their intentions, Faludi perceives all the individuals involved in backlash rhetoric as helping to create a climate where the term feminism is once again regarded with profound suspicion. Such a collision of like-minded forces is fundamentally an inevitable reaction to a force, like feminism, which threatens the status quo of post-capitalist democracy.

What is more specifically disturbing about the backlash of the 1980s and 1990s is the ways in which feminism, rather than male domination, sexism, or inequality of opportunity, were seen to be responsible for the ills of contemporary woman. In mass cultural productions, such as films, advertisements and newspaper articles 'liberated' independent women were represented less favourably than they had been at the height of feminism's popularity. This backlash against feminism seemed to come into force during the mid-1980s, characterised in political terms with the upsurge of the New Right in both the UK and the USA and the vigorous promotion of 'family values' (which often assumed a subordinate and primarily domestic role for women). The film *Fatal Attraction* (1987) might be taken as the backlash text *par excellence* – in the ways it dramatised the implicit penalties for the single career-oriented woman, and spawned a series of like-minded films.

It was and is difficult to fight such a concerted attack, because feminists never succeeded in gaining a significant foothold in the media, and much of their work had been misunderstood by the very women they were trying to reach, passed as it often was through the lens of an unsympathetic media. Moreover the backlash appeals to nostalgia on so many levels – not just the 'good old days' when men and women knew their place in the world, but also the pull of 'nature': many perspectives suggested that women were going against the grain of their own instincts. In Oakley's words, backlash texts 'return us to a world of naïve understandings about the origin of social differences between men and women' (in Oakley and Mitchell 1997: 33).

The success of the backlash lies in the fact, which Faludi rightly identifies, that women internalise the messages sent to them and long for stability: '[i]t is most powerful when it goes private, when it lodges inside a woman's mind and turns her vision inward, until she imagines the pressure is all in her head, until she begins to enforce the backlash, too – on herself' (Faludi 1992: 16). Her analysis of political trends, 'scientific' findings about infertility, women's supposed incapacity to fully compete in the world of work without health implications, etc., make fascinating though depressing reading. Yet, as Sylvia Walby reminds us, there are other ways to push women back into the home, and the movement of women isn't simply either 'in' or 'out': the conditions for women in the public sphere of work can themselves be grim, with many relying on part-time or low-paid work with poor conditions of employment or job security, particularly working-class women, women of colour or differing abilities, and any woman with less access to further or higher education (Walby 1997: 165).

For some this concept of a 'backlash' fits in with the depiction of feminism as coming and going in 'waves'. Nonetheless in our contemporary period it is certain that for many people feminism has come to be regarded as doctrinaire, puritanical and destructive, making it difficult to take a 'feminist' platform and expect to be heard without prejudice. As Whelehan has observed, '[t]hose who deal in backlash logic conveniently omit to acknowledge how important feminism has been to social progress and that feminist perspectives on rape, for example, have enabled important shifts in the legal system, police practices and the public perception of the crime' (2000: 20).

Other feminist commentators such as Rosalind Coward see the notion of backlash as oversimplifying the debates around feminism into 'for' or 'against'; she argues that what is required is a new analysis of power that does not focus so crucially on gender as its determinant. Her suggestion that women need to confront the problems men face in our changing world could of course itself be perceived as part of a backlash swing that simply can't tolerate woman-centred politics. This brings us to another problem in defining the backlash – that the term might be used to dismiss an opposing but self-declared 'feminist' viewpoint. If differing feminist perspectives themselves get caught up in the fray, the toleration of conflicting stances is buried under the more worrying assumption that there is, or could be, a single 'correct' definition of feminism.

5

**FURTHER READING**

Essential reading for this topic, needless to say, would be Susan Faludi's pathbreaking *Backlash* (1992). It is a comprehensive survey, and although her investigative journalist style has been criticised by some, it is a provocative and engaging read. Whelehan (2000) has written on the effects of the backlash in Britain in the 1990s and the emergence of 'retrosexism' in popular culture; Oakley and Mitchell's collection of essays (1997) also presents some key current debates.

# body

In the seventeenth century, the philosopher Descartes based his theory of knowledge on the idea that the human mind and the human body are fundamentally distinct from one another (a distinction that has come to be known as 'Cartesian dualism'). By the late twentieth century, some philosophers and social theorists han begun to challenge the legacy of Cartesian thinking on the mind/body split. Consequently, the concept of 'the body' now operates to identify the realm of people's bodies as an appropriate topic for philosophy, the humanities and the social sciences rather than, as implied in Cartesian thinking, being the sole preserve of the natural or physical sciences, such as biology and medicine. Within feminism and gender studies, the body has occupied a key position in a wide range of debates, including: men's control of women's bodies as a key means of subordination; critiques of dichotomous thinking; and in debates about essentialism and the theorising of difference and diversity.

Feminists have long recognised that bodies matter in social relations, but over time, there have been shifts in conceptions of what the body is, especially in relation to nature and to culture. The range of conceptions of the body present within gender studies can be grouped into three broadly defined categories: the body as nature, the body as socially constructed, and embodiment. In 'body as nature' perspectives, the body is conceptualised as a natural, biological entity that determines inequalities or differences between women and men. In Firestone's (1979) analysis, for example, inequality between women and men is based on biological differences in the body's reproductive functions. The capacity of women to conceive, carry, give birth to and breastfeed a child meant that, until fairly recently, women were at the continual mercy of their biological bodies. Hence, women became dependent upon men for their survival. For Firestone, the natural difference in bodily reproductive capacity evolved over time into other, culturally based, differences. In order to eliminate inequalities between women and men, Firestone contends that it is necessary to eliminate the bodily differences in reproductive functions. She advocates the use of advanced scientific methods, so that all aspects of the debilitating processes of natural reproduction would take place outside of a woman's body, for example, the fertilisation of eggs by sperm and the growing of foetuses in artificial wombs. Firestone regards women's natural bodies negatively, arguing that they have to become more like men's if equality is to be achieved. Other writers, who similarly rely on a conception of the body as natural and determining, take a more positive view of women's bodies, arguing that their more extensive sexual and reproductive capacities make women superior to men. Writing in the 1970s, Alice Rossi identified biological differences in the responsiveness of women and men to children. For Rossi, these biological differences, rooted in the body, made women better able to care for children than men. As a consequence, equality between the sexes should not be achieved through women devolving childcare responsibilities to others. Rather, equality should be achieved through securing proper societal recognition for women's distinctive, biologically rooted childcare abilities (discussed in Sayers 1982: 148–9). In the work of French feminist writers such as Cixous and Irigaray, sexual bodily differences between women and men are stressed, with women's bodies praised and valorised as an especial source of women's empowerment (see Tong 1998; Whitford 1991).

In contrast to 'body as nature' perspectives, those who regard the body as 'socially constructed' emphasise social and cultural practices. In 'mild' versions of social constructionist perspectives, such as socialisation theories, the natural physical body is recognised but primarily as an object of interpretation and the attribution of meaning. In sex-role theory, for example, it is argued that the appropriate behavioural roles for each sex are learnt, especially during childhood. Boys and girls learn the social roles appropriate to their sex, as this is marked by their body, through social interaction with successfully socialised adults and immersion in sex-typed culture, and reinforcement through a system of rewards and punishments. It is suggested within sex-role theory that gender inequalities can be reduced through altering socialisation into

7

sex-roles, via, for example, non-sexist childrearing practices (Weinreich 1978; Maccoby and Jacklin 1975). Thus, in sex-role theories, the social and cultural practices arising from meanings given to female and male bodies are emphasised as primarily important, rather than the natural body itself. Nevertheless, the conception of the body present with socialisation perspectives has residues of biological determinism. This tendency is clear in the account of Maccoby and Jacklin (1975), who explicitly refer to biology as the 'framework' which constrains socialisation practices, making it possible for culture only to minimise, rather than eliminate, the effects of natural biological differences between women and men. As Connell (1987: 50) explains, in socialisation theories 'the underlying image is of an invariant biological base'. The concept of the body 'hidden' within mild social constructionist approaches is that of a real, physical entity, unchanging across time and space, and which is, in and of itself, unaffected by culture. In contrast, 'strong' versions of social constructionist approaches to the body place so much emphasis on culture and representations, especially in terms of language and discourse, that the body as a real, physical entity all but disappears. Judith Butler, for example, proposes that 'the body is not a "being" but a variable boundary, a surface whose permeability is politically regulated, a signifying practice within a cultural field of gender hierarchy and compulsory heterosexuality' (1999: 177). In her theory of gender performativity, Butler argues that 'the anticipation of a gendered essence' in social and cultural life 'produces that which it posits as outside itself' (1999: xv). In other words, in acting as if sex and gender 'really' exist, we bring sex and gender into being. For Butler, the 'repetition' and 'ritual' of 'gender performances' have an ongoing outcome. They contribute to the 'naturalising' of bodies, making the 'cultural fiction' of gender appear credible and real, rather than being, as Butler contends, a corporeal (or bodily) 'style' or 'enactment', a constitution of meaning (1999: 177–8). Butler cites the example of drag (in which a person 'performs' a gender that does not 'match' their 'sex') in illustration of her argument that bodies are not 'beings' but are the effects of discourses. The 'strong' social constructionist approach epitomised by Butler has been criticised for dissolving the body as a real, material entity. For example, Klein writes, 'The bodies I have been reading about in postmodern feminist writing do not breathe, do not laugh and have no heart' (quoted in Brook 1999). Sayers (1982) uses the example of menstruation to argue that biology does have real physical effects on women's bodies and their experiences, effects not limited to the discourses circulating within a society (see also Oakley 1998).

Within 'embodiment' perspectives, the body is conceptualised simultaneously both as a natural, physical entity and as produced through cultural, discursive practices. Connell (1987) examines the interrelations of nature and culture on the body. He identifies a set of cultural practices which, in combination, act to 'negate' (or minimise) the similarities between the bodies of women and men, through over-exaggerating their differences. Clothing and accessories are an important means of achieving the negation of the body: skirts, high-heeled shoes and handbags (all with 'feminine' styling) for 'female' bodies, and trousers (with pockets), ties, and flat shoes (all with 'masculine' styling) for 'male' bodies. Connell also identifies cultural practices which 'transcend' (or transform) the body physically, making and remaking bodies so that they are more, or less, feminine or masculine. For example, the differing physicality of men's and women's bodies is brought about, in part, through cultural practices in which boys and men are encouraged, more than girls and women, to be physically strong and confident. Connell argues therefore that, rather than natural biology determining men's and women's bodies as different, masculine and feminine bodies are largely made as such through cultural practices. 'The body, without ceasing to be the body, is taken in hand and transformed in social practice' (1987: 83). Elizabeth Grosz argues for a similar conception of the body in her development of 'corporeal feminism'. She challenges dichotomous thinking that posits a split between, on the one hand, the 'real', material body, and on the other, its various cultural and historical representations (1994: 21). 'It is not simply that the body is represented in a variety of ways according to historical, social and cultural exigencies, while it remains basically the same; these factors actively produce the body as a body of a determinate type' (1994: x). For Grosz, the body should be at the centre of the analysis of women's and men's subjectivity, but not in a biologistic or essentialist sense. The concept of 'embodied subjectivity' means recognising that who we are ('female, male, black, brown, white, large or small': 1994: 19) arises from the 'corporeal' (the body), as this is itself inscribed by the cultural, within changing time and shifting space (1994: 23). Importantly, embodiment perspectives point to the status of the body as an unfinished entity. In being continually subject to on-going cultural work, the material body can only ever be apprehended through culture. Embodiment represents the current moment in conceptualising the body but the tension between the body as 'real' and the body as discursive remains a key axis of debate within gender studies.

**See also:** *dichotomy, essentialism, post-structuralism*

**FURTHER READING**

Janet Sayers (1982) provides a clear discussion of feminist and anti-feminist 'biological politics', although by virtue of when the work was published, it does not specifically address embodiment perspectives. A very useful overview of feminist perspectives on the body is provided by Brook (1999), in conjunction with a focus on such topics as dieting, plastic surgery and reproduction. A selection of key feminist writings on the body can be found in a reader edited by Price and Shildrick (1999).

# citizenship

Citizenship is a status within which the person (or 'the citizen') has the rights and/or obligations of membership of a wider community, especially a nation-state. A key reference point in the citizenship literature is T.H. Marshall's (1950) elaboration, where citizenship is seen to be comprised of three sets of rights. First, civil rights which include the right to justice, to freedom of speech, thought and religious belief, and the right to own property. Second, political rights, namely the right to take part in the exercise of political power through, for example, voting. Third, social rights including the right to economic welfare and security, and the right to 'live the life of a civilised being according to the standards prevailing in the society' (1950: 10–11). In Marshall's analysis, these rights evolved gradually in Britain between the seventeenth and twentieth centuries, with civil rights emerging first, followed by political rights and, lastly, social rights. Marshall's work on citizenship has generated much debate, not just because of the nature of his particular account, but because of the highly contentious character of the concept more generally. One important reason for the contested character of citizenship lies in the way it can operate as both an inclusionary and exclusionary mechanism (Lister 1997). Those who are deemed to be citizens are included in the benefits of that status, but this positive process of inclusion simultaneously operates negatively, to exclude other individuals from that privileged status, and the rights and responsibilities it brings. Within the field of gender studies, debates have especially centred around the exclusionary mechanisms of citizenship. Citizenship is regarded as gendered, in that men have had a fuller and/or different range of citizenship rights and

10

obligations than women. More recently, recognition has been given to the ways in which gendered citizenship can also operate to include/exclude individuals on the basis of their sexuality (for example, Richardson 1998), ethnicity, nationality and/or territorial location (for example, Yuval-Davis 1997; Yuval-Davis and Werbner 1999).

The study of gender and citizenship has developed through a range of different phases, much of the dynamics of which lie in wider sets of debates about equality and difference, and in the influence of postmodernist thinking. Initially, there was an especial concern with establishing both the historical exclusion of women from citizenship and the remaining, contemporary inequalities between women and men in terms of citizenship rights. Here, Marshall's classic elaboration of the development of citizenship has attracted a range of criticisms. As noted by Siim (2000: 13), 'Marshall's model was based on the development of rights of *men* [original emphasis] and thus failed to notice that the development of women's rights and other subordinated groups has had its own history and logic.' Several writers have challenged Marshall's account of the emergence of citizenship. For example, Pateman's (1989) re-reading of the classic texts of social contract theory shows that women were incorporated into the new social order differently from men, as beings whose sexual embodiment was seen to prevent them from having the same political standing as men (1989: 4). Walby directly criticises Marshall's concept of citizenship, arguing that the ordering of the emergence of women's rights differs from his 'universal' model. For British women, 'political citizenship was at least as often the power base from which [they] were able to win civil citizenship, as vice versa' (1994a: 385).

As explained by Lister, 'women's exclusion from citizenship has, both historically and today, elicited two main responses: either to demand inclusion on the same terms as men or to press the case for recasting of citizenship's premises so as to accommodate women's particular interests' (1997: 91). For 'equality' theorists seeking to demand women's inclusion on the same terms as men, the essential objective is a gender-neutral citizenship, where women are enabled to participate with men as equal citizens, especially in the public sphere. In Britain, this liberal–democratic conception of citizenship was the major impetus for 'first wave' feminist campaigns, especially up until 1928, when women became politically enfranchised on the same terms as men. In contrast, for 'difference' theorists, the objective is a gender-differentiated citizenship, where women's responsibilities and skills in the private sphere are recognised, valued and rewarded. Elshtain (for example, 1993) is one of the foremost

11

advocates of what has been termed a 'maternalist' conception of citizenship. Elshtain objects to the dominant understanding of politics as taking place in public space and of 'citizens' as those who inhabit that public space. In reference to its ancient historical origins, Elshtain terms this understanding of politics and citizenship 'the Greek way' and argues that it operates to exclude and debase women. For Elshtain, the private sphere is the focus of humanising activities centred around women's concern for and care of others. As such, it provides a model for reconceptualising routes to citizenship and for the practices of politics itself. 'The activation of a female participatory capacity must begin with her immediate concerns, go on to give a robust account of them, and then bring these concerns to a transformed vision of the political community' (1993: 348). (For critique, see Dietz 1998.)

Several writers, such as Prokhovnik (1998) and Lister (1997), attempt a synthesis of the above outlined perspectives. For Lister, the goals of both equality theorists and difference theorists are distorted due to their underlying dichotomous logic, and lead to a political and theoretical dead-end. A more constructive way forward, argues Lister, is a conception of citizenship that combines elements of the gender-neutral and gender-differentiated approaches, employed strategically, while at the same time remaining sensitive to the differences that exist between women. Prokhovnik proposes an understanding of citizenship as a social status based on a set of ethically grounded activities: 'Citizenship is first and foremost a moral relationship' (1998: 85). Thus conceptualised, citizenship can incorporate the range of activities people engage in, differentiated by gender (and ethnicity), within both the private and the public spheres. Prokhovnik emphasises that such a feminist rethinking of citizenship requires an associated rethinking of the dichotomy between the public and the private, and a recognition that it is the 'same fully human self' that moves between the two spheres, thereby interconnecting them. 'It is *not* that women need to be liberated from the *private* realm in order to take part in the public realm as equal citizens, but that women – and men – already undertake responsibilities of citizenship in both the public and the private realms' (1998: 84, original emphasis).

In the context of globalisation and migration across national borders, attention has increasingly turned toward the exclusionary mechanisms of citizenship arising from gender, ethnicity and territorial location. Rather than rejecting citizenship as a concept, however, the current moment is toward widening it beyond the relationship between the individual and the nation-state, so as to incorporate notions of global citizenry and

12

internationally codified human rights (for example, Turner 2001). Thus, Werbner and Yuval-Davis write, 'Our alternative approach defines citizenship as a more total relationship, inflected by identity, social positioning, cultural assumptions, institutional practices and a sense of belonging' (1999: 4). Citizenship may be a concept with ancient historical origins, but it continues to be a fertile source of debate both within contemporary gender studies, and more widely.

**See also:** *equality, public/private, sexual contract*

### FURTHER READING

Lister (1997) provides an excellent discussion of citizenship from a feminist perspective. Siim (2000) undertakes a comparative study of the processes of inclusion/exclusion of women as citizens in France, Britain and Denmark, while a volume edited by Yuval-Davis and Werbner (1999) focuses on the gendering of citizenship from a post-colonial feminist perspective.

# class

Generally, the concept of class is used in the analyses of social divisions based on the unequal distribution of economic resources. People are grouped into different classes according to their relative position in an economically-based hierarchy. For example, in the classic Marxist sense, classes are defined in terms of their relation to the means of production, being either workers who own nothing but their labour power, or capitalists, who directly own the materials, machines and settings through and within which productive activity takes place. In contemporary class analysis, a person's occupation is often used as an indicator of their class position, not least because of the relationship between level of occupation and level of pay. Arguably, there is broad agreement that classes are based, at least to some extent, on the differential distribution of economic resources. Beyond this, however, the concept of class is a highly contested one. Aside from differing views as to how class should be defined and measured, there has been debate as to the continued salience of class as the pre-eminent source of social inequality and identity in contemporary

Western industrialised societies, and relatedly, what the relationship is between class, gender and 'race'.

For many years within the various disciplines of the social sciences, social inequality was predominantly understood, if not equated with, class inequality. In British sociology, for example, social inequalities based on class have been a fundamental and enduring concern. As Crompton (1996) explains in her review of traditions in class analysis, much of this research grouped men (and their families) into classes according to the man's position in the occupational or employment structure. Analyses were then conducted of, for example, the changing class structure, poverty and inequalities in wealth and income, class mobility, class consciousness and political action. Since the 1970s, however, a number of related developments have undermined the pre-eminent position of class analysis within sociology. First, the economic and social changes of the post-war period have led some to argue that class is no longer the primary form of social inequality, nor source of social identity, nor basis for political mobilisation (for example, Paluski and Waters 1996). The restructuring of the labour market, unemployment and the rise of flexible working, together with increased political mobilisation on the basis of gender, ethnic or other interests have contributed to a shift away from a primary concern with occupationally-determined class analysis. Second, feminist writers have criticised class analysis for its tendency to 'ignore gender relations' (Walby 1990: 8) and for its resistance to incorporating the direct role played by gender, and other forms of social inequality, in the structuring of class. Third, the emergence of postmodern or post-structuralist perspectives has undermined faith in the validity of groupings based on class. In focusing attention on difference and diversity, these approaches encourage a concern with the local and the specific, and so 'undermine all notions of collectivities, such as classes' (Bradley 1996: 3), as existing other than at the level of discourses.

Elaborating on feminist critiques of class analysis usefully illustrates the impact of the above outlined developments on the study of class and gender. Initial feminist critiques of class analysis attempted in various ways to use conventional Marxist-derived class and related concepts in order to theorise gender inequality. For example, as outlined by Walby (1990), Delphy developed an argument that women as housewives constitute one class and men as husbands constitute another, by virtue of their different relations to the patriarchal mode of production, whilst Firestone located men and women in different 'sex-classes' on the basis of their relations to the means of reproduction. Such efforts to reconceptualise class, away from conventional economic indicators to incorporate explicitly

**14**

gendered inequalities, have themselves been subject to a range of criticisms (see Walby 1990 for review). Other feminist writers directly criticised class analysts for their lack of attention to gender in the definition and measurement of occupationally-determined class. For one thing, major British studies such as that by Goldthorpe et al. (1969) used all-male samples. Although at the time, this marginalisation of women's experiences was barely recognised, by the early 1980s, writers such as Goldthorpe (1983) began to respond to feminist and other criticisms directed at conventional class analysis. Bradley usefully summarises the defence of the conventional position on class and gender: 'It was argued that women took their class from husbands or fathers, that to include women would make it difficult to compare findings with other studies which had also omitted women, or that since women's social roles were primarily domestic, occupational class was not relevant to women' (1996: 15). However, such justifications have further been contested, for example, on the basis that they ignore the increasing numbers of women in paid employment. A more fundamental problem with conventional class analysis is argued to derive from the occupational classification schemes used to determine a person's class. As Crompton and Scott explain, problems arise because the occupational structure 'bears the imprint of other major stratifying factors, most particularly gender, race and age, that are difficult to disentangle from those of class' (2000: 3). Therefore, gender segregation in paid work means that occupational classification schemes are indicative of gender inequalities as well as 'purely' economic inequalities.

Arising out of the sustained challenge to class analysis, a more nuanced understanding of class as but one of a number of intersecting sources of social inequality and social identity has increasingly gained ground. However, Anthias and Yuval-Davis (1992) have cautioned against thinking about gender and 'race' merely as additional layers on top of class. For Anthias and Yuval-Davis, 'race' and gender make for a qualitatively different kind of class inequality, and are not 'additions' to it. Anthias (2001) proposes theorising class as one of three primary 'social divisions' in modern society, along with gender and ethnicity. Each involve distinctive relations of differentiation and stratification and, together, provide the formation of both life conditions and life chances (2001: 846). In her account, Anthias expands the concept of class beyond the merely economic, arguing that 'class is not in fact an economic relation per se but a social relation which involves forms of social organisation and cultural modes of expression related to production and consumption processes' (2001: 846). This approach can also be found in Skeggs's

(1997) ethnographic study of a group of white, working-class women. Skeggs argues that, in the understanding of power relations in modern societies, class and gender must be regarded as 'fused together'; class cannot be understood without reference to gender and vice versa. In her analysis, Skeggs used Bourdieu's model of class as being comprised of varying forms of 'capital', including economic capital, cultural capital, social capital and symbolic capital. For Skeggs, this framework offers the 'greatest explanatory power to understand the intersections of class and gender' (1997: 7), and is revealing of the ways in which 'the category "woman" is always produced through processes which include class' (1997: 2). Crompton (2000) points to the increased importance of the intersection of gender and class, in her study of people in middle-class occupations. Crompton found that there were patterns of difference in the 'management of the employment–family interface' between those in 'professional' occupations and those in 'managerial' occupations. Crompton therefore shows that the restructuring of the labour market may come about, at least in part, from gender processes, through strategies developed by some women (and men) to manage unpaid housework and caring, alongside their paid work.

Understandings of class as a concept, therefore, have shifted from a rather narrow concern with class location as the primary structure of inequality and source of identity within an economically stratified hierarchy, to a broader, more flexible understanding in which class is but one of one of several 'dynamics of inequality' (Bradley 1996) and resources for identity, especially gender and race, which are in constant interplay with one another.

**See also:** *gender segregation, postmodernism, race/ethnicity*

## FURTHER READING

Bradley (1996) offers an excellent account of changing patterns of inequality and identity and of efforts to theorise them. Delamont (2001) reviews a range of sociological evidence from the twentieth century in support of her argument that it is not gender but class that remains the primary form of social inequality in Britain. Jordan and Weedon (1995) examine the ways in which the social inequalities of class, gender and race are both legitimated and contested through culture, and include case studies on art and literature from Britain, North America, Eastern Europe and Australia.

16

# —consciousness raising—

Consciousness raising became one of the key activities that underpinned second wave feminism and made it distinct from its forebears, and announced the emergence of a very different kind of political organisation. Taken from the idea of 'speaking pains to recall pains' used by peasants during the Chinese revolution (see Echols 1989: 84), the idea was that women should regularly collect in small groups over an agreed period of time and give accounts of their own lives and how they 'became' a 'woman'. In this way it was hoped that all the women involved might look askance at their own lives and realise the extent to which they share experiences with other women of various backgrounds and ages; that their problems are not unique and individual, but rather all too common and produced by wider social relations and institutions. There were no hard and fast rules about how one should go about organising a consciousness raising (CR) group, but one anonymous essay, 'Consciousness Raising' (collected in Koedt et al. 1973: 280–1) offers guidelines, suggesting that the first three to six months should be taken up with looking at the members' personal experiences; then the group should move on to establish activities such as self-help and reading groups. Once each CR group has developed a rapport and understanding among themselves, they could then determine what future action they might embark upon or how they might further theorise the facts of their own oppression to advance the knowledges and purposes of the Women's Liberation Movement.

Most CR groups expected women to make the commitment to turn up regularly, so that, rather than this being a loosely defined 'club', it became a cohesive group of women who would get to know each other very well and therefore build up a strong relationship of mutual support. Each group was supposed to limit its numbers in order to help build up trust within the group and to prevent dominant personalities from taking over, and once a CR group had been firmly established, new members were generally prohibited. This is one woman's account:

> Our meetings would be closed to new members and each woman's testimony should be personal to herself so that statements of a generalising nature were to be out of order in the first part of the meeting. Only after everyone had spoken would we attempt to draw the threads together and see what we had in common as women. We

17

also decided to rotate the meetings in each other's homes. The idea here was twofold; firstly, everyone had to act out the hostess role and, secondly, even if things were a little cramped, it was important in building up a mental picture of each other that we become aware of the material conditions of our home environment. (Bruley in Feminist Anthology Collective 1981: 60)

Perhaps never before had the personal circumstances of each member of a political group been the subject of such intense scrutiny by the rest of its members, and this underlined the informal aspect of feminist politics – the sense, too, that it was in a constant process of evolution. It embodied the central edict that 'the personal is political' intended to awaken women to injustices of their social position but also to encourage them to actively reassess their personal and emotional lives – so that in a real and literal sense feminism was expected to have a life-changing effect on each of its participants.

It is hard to quantify the effects of CR in women's groups both in the USA and Europe, but it seems to be a practice that succeeded in recruiting a huge number of women to feminism, as well as being a means by which new Women's Liberation groups were created. Early on the problems with this style of 'rap group' became evident – the group's identity might become so strong that they were unable to relate their work to the wider movement; the sessions might just come to be seen as 'therapy' for the individuals concerned rather than a political means to an end; since new members were prohibited, the findings of the group may not be communicated beyond it. Carol Williams Payne's essay, 'Consciousness Raising: A Dead End?' expressed reservations with the whole process, claiming that although her group identified key problems, 'we never tried to relate these problems to the structural problems of women in society' (Payne in Koedt et al. 1973: 283). This problem would be more acute when it came to issues of race, class or sexuality given the likelihood that small groups of women would tend to meet together because of their shared backgrounds.

Nonetheless, CR groups appeared to form the backbone of local feminist 'cells' particularly in regions away from large metropolises and these groups may well have helped strengthen and galvanise feminist activism and allow each group to take on a highly individual feminist imprint of its own. Equally, conflicts within the group might be thrown into sharp relief by the highly personal nature of communication that the CR process encouraged. Echols' (1989) account of radical feminist politics in the USA, and also Brownmiller's (2000) memoir of the same period, underline how conflicts within groups could become highly personalised and intensely acrimonious.

18

CR groups also represented the move to political separatism for modern feminism and for many women that in itself was experienced as liberation. As one group from Birmingham in the UK put it, 'Women's Liberation gave us our first experience of talking to other women in a deeply personal and supportive way (i.e. talking about things other than nappies, make-up and the cost of living); our first experiences of being together of our own choice and in our own right, rather than in the usual supporting role at our men's and children's functions' ('The Monday Group', *Birmingham Women's Liberation Newsletter* 1974: 24). Yet these sentiments reveal a key contradiction in the whole CR process: as much as it was geared towards collectivising women's experiences and gaining understanding in order to provide a more global analysis of women's oppression, it made women relate to feminism as a deeply personal process. For many of them it might subsequently become difficult to decide whether their feminism was about the way it changed their own lives or about the way potentially it might change the lives of women as a whole. CR groups were unthreatening and 'easy to organize, required no skills or knowledge other than a willingness to discuss one's own experiences in life, and had very positive results from the women involved in [them]' (Freeman 1975: 117).

In a way CR groups' success provide a clue to the way in which activist women's movements gave way to more personal reflections and academic theorising in the 1980s. It is perhaps not surprising that some of the most influential books for the women's movement were the so-called 'CR' novels of the 1970s produced by women, not all of whom were actively involved in feminism, but all caught up in the debates of the time and seized by the urge to fictionalise the process of one woman's coming out of false consciousness into enlightenment. Examples of such novels include Alix Kates Shulman's *Memoirs of an Ex-Prom Queen* (1969), Erica Jong's *Fear of Flying* (1973) and Marilyn French's *The Women's Room* (1978). They often used the device of having the central character 'confess', in the form of a retrospective narrative, a diary or 'memoirs', her own shortcomings and her own coming to self-realisation and perhaps for many these fictional accounts were more accessible and less threatening than other more theoretical second wave writings, not least because the characters portrayed were always depicted as having real problems with making their personal lives gel with their feminist ideals. These novels sold in their hundreds of thousands and it is clear that they generated debates about feminism far beyond the scope of organised feminist politics and into the mainstream media (who often read them as merely titillating and erotic and therefore

19

distinctly less threatening); read alongside feminist classics such as *Sexual Politics*, *The Female Eunuch* and *The Dialectic of Sex*, they provide a fascinating series of reflections on this period of the Women's Liberation Movement.

It is the process and practice of consciousness raising that set the Women's Liberation Movement apart as uniquely different from its feminist forebears, and in these practices the tensions between the personal and the collective are tightly bound together and never resolved. Despite ongoing debates about how much CR actually contributed to feminist theory, it can be seen to be directly responsible for the groundswell of support for the Women's Liberation Movement in the USA and Europe from 1968 to the early 1980s.

**See also:** *second wave feminism*

### FURTHER READING

The essays from the US Women's Liberation Movement collected in Koedt et al. (1973) provide a fascinating range of documents from this period of feminism and there are a number of essays which directly deal with the pros and cons of consciousness raising. Echols (1989) provides a thoughtful reflection on the genesis of consciousness raising and helps to link it to the origins of second wave radical feminism in New Left and Civil Rights politics.

**20**

# cyborg

The concept of the cyborg is intended to encapsulate the extent to which advanced technological developments have blurred the boundaries between, on the one hand, 'natural' human bodies and, on the other, 'artificial', 'manufactured', 'automated' human bodies. Donna Haraway, with whom the concept is especially associated, defines cyborgs as 'hybrid creatures', composed of those 'special kinds' of organisms and machines appropriate to the late twentieth and early twenty-first centuries. 'Cyborgs are post-Second World War hybrid entities, made of, first, ourselves and other organic creatures in our unchosen, high-technological guise as information systems, texts, and ergonomically controlled labouring, desiring, and reproducing systems. The second essential ingredient in cyborgs is machines in their guise, also, as communication systems, texts, and self-acting, ergonomically designed apparatuses' (Haraway 1991: 1). The concept of the cyborg has proved influential in several substantive areas of gender studies, including in the analysis of relationships between nature, bodies and culture, and in the theorising of identity and 'difference'.

In a seminal paper first published in 1985, and entitled 'A Cyborg Manifesto', Haraway points to the potentialities presented by the compounding of organisms and machines achieved by Western scientific culture in the late twentieth century. In part, Haraway's manifesto is a refutation of the anti-technological stance evident within some feminist critiques of 'masculinist' or 'patriarchal' science and technology. It is also an important contribution to debates about the body, identity and the theorising of 'difference'. For Haraway, a full cyborg entity is, as yet, a largely mythical creature. Its importance lies more in its symbolic value, via its potential as a strategy for a postmodernist reconceptualisation of social relations previously predicated on dualisms, divisions and differences. The cyborg, as a hybrid of organism/nature and machine/culture, is a creature of 'permanently partial identities'. As such, it presents an image of 'transgressed boundaries, potent fusions and dangerous possibilities which progressive people might explore as part of much needed political work' (1991: 154), in order to move away from 'an impossible but all too present reality to a possible but all too absent elsewhere' (1991: 4). Haraway's argument is, then, that the image of the cyborg holds promise as a way of rethinking similarities and differences in social relations, via the way it focuses attention on 'specific historical positionings and permanent partialities without abandoning the search for potent connections' (1991: 1).

Geldalof (2000) provides one example of how the concept of the cyborg can be used to analyse the issue of identity. Geldalof is concerned with the way in which women are symbolically and strategically positioned within discourses and conflicts that produce national, ethnic and racialised community identities. Such positionings are problematic, in that women may be idolised as 'mothers of the Nation' through their reproductive and home-making activities and, relatedly, be the targets of rape as a weapon in inter-ethnic wars. For Geldalof, the concept of the cyborg is useful for suggesting ways to positively redefine women's embodied locatedness in relation to community identities and differences. In particular, Geldalof argues that the cyborg 'is a model that refuses the binary separation into object and subject' (2000: 349). It is a

21

concept that encourages a 'double focus' or a 'simultaneous recognition', first, of the ways in which Woman/women can be positioned as a location from which gendered, raced and national identities are constituted. Second, it allows that location to be reconceptualised, as vocal and as actively playing a part in the reconstitution of those identities, as a place of resistance and a source of instabilities within existing power relations. Following Haraway, Geldalof argues that 'what needs "recoding" is not just the binary logic that locates "Woman" and "women" as object, ground or resource, but also the conceptualisation of that ground as inert' (2000: 349).

Other writers have less of a concern with the mythical, symbolic or metaphorical value of the cyborg and instead draw on the concept in the analysis of the present reality of connections between selves, bodies and technology in contemporary Western cultures. 'Cyber-anthropology' has emerged as a specialist area concerned with the multiple fusions of bodies with science, technology and medicine, through such artefacts as contact lenses, mobile phones, air conditioning, artificial organs and limbs, and gene therapy. In this field, the aim is to use the cyborg concept as an adjective, to describe and explore a wide range of ways through which advanced technological cultures routinely contribute to the 'fashioning of selves' (Downey and Dumit 1997). A key area of cyber-anthropology, with added significance for gender studies, is the analysis of the interrelations between human reproduction and medico-technological developments in the production of 'cyborg babies' (Davis-Floyd and Dumit 1998). In the field of cultural studies, Balsamo's (1996) work on practices and representations of the gendered body in the USA draws together the cyborg themes of technology and identity. Balsamo concurs with Haraway that the ubiquity of technologies through which the body can be refashioned within contemporary culture has opened up the potential for both the practical refashioning of gendered bodies and the theoretical reconstruction of gender.

> Cyborgs are hybrid entities that are neither wholly technological nor completely organic, which means that the cyborg has the potential not only to disrupt persistent dualisms that set the natural body in opposition to the technologically recrafted body, but also to refashion our thinking about the theoretical construction of the body as both a material entity and a discursive process . . . The cyborg provides a framework for studying gender identity as it is technologically crafted simultaneously from the matter of material bodies and cultural fictions. (1996: 11)

In Haraway's original formulation, the cyborg was a mythical hybrid, regarded optimistically as a symbol for the development of analytical as well as practical political strategies for diminishing social relations of domination. Critics of the cyborg concept are more concerned with the realities of actual 'cyborgification' in the here and now, and are much less optimistic than Haraway. Davis-Floyd (1998) invokes the 'shadow side of the cyborg story' in her account of birthing technologies such as caesarian sections. Her argument is intended to counter the view that the cyborgification of 'natural' processes is enhancing and empowering, through addressing the ways in which reproductive technologies can be mutilating and disempowering for women. Davis-Floyd contends that, at least in the case of birthing technologies, 'the forces of cyborgification' are powerfully aligned with already dominant, hegemonic cultural forces. In evaluating the potentials of cyborgification, Davis-Floyd therefore points to the importance of addressing issues of interests, ownership and control. Balsamo (1996) also locates cyborgification in the nexus of existing relations of power and control. The possibility may exist within cyberculture to refashion gender, including through reproductive technologies, but for Balsamo, the evidence suggests that gender boundaries are in fact being vigilantly guarded. In her analyses of practices and representations of the gendered body in North American culture, Balsamo aims to describe how technology is ideologically shaped by 'gender interests', and how, consequently, conventional gendered patterns of power and authority are reinforced. She argues that contemporary discourses of technology continue to rely on a logic of binary gender-identity as a underlying organisational framework, and so the revisionary potential of cyborg technologies are significantly limited (1996: 9–10). In a general critique of cyberculture and cybersociety, Robins (1995) concedes that new technologies do open up experiences that take individuals away from their social and spatial locations. However, he argues that it is necessary to 'de-mythologise' cyberculture and to recognise that we continue to have physical and localised experiences, with all the disadvantages and limitations these foist on us. 'We should make sense of [the new technologies] in terms of [the] social and political realities of [this world], and it is in this context that we must assess their significance' (1995: 137). Whether as a source of inspiration or as a target of criticism, Haraway's concept of the cyborg has become a central reference point within a range of debates, centring around the impact of scientific, technological developments for our understandings of our selves, our bodies and our relations with organic and inorganic others.

**See also:** *body, postmodernism, reproductive technologies*

**FURTHER READING**

Haraway's original arguments are elaborated in her later works, including *Primate Visions* (1992) and *Modest_Witness* (1997). *The Cyborg Handbook* (Hables Gray 1995) remains a substantive and wide-ranging collection of writings on cyborgification. Perhaps unsurprisingly, the Internet is a good source of material for work that engages with the cyborg concept, for example http://www.thecore.nus.edu.sg/landow/cpace/cyborg/cyborgov.html.

# dichotomy

A dichotomy means a division into two. The concept is especially used when a firm or polarised distinction is made between two entities. In the seventeenth century, Descartes based his philosophy of knowledge on the idea of a fundamental difference between mind and body, a distinction that has become known as 'Cartesian dualism'. This philosophical principle is widely regarded as having a crucial influence on the development of Western theories of knowledge, where reality is understood as if it were comprised of sets of 'either/or' pairings. Some examples of dichotomous (or, as it is sometimes called, binary) thinking are reason/emotion, true/false, normal/deviant, culture/nature or science/nature, public/private, hard/soft, knowledge/experience, self/other, objectivity/subjectivity, and male/female.

Prokhovnik (1999) identifies four key features of dichotomous thinking. The first feature of dichotomy is the extension of a *difference* between two entities, into an *opposition*. Each part is dependent on the other part for its position, and each part is defined by its not being the other. A second feature of dichotomy is the hierarchical ordering of a pair. The part ranked or valued more highly has gained its position through the prior exclusion of the subordinate part. The third feature is the assumption that, between them, the dichotomous pair encapsulate and define a whole. In other words, together they sum up the range of possibilities. Fourth, a key feature of dichotomous thinking is that the subordinate entity can only gain value or move upwards by transcending itself. In other words, by becoming like the dominant part of the dichotomy.

**24**

In their survey of contemporary debates in feminist theory, Barrett and Phillips note that the 'critique of dichotomies, of dualisms, of falsely either/or alternatives has become a major theme' (1992: 8). Feminist writers have been at the forefront of the critique of dichotomous thinking, because of their broader concern to develop new understandings of what counts as knowledge. A general criticism of dichotomous thinking is that it 'forces ideas, persons, roles and disciplines into rigid polarities' and thereby 'reduces richness and complexity in the interest of logical neatness' (Sherwin 1989, cited in Oakley 1992: xi). Oakley argues that 'the habit of thinking in dichotomies' puts 'an embargo on both/sometimes-the-one, sometimes-the other, possibilities' (1992: xi). In other words, it operates to preclude the recognition of plurality and heterogeneity. Feminist writers are especially critical of dichotomous thinking because of the tendency for the dominant element of any dichotomous pairing to be associated with masculinity, while the subordinate element is associated with femininity. In the above list of examples, the first terms of the dichotomies are conventionally regarded as masculine attributes, and as having high status, and the second terms as feminine attributes, with a low status. As Prokhovnik explains, dichotomous thinking inherently underlies a range of social practices and cultural values that result in the subordination of women (1999: 37). For feminist writers, then, the habit of thinking in dichotomies is not a neutral or benign way of understanding the world. Rather, it is a way of thinking within which patriarchy, and other relations of domination, are fundamentally embedded. 'In short, the political significance of dichotomous thinking is that it maintains inequalities of power' (Squires 1999: 127).

A number of theorists have sought to develop new, non-dichotomous ways of thinking. Although varying in detail, such theories have in common an emphasis on thinking *relationally*. The relational mode of theorising 'argues for the intellectual and social benefits of recognising that within each dualism ... the relationship, the connection, the interdependence between the two parts is crucial to the character of both parts' (Prokhovnik 1999: 13). Moreover, it recognises complexity, plurality and heterogeneity (or 'difference'), rather than simple, mutually exhaustive dualisms. One example is the work of Stanley and Wise (1993). Their 'feminist ontology' (or theory of reality) is concerned with ways of understanding the relations between the body, the mind and the emotions, as an alternative to Cartesian ontology in which mind and body are dichotomised. Stanley and Wise argue that their feminist ontology challenges 'masculinist' Cartesian dualism in a number of ways, including

25

through recognising and valuing difference, conceived in non-oppositional terms, and through understanding the body as 'embodiment', a cultural process through which the body becomes a site of culturally ascribed and disputed meanings, feelings and experiences (1993: 194–6). The work of Judith Butler (1999) is at the forefront of efforts to reject dichotomous thinking, particularly in relation to the distinction between gender and sex. In developing her arguments, Butler follows a post-structuralist approach in which the material (nature, the body, sex) is seen to be interrelated with the discursive (culture, embodiment, gender). One of Butler's key points is that sex itself is a social construction, because of the ways cultural values and practices interrelate with 'natural' biology, and so inherently effect the classification of bodies as either 'male' or 'female'. She writes that gender 'ought not to be conceived merely as the cultural inscription of meaning on a pre-given sex; gender must also designate the very apparatus of production whereby the sexes themselves are established. As a result, gender is not to culture as sex is to nature; gender is also the discursive/cultural means by which "sexed nature", or "a natural sex" is produced and established as "prediscursive", "prior to culture"' (1999: 11). Prokhovnik (1999) develops a critique of dichotomous thinking that locates reason or rationality in the (masculine) mind and emotions or relegates irrationality to the (feminine) body. She aims to challenge the priority this way of thinking gives 'to a narrow cognitive understanding of the mind as separate from lived and inscribed corporeality' (1999: 9). Prokhovnik claims to undermine the mind/body dualism, through developing her argument that emotions are located principally in the mind, which is itself part of the body.

**See also:** *body, (the) Other, public/private*

### FURTHER READING

Preves (2000) reports on her research with 'intersexed' people (those whose anatomies exist outside of the male/female sexual dichotomy), and argues that her findings demonstrate the inadequacy of the current binary classification of gender/sex. Prokhovnik (1999) provides a detailed critique of dichotomy from a feminist perspective, while a volume edited by Jenks (1998) provides a more general discussion of dichotomies.

# difference

The debate over difference takes us to the heart of feminist conceptions of equality, and how it might be achieved. It reminds us that equality is itself not a straightforward aim in a world riven with inequalities between genders and across ethnicities and social arrangements, and gradually feminists have acknowledged that there cannot simply be one model of equality. When early second wave feminists talked about equality, it was about imagining a world where women had equal access to the power and autonomy that all men notionally had by virtue of being men. Equality was also breaking down traditional gendered binaries that suggested women were incapable of certain tasks or holding positions of responsibility because of their sex. Gradually this aim for equality would be held up to account and its critics would ponder whether women strive to be 'equal' to men when what are currently considered to be dominant traits of 'masculinity' are hardly the most desirable, and certainly don't gel with some of the aspirations of second wave feminist politics.

In any case the question had to be asked about which men feminists should strive to be equal to. If it was about having access to the power of the most privileged men, this would just presumably perpetuate the social system that propagates free market capitalism. Additionally, even if it is the case that women are more than capable of performing most tasks usually allotted to men, there are still differences that have to be acknowledged, even if it is simply the fact that many women and no men give birth. These exceptions to notional equality prompted more of an 'equal but different' inflection to the argument. Modern feminism from the outset drew a distinction between biological and cultural differences – biological ones having been so important in the subordination of women in the past – and focused much more on the cultural. Thus in early feminist debates, 'sex' was taken to refer to biological differences and 'gender' to those constructed by society – this was useful as a way of showing that masculinity and femininity said very little about essential qualities of sexual difference but rather only about the ways they are used to encourage people to take up 'appropriate' forms of behaviour

Gradually the term 'difference' within feminist theory took on a number of varied meanings. The concept of gender difference lay at the heart of feminist politics; but increasingly it needed to pay more heed to the differences between women and the meanings we attach to them.

27

Opinion remained divided over whether the differences between women make the assumption of shared concerns less credible, or whether such differences can strengthen associations between women by demonstrating the breadth of female experience and their potentiality for greater achievement. When the Women's Liberation Movement was in its infancy, the notion of a 'sisterhood' with global reach was compelling and suitably optimistic. But effectively from the moment the concept of 'sisterhood' was being developed, the differences between women – ethnicity, class, family circumstances, sexual orientation, were also viewed as crucially shaping experience.

When it comes to sexual difference there are swings between what Nancy Cott calls 'difference' and 'sameness' debates in feminism and a point midway where it is argued that women have the same intellectual and rational qualities as men, but that women also possess special characteristics. This means that the 'definition of women as a sex/class, which is a major, perhaps the major, contribution of recent feminist theory, has been pulled in two directions: towards the elimination of gender roles ("sameness" argument) and toward the valorization of female being ("difference" argument)' (Cott in Mitchell and Oakley 1986: 59). One may want to claim that, particularly in our technological society, the physical differences between men and women should not adversely affect their ability to take on roles more traditionally associated with one sex or the other, yet there may be reasons why it is deemed necessary to acknowledge that 'natural' effects of female identity (such as childbirth) result in the occasional need for different treatment of women. Moving on to the 1980s, Cott observes that 'the value accorded to "sexual difference" in feminist theory has increased at the same time that the universality of the claim for sisterhood has been debunked. Ethnic, racial and sexual diversity among women is stressed more than ever before in feminist theory, but so is the emphasis on how women (as a whole) differ from men (as a whole)' (Cott in Mitchell and Oakley 1986: 59).

Writing in the late 1980s Lynne Segal feels that there was a turn towards an acceptance of fundamental differences between men and women, even though she and others would have characterised the onset of second wave feminism as based on a denial that biological difference had any significant effect on the social capabilities of men and women (Segal 1987: x). For her the tendency to present women as being more pacifist, nuturant and generally more humane (e.g. the representation of Greenham Common protestors and the setting up of a Women's Peace Camp in 1981) is a sign that the feminist agenda is increasingly taken over with questions of male violence and aggression. Segal asserts that there was a growing hegemony of cultural feminism in the 1980s that exploited this notion of essential difference and drew strength from the work of women such as Mary Daly. Certainly it is true that radical feminism in its original form seemed to become subsumed by cultural feminism and, as Echols observes, 'cultural feminism with its insistence upon women's essential sameness to each other and their fundamental difference from men seemed to many to unify a movement that by 1973 was highly schismatic' (1989: 244). For Echols this move to cultural feminism was in response to a backlash, but it is also a conservative rejection of 1960s' radicalism.

The difference and sameness debate re-emerged in the late 1980s and coincided with more feminists embracing post-structuralist and post-modern ideas. Theorists have commented that to argue for equality on the basis of sameness is to insert women into male-oriented structures that assume male experiences and norms at their heart. As Anne Phillips explains, 'women can say they want to be treated the same – but this means being treated as if they were men; or they can demand laws that are specific to their needs – but this means being compensated for their lesser abilities or role. The fact is that the norm is already sexually specific . . . [w]e should think rather of a plurality of many differences, so that equality becomes compatible with diversity instead of forcing us into the self-same mould' (Phillips in Barrett and Phillips 1992: 20). From a post-structuralist perspective this means interrogating the binary opposition of 'difference' and 'sameness' and looking at how 'bodies become invested with differences which are then taken to be fundamentally ontological differences' (Gatens 1996: 73) – which is to say that the means by which culture, historical context, custom and gender construct the sexed self do have a real impact on human experiences in ways that can't be separated into 'mind'/'body' experiences.

For some this has meant a problematising of the term 'woman' and concern about its effectiveness as a political organising concept. Yet Bryson reminds us that 'of course society *does* treat certain biological differences as highly significant: every individual is legally classified at birth as a biological male or female, and a whole set of gender expectations are mapped onto this primary sex distinction . . . we need to be able to see ourselves as women if we are to resist our current construction as women' (1999: 49). For Jana Sawicki it is vital for women to value difference between them so they can define 'the common interests of a diverse group of people' (1991: 46) rather than attempt to homogenise experience to fit a predetermined model. Instead of perceiving difference as an obstacle to resistance (because of the lack of a collective identity) Sawicki suggests that '[d]ifference can be a resource insofar as it enables us to multiply the

29

sources of resistance to the many relations of domination that circulate through the social field. If there is no central locus of power, then neither is there a central locus of resistance. Moreover, if we redefine our differences, discover new ways of understanding ourselves and each other, then our differences are less likely to be used against us' (Sawicki 1991: 45). In her thorough and wide-ranging exploration of the difference debate in 1997, Rita Felski concludes that:

> [R]ather than endorse a metaphysical vision of woman as invariably and eternally other, feminism can more usefully conceptualize the position of women in terms of a difference within sameness and a sameness within difference, a form of interference with the purity of such categories that is variously and contingently actualized. Such a perspective remains more open to the multiple and mutable concerns of feminism than does the appeal to incommensurability and otherness, an otherness that necessarily leaves the realm of the same untouched. (Felski 1997: 21)

At a time when feminism has been castigated for losing sight of the interests of 'ordinary' women, a position of radical pluralism might be one of the better ways forward.

**See also:** *equality, essentialism, gender, post-structuralism*

### FURTHER READING

Cott's essay in Mitchell and Oakley (1986) helps to contextualise the difference/sameness debate in feminism over the past century as does her book on American feminism during the first two decades of the twentieth century (1987). Barrett and Phillips (1992) provide a reasonably accessible account of the increasingly 'postmodern' turn in feminist thought. A more theoretically articulated account is that of Felski (1997).

30

# domestic division of labour

The domestic (or household) division of labour refers to the distribution between family members of those responsibilities and tasks necessary for the ongoing maintenance of a domestic home and of the people who live in it. Sometimes, the concepts of the 'sexual' division of labour or the 'gendered' division of labour are used in recognition that, historically and currently (especially in many Western industrial societies), there are marked differences between women and men in responsibilities for and the performance of the tasks necessary for daily living in a family household. Developing especially since industrialisation, a 'traditional' domestic division of labour is that in which men have primary responsibility for the necessary financial provision of their family household (via labouring/working outside the home in exchange for a wage), and women have primary responsibility for the management and performance of housework and caring work (such as cleaning, laundry, shopping, cooking, and caring for children). This domestic work/labour undertaken by women is unpaid, is mostly (though not always) performed within the home, and is necessary for the day-to-day maintenance of the household and of its members.

The concept of the domestic division of labour especially came to prominence in academic debates in the 1970s. Using Marxist theories, feminists argued that what women do within the home, although unpaid, is 'work' or 'labour'; in other words, a form of productive activity like men's waged labour. A range of feminist theories developed in an attempt to explain the traditional domestic division of labour. For example, Della Costa (1972, cited in Delphy and Leonard 1992) suggested that the domestic division of labour benefits capitalism. Unpaid housework and caring work replenish labour power on a daily and generational basis, and in this way contributing to the production of surplus value, sustain the capitalist dynamic. Other theorists emphasised the connections between capitalism and patriarchy. For example, Hartmann (1982) argued that before the development of capitalism, a patriarchal system was established in which men controlled the labour power of women and children in the family. Through this, men learned the techniques of hierarchical organisation and control which, as capitalism developed, they then used to segregate paid work to their own advantage. Job segregation invariably means that it is men who hold the jobs with greater material rewards, not least relatively high wages, compared to women. According to Hartmann, the lower wages earned by women in their jobs 'keep women dependent on men because they encourage women to marry. Married women must perform domestic chores for their husbands . . . This domestic division of labour, in turn, acts to weaken women's position in the labour market. Thus, the hierarchical domestic division of labour is perpetuated by the labour market, and vice versa' (1982: 448). In

Hartmann's account, there is a 'mutual accommodation' between patriarchy and capitalism, which results in a 'vicious circle' of disadvantage for women. In contrast to Hartmann's 'dual system' identification of both capitalism and patriarchy, Delphy and Leonard (1992) focus on patriarchy in their explanation of the domestic division of labour. They claim that 'women's continuing subordination in Western society is due in large measure to men's exploitation of women's domestic labour' (1992: 29) and that 'women's oppression is directly beneficial to men and perhaps only indirectly beneficial to capitalism' (1992: 35). In Delphy and Leonard's approach, the 'practical, emotional, sexual, procreative and symbolic work done by women for men within family relationships' (1992: 23) takes place within a domestic or patriarchal 'mode of production'. Men exploit (or 'appropriate') women's unpaid domestic labour and benefit directly from it: they do not take responsibility for or perform much of the routine and never-ending domestic work themselves; and thereby gain an advantage in the labour market, being 'freer' than women when it comes to selling their labour power to employers.

A further area of debate is the extent to which changes have occurred in the domestic division of labour. From the beginning of the twentieth century up until the 1960s, British census data indicates that women made up less than one-third of the total paid labour force (Hakim 1979). After the 1960s, however, women's representation in the labour force began to rise, and by 2001, women were 44 per cent of the working-age labour force (Twomey 2002). Women significantly increased their representation in paid work in Britain during the second half of the twentieth century, but does this mean that the 'traditional' domestic division of labour also changed? Studies on family life in the 1960s and 1970s did begin to suggest that the domestic division of labour was becoming more equal, in that more married women were engaging in paid work outside the home and more married men were doing housework and caring work within the home (for example, Gavron [1966] 1983; Rosser and Harris 1965; Young and Willmott [1973] 1975). However, later studies show that despite their involvement in paid work, women remain responsible for the bulk of unpaid housework and caring work (for example, Edgell 1980; Mansfield and Collard 1988; Oakley 1974; Warde and Hetherington 1993). Women's major responsibility for unpaid household work has been shown to continue, even when their men partners are themselves unemployed (Morris 1985; Wheelock 1990), or when both partners work full time (Brannen and Moss 1991; Gershuny 1997; Kiernan 1992; Pahl 1984). A study by Sullivan (2000) used nationally representative data collected in 1975, 1987 and 1997 to address the issue of change in the division of domestic labour in Britain. She found that in 1997, women still performed the bulk of domestic work (as measured in terms of time contributed). However, men had significantly increased their participation in domestic work and there was also a substantial increase in more 'egalitarian' couples, especially among the full-time employed. Over time, then, men have been gradually increasing their share of household work but, as suggested by Gershuny, Godwin and Jones (1994), men are 'lagging behind' women, being slower to respond to women's changed attitudes and practices (Kiernan 1992; Witherspoon and Prior 1991). Despite women's increased involvement in paid work, the 'traditional' pattern of the domestic division of labour has proven quite resilient. Some studies suggest that, when both partners undertake full-time paid work, a solution increasingly favoured is to pay someone else (usually a woman) to do the housework (for example, Gregson and Lowe 1994).

Given the slow rate of change in the traditional domestic division of labour, attention has turned to understanding the reasons for its persistence. A number of factors have been identified as helping to explain women's continuing responsibility for housework and caring work, including their greater time availability, their lack of economic power relative to their partner due to gender segregation in paid work, and beliefs about gender roles (see Pilcher 1999 for an overview and critique). More recent research has focused on men's and women's subjective perceptions of their particular domestic divisions of labour, in terms of whether or not they perceive it to be 'fair'. For example, Baxter (2000) uses data from a national Australian survey to explore husbands' and wives' perceptions of the fairness of the domestic division of labour. Baxter found that 59 per cent of the women reported that the domestic division of labour in the home was fair, even though they also reported that they themselves were responsible for doing the bulk of it. Baxter argues that this is because perceptions of fairness were primarily based, not on the amount of time spent doing tasks, but on which tasks got done by whom. 'In terms of housework, the tasks which influence perceptions of fairness include those typically associated with traditional areas of women's work within the home, such as cleaning, cooking, laundry and shopping. For women, men's involvement in these areas enhances women's perceptions that tasks are shared fairly' (2000: 626). Baxter concludes that women's perceptions of fairness probably reflect the unattainability of the goal of men taking on a more fully equal share of time spent on unpaid domestic work. Therefore, it is likely that further and more substantial changes in the domestic division of labour will occur only very slowly.

### FURTHER READING

Pilcher (2000) provides an overview of research evidence on the domestic division of labour in the twentieth century, while Laurie and Gershuny (2000) discuss the gendered division of work and money using data from a longitudinal study of British families. Bhopal's (1997) study usefully cautions against stereotypical depictions of domestic divisions of labour among British women of South Asian ethnicity.

# double standard

In social life, behaviour is governed by informal norms and rules, as well as formal laws. In feminist analyses, men's power to define the content of formal and informal behavioural cultures means that the criteria or standards used to evaluate and regulate women often differ to those used for men. In other words, rather than a single standard of behaviour for all, there exist two-fold, or 'double standards', one relating to men and the other to women. In the context of an androcentric culture, double standards most often benefit men rather than women.

In a general sense, feminism has long been concerned with problematising the existence of double standards. In striving for formal legal equality between women and men (the right to vote, or equal pay, for example), feminists have argued that women should enjoy the same citizenship rights and rewards as men. The concept of the double standard is, though, more recently associated with the analysis of informal norms and rules of behaviour, particularly within sexual culture. Despite a degree of social change in Western societies, as sexuality has become more liberal, sociologists have argued that there continue to be marked differences between the norms and rules governing men's sexuality and women's sexuality (Hawkes 1996). The double standard of sexuality means that sexual behaviour deemed inappropriate in a woman, and for which she is shown social disapproval, may be regarded as appropriate and as praiseworthy in a man.

There are a number of sources of evidence on the existence of a double standard of sexuality. For example, in a nationally representative survey

34

of the British population, men said that they had had a higher number of heterosexual partners, compared to women. This finding was argued to reflect a tendency for men's prolific sexual activities to be condoned, while women with many sexual partners are viewed much more negatively. The survey also found marked differences between women and men in attitudes to casual sex. While 63 per cent of women surveyed said that 'one night stands' were wrong, only 36 per cent of men said so (Wellings et al. 1994). Studies of young people's sexuality show the resilience of the sexual double standard in contemporary Britain, several decades after sexual liberalisation and its supposed effects on traditional sexual morality. Lees's (1989) research revealed a double standard of sexual reputation within the sexual cultures of young people. 'A girl's standing can be destroyed by insinuations about her sexual morality, a boy's reputation in contrast is usually enhanced by his sexual exploits' (1989: 19). Terms like 'slag' and 'tart' were especially important ways through which girls' sexuality was socially controlled and regulated. Lees found that this language of sexual reputation was applied exclusively to girls and there was no equivalent label set applied to boys. In their efforts to avoid being labelled as a slag or a tart, girls had permanently to monitor and check their sexuality, including their style of dress, their friendliness with boys and their number and frequency of sexual encounters. Research by Holland and her colleagues (1996) also revealed that similar sexual behaviour by young women and young men tends to result in different sexual reputations. In the words of one of the young women interviewed, 'If you sleep around you're a slag, if a bloke sleeps around he's lucky' (1996: 242). On the basis of their findings, Holland and her colleagues argued that both young women and young men constructed their sexuality in response to the rules of masculine-dominated heterosexuality. Young women had to safeguard their sexual reputation and avoid being labelled as sexually promiscuous, while young men had to demonstrate their sexual reputation in order to enhance their standing with their masculine peer group.

The concept of the double standard has also been used in the analysis of the ageing process. Sontag (1979) has argued that, as they grow older, men and women are evaluated by different standards, and this is advantageous for older men. The qualities and attributes that women are valued for, especially their youthful physical attractiveness, are threatened by growing older. Men's value depends less on how they look and more on what they do, particularly economically. Sontag also points to the ways in which signs of ageing in men are less heavily penalised than they are in women. In men, wrinkles and grey hair may be valued as a sign of experience and be described as 'distinguished'. In contrast, women are more strongly encouraged to conceal signs of ageing on their faces and their bodies, due to the importance of youthful attractiveness to women's sexual candidacy. Support for this analysis of the double standard of ageing can be found in survey data. Older women may experience 'sexual redundancy' in that they are more likely than older men to have no sexual partner. Men, on the other hand, are more likely to form a sexual relationship with a younger woman (Wellings et al. 1994). Moreover, a sexual relationship between an older woman and a younger man is more likely to attract social disapproval than vice versa.

As a concept, the double standard is most often used to describe a disparity between the experiences of women and men, which is to the benefit of men. More rarely is it used to draw attention to a disparity in which men are disadvantaged. An example of a 'reverse' double standard (where the discrimination is against men) is provided by the issue of winter fuel payments by the state to those of pensionable age in Britain. Because men's state pension entitlement begins at age 65 and women's at age 60, this meant that women also received the winter fuel payment at an earlier age then men. This policy was challenged by a retired man, who took his argument that men should be entitled to the payment at the same age as women to the European Court of Justice. It ruled in his favour and the policy has subsequently been changed so that women and men now receive the benefit at the same age (*The Guardian*, 17 December 1999). In informal codes of expected behaviour, 'reverse' double standards may also be identified. For example, criminologists have drawn together a range of evidence which suggests that gender stereotypes held by criminal justice professionals influence the treatment of offenders, with the result that women offenders are often treated more leniently than men (see, for example, Gelsthorpe and Loucks 1997). However, as argued by Morris, the lenient treatment of women within the criminal justice system is dependent upon their conformity to particular models of femininity. It is likely, therefore, to be reserved for 'passive, unaggressive, remorseful, white, middle class women' (1987: 82).

As understandings of gender relations have become more sophisticated, it has been recognised that double standards are often far from uniform in their application or effects, but vary in the context of class, ethnicity and sexuality, for example. In Connell's analysis of the gender hierarchy of power (1987; 1995), a particular form of masculinity (hegemonic masculinity) is suggested as the dominant force in the production and reproduction of double standards. Those men who do not

**36**

live up to the hegemonic masculine ideal (particularly gay men) may find themselves disadvantaged by the operation of double standards. Heterosexuality is an important component of hegemonic masculinity and gay men's sexuality is evaluated in relation to it. Thus, while prolific sexual activity by heterosexual men may be condoned, the alleged prolific sexual activity of gay men is vilified and forms an important part of homophobic discourse. Just as some men may be disadvantaged by double standards of sexuality, some women may be able to draw on resources (such as their education or economic status) to minimise the restrictions on their sexual lives they might otherwise face.

**See also:** *(the) Other, sexuality*

### FURTHER READING

The various publications of the Equal Opportunities Commission report on all aspects of the more formal double standards that continue to exist between women and men in Britain. See their web pages at http://www.eoc.org.uk/ for current publications. The volume edited by Weeks and Holland (1996) reports on a range of sexual cultures in contemporary Britain, while that edited by Arber and Ginn (1995) examines the relationship between gender and ageing.

# equality

Equality can be defined as a state or condition of being the same, especially in terms of social status or legal/political rights. (Although satisfactory as an initial definition, the idea of equality as sameness has become a subject of debate in gender studies; see below.) Historically in Western societies, men have had a higher social status and more extensive legal and political rights than women. In late nineteenth- and early twentieth-century Britain, for example, 'equal rights' feminists campaigned to extend to women the key rights and privileges (in relation to education, property, employment, the vote) previously enjoyed by men. By the late twentieth century, a range of legislation was in place (including the Sex Discrimination Act and the Equal Pay Act) that aimed to facilitate equality between women and men, through the prohibition of discriminatory practices. Gay men and lesbian women have also campaigned for social acceptance and for legal rights, including the age of consent and spousal or 'marital' rights, equivalent to those enjoyed by heterosexuals.

Behind the scenes of the historical struggle for gender equality lie long-standing, and ongoing, debates about the meaning of equality. Does the achievement of equality require the provision of equality of opportunity, or does it mean securing equality of outcome? What is the nature of the difference between men and women and how does this relate to the attainment of equality between them? What is the standard by which the achievement of gender equality is to be judged? Does equality mean that women have to take on masculine norms, values and lifestyles? How does gender equality relate to ethnicity, and sexuality? With whom are black women to become equal – white men, or black men, or white women? One early illustration of the problematical status of the concept of equality for feminism is provided by the tensions that existed between British feminists in the 1920s and 1930s. The so-called 'new feminists' of this period concentrated on winning special measures for women, such as family endowments (a form of child benefit, to be paid to women as mothers), birth control and protective employment legislation. Priorities such as these were an anathema to the 'equal rights' feminists. Rather than securing special measures or privileges for women, they were instead concerned to re-orientate women away from the private, domestic sphere and to achieve parity with men in the public sphere. In the eyes of the equal rights feminists, the campaign for protective legislation implied a fundamental difference between women and men, 'but also female weakness and dependence and to this extent at least female inferiority' (Banks 1981: 115).

The issue of whether equality requires all women being treated the same as all men, irrespective of their differences, or whether equality requires that differences between women and men be recognised and provided for, remains central to feminism and to gender studies. It is possible to identify three perspectives in what has become known as the 'equality/difference' debate (Squires 1999). First, the 'equality perspective', an example of which are the British 'equal rights' feminists of the late nineteenth and early twentieth century. Here, the concern is to extend to women the same rights and privileges that men have, through identifying areas of unequal treatment and eliminating them via legal reforms. Phillips (1997), for example, argues for 'strict equality' between women and men, because gender equality in the labour market will not be achieved without gender equality in the allocation of household and caring work between women and men. Williams (1997) focuses on contemporary issues that pose key questions about gender equality, including women in military combat roles. In Williams' view, women should not be exempt from combat roles, because this represents special treatment for women, and so allows the state to 'mark off' women as different in other ways. In the equality perspective, therefore, gender is regarded as an attribute that should not be significant in the distribution of social value or social rights. Equality is to be achieved through gender neutrality or androgyny. However, this can mean that the goal of equality is achieved through the assimilation of subordinated groups (women, gay men) to the values, institutions and life-styles of dominant groups (men, heterosexuals).

In contrast to the androgyny or gender neutrality often implied by the equality perspective, those within the 'difference perspective' insist on the recognition of and valuing of the ways in which women are different from men. For example, in the work of French post-structuralist feminists such as Irigaray (see Whitford 1991), women's experiences, their cultural, bodily and sexual differences from men, are celebrated and valorised. Other 'difference theorists' draw on the work of writers such as Gilligan (1982) to argue that women's distinctive morality requires that equality is 'gender-differentiated'. For example, Ruddick (1997) suggests that feminine (maternal, caring) values are qualities that need centring, replacing masculine values. In what is often called the 'maternalist perspective', the emphasis has been on enhancing the political position of women-as-mothers and on 'projecting their values into political life as a legitimate basis for women's citizenship from a basis of moral superiority' (Lister 1997: 95). Difference theorists, then, are critical of equality strategies where the masculine is the norm against which women are judged, and where femininity is positioned as something to be transcended in order for equality to be achieved. The strategy of proclaiming difference, though, can be a risky one, providing a justification for the continuation of patterns of social inequality and for practices of discrimination by more powerful, dominant groupings.

A third perspective in the equality/difference debate involves 'going beyond' the dichotomy represented by the previous two perspectives (Squires 1999). 'Diversity' theorists criticise both the equality and difference perspectives. 'The "equality" perspective fails to recognise the socially constructed and patriarchal nature of the criterion of evaluation deemed pertinent to social inclusion. The "difference" perspective . . . fails to theorise the extent to which "maleness" and "femaleness" are themselves socially constructed and also underplays the significance and

39

plurality of other forms of difference' (Squires 1999: 131). The perspective of 'diversity' involves deconstructing the choice of *either* equality *or* difference (Scott 1997). Lister's (1997) work on citizenship provides an example. Given that the original notion of a citizen was masculine, feminists have struggled with how women can best attain citizenship. As Lister explains, for equality theorists, the goal has been gender-neutrality, where women are enabled to participate with men as equal citizens in the public sphere. For difference theorists, the goal has been a gender-differentiated citizenship, where women's responsibilities and skills in the private sphere are recognised and valued. For Lister, both goals are distorted by their underlying dichotomous logic, and lead to a political and theoretical dead-end. For Lister, a more constructive way forward is a conception of citizenship that combines elements of the gender-neutral and gender-differentiated approaches, employed strategically, while at the same time remaining sensitive to the differences that exist between women. Diversity theorists, then, question the assumption implicit in the equality/difference debate that equality and difference are mutually exclusive opposites. For diversity theorists, 'equality and difference are not incompatible; they only become so if equality is understood to mean sameness' (Lister 1997: 96). To do so is a misrepresentation, however, because 'the whole conceptual force of "equality" rests on the assumption of differences, which should in some respect be valued equally' (Squires 1999: 97).

The connections between equality and difference, rather than their incompatible opposition, are explored in the work of Iris Marion Young (1990). Young argues that the concept of equality needs to be re-conceptualised. In what Young calls 'the politics of difference', group differences are not neutralised or transcended. Equality exists among socially and culturally different groups, arising out of their mutual respect for each other and affirmation of one another in their difference. 'Difference now comes to mean not otherness, exclusive opposition, but specificity, variation, heterogeneity' (1990: 171). In place of universally formulated and 'neutral' equality policies, Young advocates equality strategies such as 'group-conscious policies' (e.g. affirmative action or positive discrimination) and the guaranteed representation of oppressed groups in democratic decision-making bodies. For Young, then, it is unrealistic and undesirable to pursue equality through the neutralisation of group differences. 'Instead, justice in a group-differentiated society demands social equality of groups, and mutual recognition and affirmation of group differences. Attending to group-specific needs and providing for group representation both promotes that social equality and provides the recognition that undermines cultural imperialism' (1990: 191). Young's work itself is open to criticism (see, for example, Phillips 1993), but it is these efforts at 'going beyond' the dichotomy of equality/difference 'that most clearly characterises the present moment of gender theorising' (Squires 1999: 116).

**See also:** *citizenship, dichotomy, difference*

### FURTHER READING

A text edited by Bock and James (1992) aims to contextualise the different meanings of equality and difference through examining how they have been employed in different historical and social contexts. *Feminist Social Thought: A Reader* (Meyers 1997) usefully includes three contrasting arguments on equality and difference, by Williams, by Littleton, and by Scott. A detailed overview of the equality/difference debate is provided by Squires (1999).

# essentialism

Essentialism was originally identified by second wave feminists as the mode of thinking that assumes that all manifestations of gender difference are innate and transcultural and historical. Essentialism in this formulation makes constant reference back to biological differences between the sexes, using this logic to explain wider manifestations of sexual difference. This form of biological essentialism was largely rejected by the majority of feminists in favour of a social constructionist view of gender relations. More recently, feminists have further questioned the nature of the relationship between sex and gender and the wisdom of implicitly replicating the binary opposition between nature and culture. It is also questioned whether the issue of how we understand the natural has been fully interrogated. From the point of view of postmodernism, some feminists further question the validity of categories of gender since they argue that they can only be defined in relation to each other without any reference to an exterior truth. Judith Butler's model of gender as performative seems to wipe away the last vestiges of essentialism in her argument that we produce gendered identity by the process of naming/citation – the pronouncement that 'it's a girl' on the birth of a child.

41

The ways in which biological essentialism has crept into feminist debates has varied enormously. One good example is the work of Shulamith Firestone in *The Dialectic of Sex* (1970) and her assertion that women are materially oppressed by the fact of their biological capacity to give birth and that the only solution to female oppression is to liberate women from the shackles of childbirth through reproductive technologies. Cultural feminists such as Mary Daly represent biological femaleness as essentially superior to biological maleness – in that 'feminine' virtues tend to be seen as solely lying with the female sex. For the essentialist of this kind, patriarchal perspectives on femininity act to distort women's real capacities, but underneath that there is an authentic femaleness which can be celebrated. This kind of essentialism seems to have been favoured by white middle-class women and some lesbians: for women of colour essentialist arguments and the means by which they might translate across to issues of race are not so palatable. For Alice Echols the line between radical and cultural feminist is a straight binary opposite: 'radical feminists were typically social constructionists who wanted to render gender irrelevant, while cultural feminists were generally essentialists who sought to celebrate femaleness' (Echols 1989: 6).

It seemed for a while that social constructionist perspectives were to be favoured by the majority of feminists with a more theoretical turn but during the late 1980s writers such as Diana Fuss questioned whether the stark binary of essentialist/social constructionist was tenable, suggesting that 'in and of itself, essentialism is neither good nor bad, progressive nor reactionary, beneficial nor dangerous' (Fuss 1989: xi). Additionally, the idea of essentialism 'as a belief in the real, true essence of things' (Fuss 1989: xi) can be mobilised in many contexts and to many uses. Fuss gives examples of crossovers between social constructionists and essentialists, arguing that although social constructionists looking at gender will demand a historically specific and contingent methodology, 'the categories "man" and "woman" still remain constant' (Fuss 1989: 4) as terms of reference. Fuss makes the point that within the discipline of women's studies 'the category of "female experience" holds a particularly sacrosanct position' (1989: 113), even though it is impossible to posit this experience as universalised or knowable, she suggests that as a category it still holds some essence of use to the field of study.

For Tania Modleski the postmodernist denial of any coherent identity which one can lay claim to reaches the point of absurdity when attempting to deny the credibility of feminist politics because it uses the universalising category of woman – 'The once exhilarating proposition that there is no "essential" female nature has been elaborated to the point where it is now often used to scare "women" away from making *any* generalizations about or political claims on behalf of a group called "women"' (Modleski 1991: 15). The denial that one can make political statements for a grouping under the category of woman or gay man or African-American lesbian, etc. is for many a denial of political agency, and those who feel uncomfortable with the use of categories 'may be on the slippery slope to abandoning the use of all terms indicating common sources of and forms of oppression. The strategy, then, may be conservative and individualist in effect' (Assiter 1996: 112). Gayatri Spivak has, however, argued for the usefulness of a 'strategic' essentialism when embraced from the position of an oppressed group who may seek a more positive and challenging identity from such a stance. Assiter, Modleski and Spivak here seem to be in tacit agreement that while universalising experience and making appeals to the essence of a thing may be negative, it may also be positive and necessary to come to any shared understandings about what our position as 'women' means to us in the current world order, even at the risk of some false generalisation. As Modleski teasingly suggests, 'In the final analysis it seems more important to struggle over what it *means* to be a woman than over whether or not to be one' (1991: 20).

**See also:** *difference, identity politics, post-feminism, postmodernism*

### FURTHER READING

Fuss (1989) offers an intelligent and thorough account of recent debates on essentialism and constructionism with useful glosses on figures such as Derrida, Lacan, Irigaray and Wittig. Assiter (1996) looks at why feminists should return to a 'modernist' viewpoint to counter some of the more alienating effects of the postmodern theory of the subject, sex and gender. Firestone (1970) offers an example of the radical feminist kind of essentialism.

43

# the family

As feminist knowledge developed and became more sophisticated throughout the 1970s, the family came to be an important object of analysis. For many, it was the crucial site of women's oppression, the space where, unheeded by the world outside, women were at the mercy of fathers or husbands; where the law of 'patriarchy' held its most primitive form. Feminism's scrutiny of the 'private' sphere was one of the things it considered to be unique about 'sexual politics'; that social arrangements notionally based on kinship and romantic love could be viewed askance as part of patriarchy's repressive regime.

Feminists analysed the family in two keys ways: first as a social arrangement subject to historical shifts in definition, but located primarily on the basis of close kinship ties; and second as an ideology that communicates a preferred form of organisation which is internalised by everyone. It is clearly important to keep these two prongs of the argument separate, since one allows us to look at how families have *actually* been arranged in any given historical period in any given cultural framework and the other allows us to look at how 'the family' operates at the level of representation. In the case of a familial ideology it is useful to be able to recognise how this works upon the emotional responses of the individual in order to enforce a particular family 'norm' regardless of how little relationship it might bear to people's lived experiences of the family. It is also the ideology of 'the family' which is utilised to effect by politicians when they want to be seen to champion the family from perilous erosion by the forces of change.

The bonds of kinship make family relationships potentially more oppressive than anything else we experience; family both protects us from the outside world and socialises us into it. It is generally through our parents and siblings that we come to understand the meanings of gender difference and where messages about morality and normality we learn at school are reinforced (or not). As Freud made clear, the family is also the place where we receive our neuroses and phobias; where we grow up sexually well- or mal-adjusted. A happy family life can provide an individual with a long-lasting cushion against periods of alienation in social and professional life; but it is also the case that most sexual abuse takes place within the family and that most murder victims are killed by someone they are close to.

Michèle Barrett and Mary McIntosh declared in their influential socialist-feminist critique of the family that '[a]lthough we have used a rather impersonal style, no author or reader can be completely detached from the personal implications of the arguments. But personal life is at one and the same time the story of our own lived experiences – the context of our deepest motivations, rewards and frustrations – and also the product of a particular moment in history and a particular structure

44

of society. So we are often divided between subject experience on the one hand and political analysis on the other' (Barrett and McIntosh 1982: 9). Here the authors illustrate the tensions involved for all feminists in analysing structures which have real individual emotional investments for them and the moral panic that such critiques can evoke. Unpalatable or difficult as it is, feminists asked questions about the so-called 'private' sphere which had previously remained more or less taboo, and in doing so suggested that there might be other ways of arranging family life – or at least of adjusting relations of power within the existing dominant family form.

As Barrett and McIntosh note, the nineteenth-century family ideal is still held up as the model in contemporary society: '[i]t has an orderly division of labour between husband and wife, and a firm but kindly style with the children that will be good for them in the long run. It is today's equivalent of the nineteenth-century bourgeois ideal. It appears in child-care manuals, in advertisements for cars and insurance policies, in the formal and the "hidden" curricula of schools, in the catalogues of Mothercare and the brochures of travel agents . . . Few people wish their children to be deviants, misfits, delinquents or suicides' (Barrett and McIntosh 1982: 29). Moreover, sitcoms and soap operas are popular dramatisations of family life which enforce certain norms: even when families are portrayed as actively dysfunctional, the ideal of benign family life is held up. The head of the household is generally still unthinkingly presumed to be a man, supposed to be capable of catering for the material needs of wife and children, while the wife and mother provides nourishment and nurturance.

Needless to say, many feminists went beyond offering critiques of the family and preferred alternative arrangements as more desirable such as communal living – something which lies at the heart of Firestone's radical treatise (1970). Feminists of all political persuasions were clear that the sheer volume of domestic labour necessitated by the maintenance of the nuclear family was exhausting, repetitive, lacking any spiritual and, more to the point, financial rewards. In addition, it is clearly wasteful for every family unit to be doing laundry, cooking and cleaning for a small number of people on a daily basis. Again, it was suggested that domestic labour of this kind could be 'socialised' among a wider community group, along with childcare and other activities. Feminists were inevitably keen to disaggregate domestic labour with women's roles, or else to have it financially rewarded, but the latter 'wages for housework' movement became unpopular, because of the risk of associating housework with women's work. The principle of the campaign was an inspired one,

45

*the family*

however, since it tried to compare the work done in the home with that performed for pay in the workplace in order to demonstrate the injustice of the traditional social role of wife and mother.

Many of the difficulties of family life for women were financial in that traditionally men had been expected to earn a 'family wage' regardless of their actual circumstances. As divorce rates increase and more single families are in evidence, it is clear that single mothers need an equal opportunity to be 'breadwinners'. To displace the ideal of the nuclear family as the central determinant of social existence would, it was felt, release women from some of its inevitabilities and make such a structure 'less necessary' (1982: 159) rather than find something to take its place. Barrett and McIntosh also view the 'present ideology of the family to be so steeped in heterosexism that any realistic engagement with familialism must locate the discussion within that framework' (Barrett and McIntosh 1982: 9). The importance of the ideal-type family is of course embedded in mainstream politics when all the main parties vie for the title of 'family party'; moreover, the endorsement of its heterosexualism is witnessed by a glimpse at the wording of the UK's Section 28 of the Local Government Act 1988 where homosexuality is defined pejoratively as a 'pretended family relationship'.

Despite the success of single-parent family pressure groups, there are still waves of reaction against modernising the family model to reflect the varieties of family life experienced by people today. With a strong investment still in marriage over common-law cohabitation, attempts to widen the image of the model family further have as yet met with strong rejection. Recently there have been attempts to broaden the range of individuals eligible to adopt to single people and gay and lesbian couples, which has prompted inter-party strife and disproportionate amounts of moral panic in the tabloids. Family as a concept is still appealed to in all debates about the erosion of social values and in a period where so many families break up, more is made of both the mother *and* father's role – even though the enlightened attitude this implies is underpinned by the reality that women still do the lion's share of domestic tasks. Although they may be full participants in paid employment, they are effectively doing a 'double shift' of work and domestic labour and caring in the home.

Family defenders more often than not seek to blame feminism for evidence of social deterioriation, and obviously to some extent it is correct to see feminism as gnawing at the foundations of the nuclear family. Yet during the 1980s and 1990s feminists became quite sharply divided over the issue of the family. For black feminists in particular the dominant conception of the family reflected white values and experiences and failed to take into account, for instance, the fact that for many black women and men the family was an effective haven from racism. In addition, as bell hooks points out, research on black African-American families produced a matriarchy thesis because they couldn't comprehend the fact that the women were active providers and decision-makers in the home: 'they chose to see the independence, will power, and initiative of black women as an attack on the masculinity of black men . . . They argued that the black woman's performance of any active role in family life both as mothers and providers had deprived black men of their patriarchal status in the home' (hooks 1982: 75-6). Patricia Hill Collins further exposes the narrowness of the white feminist analysis of the family when she talks of the African-American extended family and existence of othermothers – 'women who assist bloodmothers by sharing mothering responsibilities' (Collins 1990: 119). Her argument is not only that the white Western model of the family doesn't fit all experiences, but that white feminists could learn from the sense of community – 'African-American women may find it easier than others to recognize connectedness as a primary way of knowing, simply because we are encouraged to do so by a Black women's tradition of sisterhood' (Collins 1990: 212).

A liberal view of the family still remains dominant and sees it as the unquestioned core of social life in civilised society, to be kept separate from the public sphere and closed to interference. This makes it difficult to analyse how women remain disempowered within their families or become victims of domestic violence, and precludes discussion about the real structures of changing family forms across cultures. This view appeals to us as individuals and encourages us to view any challenges to the family as unnatural, personally threatening and possibly a threat to our privacy. For Melissa Benn, contemporary politics is still unequal to the task of re-envisioning the family or supporting women's changed roles within and outside it: 'they are more concerned to resurrect a mythical family of old than pay attention to the detail of new family formations' (Benn 1998: 245). While successive governments are still reluctant to acknowledge the value to society of childrearing, the material significance of what for many is painted as a choice based on love and kinship remains obscured.

**See also:** *domestic division of labour*

### FURTHER READING

Barrett and McIntosh (1982) is one of the earliest full-length feminist texts on the family and explains why socialist feminists in particular analysed the family form in some depth. Jackson's essay (in Robinson and Richardson 1997) is clear and helpful as a summary of the key points and books such as hooks (1982) and Collins (1990) offer an African-American perspective on the analysis of the family.

# feminisms

The word 'feminism' itself originated from the French word *féminisme* in the nineteenth century, either as a medical term to describe the feminisation of a male body, or to describe women with masculine traits. When it was used in the United States in the early part of the twentieth century it was only used to refer to one group of women: 'namely that group which asserted the uniqueness of women, the mystical experience of motherhood and women's special purity' (Jaggar 1983: 5). It soon became understood to denote a political stance of someone committed to changing the social position of women. Since then the term has taken on the sense of one who believes that women are subjugated because of their sex and that women deserve at least formal equality in the eyes of the law. Despite the fact that the usage of the term is relatively recent, it has become common practice to refer to early writers and thinkers – for example the eighteenth-century writer Mary Wollstonecraft – as 'feminist' in acknowledgement of the connections between their arguments and those of modern feminism

Feminist writers and activists, even those who were in existence long before the term feminism came into popular usage, shared the will to imagine a world where women were able to realise their potential as individuals. In doing this, they had to conceptualise ideas that were, when women had no legal identity as individuals, literally unknowable. Feminist knowledge, then, has long been regarded as informal or illegitimate in some way and for modern feminists it became important to make feminist ideas legitimate by circulating their ideas as widely as possible and inviting the contributions and responses of other women. It was also important that other women would not encounter boundaries in terms of gaining access to feminist ideas, especially by feeling they lack the entitlement to call themselves 'feminist' for any reason. This assumption that, effectively, any woman who chooses to call herself feminist is one, disallows the production of a feminist dogma or unitary position and it also accounts for the multiplicity of positions that can be held under the umbrella of this title. For good and bad reasons it becomes ultimately impossible to talk about feminism in terms other than the plural.

Since the 1980s it has become common to use the plural form when talking about feminism in order to signify that although all feminists may share a basic commitment to ending female oppression, they do not always approach this problem from the same philosophical or political base. It is also an acceptance that part of the richness of feminism's legacy is this diversity and heterogeneity of positions. We can say that all feminists agree that women suffer social and/or material inequities simply because of their biological identity and are committed to challenging this, but the means by which such challenges might be made are many and various. This inevitably means that feminism as a term becomes rather unwieldy and overburdened with meaning. Given that all feminists agree on the central fact of women's subordination, most feminists regard feminism's heterogeneity as a sign of healthy debate – although feminism's detractors tend to see it as a sign of feminism's inbuilt weakness. It is clear, too, that although some critics associate this fragmentation with modern feminism, feminists have always emerged from diverse cultural and political perspectives and focused on issues germane to the time and location they inhabit.

Despite the fact that feminism can be used to reflect a personal political position (and perhaps this tendency is becoming more apparent in the twenty-first century), there are dominant strands that make up modern feminist thought as we encounter it today. Liberal feminism draws on the diversity of liberal thought dominant in Western society since the Enlightenment, and affirms that women's subordinate social position can be addressed by existing political processes under democracy. For liberals the key battle is access to education; following Mary Wollstonecraft, it is argued that if men and women are educated equally, then it follows that they will get equal access to society. Liberal feminists would be loath to use the language of 'revolution' or 'liberation' favoured by radicals and socialists, in their belief that democracy itself is naturally adaptable to equality for both sexes. This liberal position is broadly held to be the dominant, 'common-sense' stance on feminism, applicable to the majority of women who identify as 'feminist' in some way, but don't want to overturn the social status quo in order to achieve better social conditions for women. In addition, liberal feminists would be more likely to accept in limited terms that women and men might well be suited to the separate spheres of home and the workplace and simply lobby for greater recognition of housework and caring (the wages for housework debate in the 1970s emerged largely from this position).

Socialist or Marxist feminism (for further discussion of the differences and similarities, see Whelehan 1995) links changes in women's social conditions with the overthrow of industrial capitalism and changing relations of the worker to the means of production. For them, revolution is the only answer, although as time has gone on socialist feminists have become more cynical about the prospect of a socialist revolution effecting a change in the lives of women, given the tenacious ideological grip of the current meanings of gender differences. Nonetheless socialist/Marxist feminists are always mindful of the ways society is riven by class and race distinctions as well as those of gender and that it is more useful to consider oppression as multi-pronged and inter-related rather than arguing that one form is more destructive than others. In common with liberal feminism, socialist feminism, because of its links to Marxist thought, suggests a necessary link with men and an acceptance perhaps that men are part of any movement for change.

This assumption that men as part of the problem should be part of the solution was a theme in early radical feminism, even though radical feminism is usually associated in the popular consciousness with separatism and man-hating. Radical feminists, particularly in the USA, emerged largely from new left and civil rights political groupings. Their politics was broadly radical left, but they became hugely disenchanted with the male-dominated power play witnessed in left-wing radical groupings and formed the Women's Liberation Movement in order to allow a space for the consideration of women's oppression outside of the confines of male-oriented knowledge and politics. Their conviction that a woman-centred politics could only be devised in a woman-only space led to a policy of separatism, at least at the level of policy-making and meetings. This politics of radicalism, while drawing political lessons from the new left and civil rights movements, wanted a political formation freed from the taint of maleness and therefore espoused leaderless groupings, job-sharing and structurelessness – well beyond the parameters of contemporary democracy. Many of their aspirations have been ridiculed or misunderstood by others and radical feminists are all too often sent up as dungareed, man-hating lesbians, totally obsessed with the politically correct, partly because the way in which they wanted to shape their own movement was intended to reflect their rejection of anything that smacked of the male political imperative.

Feminist groupings have always contained representations from women of colour, working-class women and lesbian/bisexual women; yet many became increasingly disenchanted by the ways in which their involvement in the movement rendered their own identities and concerns invisible, despite the rhetoric of reflecting the needs of all women. For example the Combahee River Collective's 'A Black Feminist Statement', first published in 1979 (see Hull et al. 1982) demonstrates a sense of belonging to feminism and yet being alienated from some of the principles embraced – such as separatism, but also the sense that gender determines oppression more than race, class or sexual orientation. This sense of inclusion and marginalisation simultaneously, the need to make one's own feminism to counteract the blindness of the mainstream became a commonplace in 1970s' and 1980s' feminisms – testimony to their own epistemological richness as well as less positively to the ways in which identity politics prevented feminist groups from speaking to each other and moving on.

Postmodern and post-structuralist interventions in the field bring to bear even greater diversity to what can be understood as 'feminist'. Core ideas about being a 'woman' and 'inequality' are held up for scrutiny as the idea of an essential female political identity or a transparent oppressor/oppressed relationship of power are problematised by broader questions about how meanings and truths are generated in social discourse. Throughout all these discussions feminism as a term has endured and been found useful and the fruits of feminist challenges to the social order are evident in social policy-making today. For these reasons the plurality of discourses which can be held to be 'feminist' today may be the key to its strength – its refusal to be pinned down, condensed to a single set of ideas or dogma, is what make feminist knowledge abiding in its appeal to women as well as a source of support in their daily material existence.

**See also:** *first wave feminism, identity politics, second wave feminism, third wave feminism*

## FURTHER READING

There are a number of introductions to feminism that attempt to offer definitions of what the various 'strands' of feminism mean. They all offer different nuances and, in keeping with the debates within feminism, often disagree among themselves. For this reason it is worth reading widely. Jaggar (1983) offers a political philosophical analysis of liberal, radical and socialist feminism which enables anyone with only a slim grasp of political thought to gain a solid understanding of the roots of modern feminisms. Donovan (1992) offers an account of feminism's intellectual tradition with the sad conclusion that 'feminists have reinvented the wheel a

51

number of times' (Donovan 1992: xii). Imelda Whelehan's *Modern Feminist Thought* (1995) is explicitly intended to help the reader understand what different feminisms can mean since 1968. For a fairly recent update on key debates in feminism today, Bryson (1999) is thorough and accessible.

# first wave feminism

The historical development of feminism (especially in Britain and the USA) is commonly divided into several key periods, some characterised by a relative absence of feminist thought and mobilisation, and others by the sustained growth both of feminist criticism and of activism with a high public profile . The apparent pattern of rise and fall of feminism over time has led to the 'wave' analogy; the peaks and troughs of the feminist movement are characterised as following the motion of tidal water, with its ongoing cycle of gradual swelling, eventual cresting and final subsiding. The wave analogy developed along with the resurgence of feminism in the 1960s, which had been immediately preceded by a period of relative dormancy. A distinction was drawn between the resurgent feminism dating from the 1960s and an earlier period of similarly prolific, high-profile feminist analyses and political activism. The earlier period (dating from at least the mid to late nineteenth century up until about the 1920s), became 'first wave' feminism. In turn, the resurgent feminist analyses and activism dating from the 1960s became 'second wave' feminism.

In broad historical terms, the period of first wave feminism may be dated to include pre-nineteenth-century expressions of concern about the rights of women. In particular, the French Revolution of 1789 is often identified as the arena in which the first concerted demands for women's rights were made. Moreover, it was an important influence on Mary Wollstonecraft, whose *Vindication of the Rights of Women*, published in Britain in 1792, is widely recognised as the first substantial and systematic feminist treatise. However, first wave feminism (in Britain and the USA) is most often dated as occurring between c.1880s and the 1920s. It had as its principal concern women's attainment of equality with men and therefore feminist analyses and campaigning centred around securing legislational change. Walby (1990) is not alone in her view that the first wave feminist movement in Britain was of central importance in bringing about a change from 'private' to 'public' patriarchy, via the struggle for the vote, for access to education and the professions, to have legal rights of property ownership, rights in marriage and divorce and so on.

In Britain, the origins of first wave feminism lay in the widespread social and economic changes of industrialisation, one aspect of which was the extension of constitutional rights to wider sections of the (male) population. 'The most significant feminist statements of the period [1750–1850] were direct responses to new legislation granting men rights which were not being extended to women' (Caine 1997: 11). In Britain, the 1840s saw the spread of feminist ideas among middle-class women and feminism as an organised movement first emerged in the mid-1850s, centred around a small group of women based in London ('the Langham Place group'; see Banks 1981). This early feminism was concerned with the education and employment rights of women and with improving the legal rights of married women. The question of suffrage (or the right to vote) came to prominence in the mid-1860s, particularly after J.S. Mill's attempt to get women included under the provisions of the *1867 Reform Act*. Banks (1981) identifies two other main strands of first wave feminism, in addition to this long-standing tradition of 'equal rights' feminism. 'Evangelical' feminism developed out of religious evangelical movements. Its adherents sought to protect and morally reform those less fortunate than themselves, such as working-class women, 'fallen' women, children and the poor. The other main strand of feminism identified by Banks is 'socialist feminism'. Randall (1982) describes as 'social feminism' the branch of nineteenth-century feminism concerned with social and legal reform, and gives as an example Josephine Butler's campaign against the *Contagious Diseases Act*. Although less influential than either evangelical feminism or equal rights feminism, this was (according to Banks) the most wholeheartedly feminist of the three traditions: it questioned current forms of marriage and the family and advocated the collectivisation of child care and housework (see also Dyhouse 1989).

By the early twentieth century, the question of the suffrage was the predominant concern and it was the issue on which public campaigning activity was focused. The issue of the vote, seen as the key to placing the equality of women on the legislational agenda, united almost all feminists into a single campaign. There emerged, however, a fundamental difference of opinion over tactics. The National Union of Women's Suffrage Societies was formed in 1897, with Millicent Fawcett as the President, and consisted of mainly well-connected middle-class women. In 1903, the Pankhursts set up a separate organisation, the Women's Social and Political Union, which employed more militant tactics. Thousands of suffragettes were imprisoned; many went on hunger strike and were subjected to force feeding. The outbreak of World War One in 1914 put an end to the militant activities of the suffragettes and further diversified the women's movement, since some of its leaders supported the war while others followed a pacifist line (Alberti 1989). The war itself is generally thought to have broken down many traditionally held views about women, following their being drawn into the labour force as replacements for the absent men. The ending of the war brought expectations for change in many spheres of life and in 1918, the *Representation of the People Act* widened suffrage to include all men over 21 and women over 30 who were householders, or the wives of householders or had been to university.

British first wave feminism did not focus exclusively on the suffrage question (see Dyhouse 1989; Ryan 1978) but its importance as an issue is apparent from the effect it had on the women's movement in the post-First World War period. For example, Banks has argued that the struggle for the vote bestowed a façade of unity upon the women's movement and in doing so, 'disguised the differences between them that were to become all too evident in the years after the vote had been achieved' (1981: 116). Kent (1988) describes the posture of the feminist movement during and after the First World War as 'defensive', a sharp contrast to the confidence and assertiveness which it had displayed in the pre-war era. Kent argues that at least two developments contributed to the decline of feminism as a mass movement in the inter-war years. First, the rise of anti-feminism in Britain, which focused on women and work and was concerned with 'persuading' women that they should give up their war jobs and return to their traditional roles. Second, the ideological and institutional divisions within the ranks of organised feminism itself. Following the partial granting of the vote to women in 1918, the National Union of Women's Suffrage Societies underwent reorganisation. It changed its name to the National Union of Societies for Equal Citizenship (NUSEC), and under the leadership of Eleanor Rathbone, it shifted its priorities and embodied the belief that the equality of women with men had been achieved. Feminists could now turn to the needs of women as women and thus issues such as family allowance or endowment, birth control and protective legislation were on the agenda. The 'new feminist' demands thus centred on the role of women in the home and their roles as mothers. Such priorities were an anathema to traditional 'egalitarian' or 'equal rights' feminists, who wanted women to broaden their horizons and look beyond the home. They opposed all protective legislation, including maternity leave, on principle (Lewis 1980).

The issue of protective legislation finally split the first wave women's movement, largely along class lines, with middle-class feminists opposing protective legislation and working class feminists supporting it (Banks 1981). By the end of the 1920s, equal rights feminists were no longer dominant within the women's movement. However, throughout the 1920s, the NUSEC acted with the Women's Freedom League and the Six Point Group to ensure that women's issues were constantly brought to the attention of Parliament. They continued to fight for equal suffrage, and also for the equal guardianship of children, the opening of the legal profession to women, equal pay, equal standards of morality, and a widow's pension plan (Banks 1981: 163–4). In the context of the 1930s, a decade of depression and unemployment and concerns over a declining population, it was the 'new feminism' that gained pre-eminence, with its emphasis on women's maternal role and the contribution this enabled them to make to social welfare (Randall 1982; Lewis 1980). This divergence of the two feminisms in the 1920s and 1930s marks the 'subsiding' of the first wave in Britain.

This account of developments in late nineteenth- and early twentieth-century British feminism suggests that the analogy between the action of waves and the rise and fall of feminism has its uses. It draws attention to the trough and peak, and further trough, of feminist thought and activism during this period. However, the wave analogy should not be used uncritically. It can lead to attention being overly focused on the 'crest' of the wave, on the periods of successful growth and mass activity, at the expense of the recognition due to important feminist analyses, feminist activists and real achievements that occurred both before and after the first wave, and before the onset of the second wave in the 1960s (Spender 1983). Further, the wave analogy may encourage an understanding that the cycle of rise and fall of feminism is, for whatever reason, an inevitable and unbreakable one (Code 2000).

**See also:** *feminisms, second wave feminism, third wave feminism*

### FURTHER READING

A first-hand account of British feminism of the first wave is given by Strachey (1978 [1928]), whilst Liddington and Norris' (1978) account has the benefit of a longer historical perspective. Bolt (1995) looks at first wave feminism in England and the USA, while international developments in first wave feminism are covered in volumes edited by Daley and Nolan (1994) and Sarah (1982).

# gender

The concept of gender, as we now use it came into common parlance during the early 1970s. It was used as an analytical category to draw a line of demarcation between biological sex differences and the way these are used to inform behaviours and competencies, which are then assigned as either 'masculine' or 'feminine'. The purpose of affirming a sex/gender distinction was to argue that the actual physical or mental effects of biological difference had been exaggerated to maintain a patriarchal system of power and to create a consciousness among women that they were naturally better suited to 'domestic' roles. In a post-industrial society those physiological sex differences which do exist become arguably even less significant, and the handicap to women of childbirth is substantially lessened by the existence of effective contraception and pain relief in labour. Moreover, women are generally long outliving their reproductive functions, and so a much smaller proportion of their life is defined by this. Ann Oakley's pathfinding text, *Sex, Gender and Society* (1972) lays the ground for further exploration of the construction of gender. She notes how Western cultures seem most prone to exaggeration of gender differences and argues that 'the "social efficiency" of our present gender roles centres round women's role as housewife and mother. There is also the more vaguely conceived belief that any tampering with these roles would diminish happiness, but this type of argument has a blatantly disreputable history and should have been discarded long ago' (Oakley 1972: 192).

This was not the first time that such distinctions had been made – indeed they were very much the stuff of anthropology, psychoanalysis and medical research; significantly for feminism, Simone de Beauvoir had explored this distinction in *The Second Sex* two decades previously with her statement that 'One is not born, but rather becomes, a woman' (de Beauvoir 1972: 295). De Beauvoir's discussion makes clear the ways in which gender differences are set in hierarchical opposition, where the masculine principle is always the favoured 'norm' and the feminine one becomes positioned as 'Other'. For de Beauvoir femininity can only be defined as lack – 'between male and eunuch' (de Beauvoir 1972: 295), so that civilisation was masculine to its very depths, and women the continual outsiders.

The majority of feminists in the 1970s seemed to embrace the notion of gender as 'construct' and popular youth culture seemed to endorse this in the 1970s' passion for 'unisex' clothing. However, Shulamith Firestone is one exception who suggested in *The Dialectic of Sex* (1970) that patriarchy exploits women's biological capacity to reproduce as their essential weakness. The only way for women to break away from the oppression, she argues, is to use technological advances to free themselves from the burden of childbirth. Moreover, she advocates breaking down the biological bond between mothers and children and establishing communes where monogamy and the nuclear family are things of the past.

Few feminists were ultimately sympathetic to Firestone's view of childbirth and the mother–child bond – not least because technology and its uses were and still are firmly in the hands of men. Those feminists, such as cultural feminists, who questioned whether all key differences are an effect of culture rather than biology, preferred to value and celebrate the mothering role as evidence of women's 'natural' disposition towards nurturance and pacificism, and would be loath to relinquish it even if they could.

As feminism matures, 'gender slips uneasily between being merely another word for sex and being a contested political term' (Oakley in Oakley and Mitchell 1997: 30). Oakley argues that backlash writings return gender to a close association with the biological or natural, in order to suggest that much of feminist discourse was straining against forces that were, after all, ineluctable. For her the conceptualisation of gender is the key cornerstone of second wave feminism and its major strength – attempts to discredit it are at the heart of backlash agendas precisely *because* of its success as an analytical term. In colloquial usage, however, there is a constant slippage between sex and gender so that, for example, people are generally asked to declare their 'gender' instead of sex on an application form (Oakley in Oakley and Mitchell 1997: 51).

Recent writings on sex and gender suggest that feminism has relied upon too great a polarisation of the sex/gender distinctions, observing that the meanings attached to sex differences are themselves socially constructed and changeable, in that we understand them and attach different consequences to these biological 'facts' within our own cultural historical contexts. More recent gene research also attempts to argue that biology does contribute to some behavioural characteristics and the example of research on transgendered individuals reinforces this (given that many transgendered people characterise their sense of something being wrong with them as being trapped in the wrong body).

Moira Gatens makes the point that evidence 'that the male body and the female body have quite different social value and significance cannot help but have a marked effect on male and female consciousness' (1996: 9). Certain bodily events, she argues, are likely to take on huge significance, and particularly so if they only occur to one sex: she cites the example of menstruation. She also makes the point that masculinity is not valued *per se* unless being 'performed' by a biological male: hence the male body itself is imbued in our culture with the mythology of supremacy, of being the human 'norm'. Judith Butler's theorisation about gender introduces this notion of performativity – the idea that gender is involuntarily 'performed' within the dominant discourses of heteroreality, which only deliberately subversive performances like drag can successfully undermine. Butler's conception of gender is perhaps the most radical of all, taking as she does a Foucauldian model, and asserting that all identity categories 'are in fact the *effects* of institutions, practices, discourses with multiple and diffuse points of origin' (Butler 1990: ix). She argues further that 'the sex/gender distinction suggests a radical discontinuity between sexed bodies and culturally constructed genders. Assuming for the moment the stability of binary sex, it does not follow that the construction of "men" will accrue exclusively to the bodies of males or that "women" will interpret only female bodies' (Butler 1990: 6).

This approach questions the whole way we make appeals to identity. The concept of gender as performance suggests a level of free play with gender categories that we enter into socially. The result is that individuals have the potential to create 'gender trouble' and challenge the way discourse establishes and reinforces certain meanings and 'institutions', such as that of 'compulsory heterosexuality'. Butler's most radical deconstruction of the sex/gender distinction has been embraced in particular by queer theorists and third wave feminists. However, Butler has more recently denied that performativity allows the degree of 'free play' with gender that some of these theorists have suggested (Butler in Phelan 1997). In the wider world, there remain constant shifts between conceptualisations of the human being as controlled by either predominantly biological or social forces. This is most marked by a return of popular science tracts which, using a quasi-Darwinian logic, suggest powerfully that our biology is once again our destiny. The substantial shifts in women's lives and expectations since the 1960s show just how malleable the category of femininity is; whether masculinity has shown itself to be quite so elastic, is open to question.

**See also:** *body, gendered, gender order, queer theory, third wave feminism*

### FURTHER READING

Ann Oakley's pioneering study *Sex, Gender and Society* (1972) still makes for fascinating reading and subsequent work such as her chapter in Oakley and Mitchell (1997) updates key debates. Firestone's provocative *The Dialectic of Sex* (1970) is an example of how sex/gender debates could take on a quite different hue within radical feminism. For recent theoretical perspectives, Gatens (1996) and Butler (1990; 1993) are challenging but worthwhile reads.

# gendered

In simple terms, something is 'gendered' when its character is either masculine or feminine, or when it exhibits patterns of difference by gender. Pink and blue, for example, are gendered colours, the former regarded as 'feminine' and the latter as 'masculine'. Paid work is a gendered institution, in that women and men undertake different forms of paid work (women tend to work part-time, men tend to work full-time), in different types of paid work (say, women in nursing, men in construction), and have different average earnings from paid work; see Crompton 1997). In this sense, to say something is 'gendered', is a way of *describing* it. 'Gendered', though, is also used as a *verb* and therefore gives expression to action, or 'the doing of' gender. As noted by Davies (1996), the shift to using gender as a verb ('to gender', 'gendered', 'gendering', 'engender') is a reflection of changed understandings of gender as an active ongoing process, rather than something that is ready-made and fixed. In this sense, then, something is gendered when it is, in and of itself, actively engaged in social processes that produce and reproduce distinctions between women and men. 'Gendering' and 'gendered' are concepts which 'signify outcomes that are socially constructed and give males advantages over females. They describe the production of assumptions about gender as well as the institutions that

59

are shaped by those assumptions' (Reskin and Padavic 1994: 6).

There are many examples of studies that describe the gendered character of the culture, institutions and organisations of contemporary Western societies. For example, Pilcher (1999) draws together a range of British research evidence that shows the gendered character of education and training, paid work, household work and caring, love and sexuality, body-related technologies, popular media culture, crime and criminal justice, and politics. Lisa Adkins' (1995) study is an example of an approach that focuses more on the processes or practices which make an institution recognisably 'gendered' in its character. Adkins describes her research as concerned with the 'gendering' of the contemporary labour market. 'That is to say, it has as its focus the processes through which power relations between men and women in employment are constituted, and how "advantage and disadvantage, exploitation and control, action and emotion, and meaning and identity are patterned through and in terms of a distinction between male and female" (Acker 1990: 146)' (Adkins 1995: 1). Using the hotel management and leisure park sectors of the British tourist industry as her case studies, Adkins' specific aim is to explore the significance of the family and of heterosexuality in the process of gendering. One of Adkins' main findings was that the very practices of production are themselves gendered. Women and men working in the leisure parks, for example, were required to perform differently in their work, even when they were ostensibly doing the same job. Women, in addition to the tasks they were directly paid to do, also had to be what Adkins calls 'sex-workers', working both for the public and for their male colleagues and bosses. In other words, they were 'required to fulfil conditions which related to the production of an "attractive" female workforce' (1995: 145). This gendering of production practices meant that women and men employed in the leisure parks were *qualitatively* different kinds of workers: 'To be workers, women had to be "attractive" workers and carry out forms of sexualised work, whereas men did not have to do this' (1995: 147). Adkins argues that her research shows that the labour market was gendered *prior* to jobs being differentiated. In other words, women workers in the leisure parks had to fulfil the conditions of being sexualised workers *regardless* of their specific occupation.

The move from thinking about gender as a noun, to a focus on the way distinctions between men and women are actively reproduced through 'gendering' processes and 'gendered' practices has usefully encouraged the sort of analyses represented by Adkins' work. However, more remains to be done on gendering, including variations by sexuality, social class, and 'race'. While the concepts of 'gendering' and 'engender(ed)' give a clear emphasis to the ongoing, processual quality of gender relations, a more cautious use of 'gendered' might be advisable. It suggests an action already taken place, in the past, and so may work to damage the understanding of gender relations as not being 'ready-made', fixed and unchanging.

**See also:** *gender, gender order, gender segregation*

### FURTHER READING

Kirkham's (1996) *The Gendered Object* examines the ways objects of everyday life are made 'appropriate' for women and for men. For an account of gender as practice and process, see Connell (1987).

---

# gender order

---

The gender order is a patterned system of ideological and material practices, performed by individuals in a society, through which power relations between women and men are made, and remade, as meaningful. It is through the gender order of a society that forms or codes of masculinities and femininities are created and recreated, and relations between them are organised.

The concept of the gender order was first developed by Jill Matthews (1984), in her study of the historical construction of femininity. According to Matthews, the idea of the gender order gives recognition to the fact that every known society distinguishes between women and men, while allowing for variations in the nature of the distinctions drawn. 'As systematic ways of creating social women and men, and of ordering and patterning relations between them, it is not logically necessary that gender orders should be hierarchical, inequitable or oppressive' (1984: 13). Matthews draws an analogy with the concept of the economic order or mode, which as a systematic ordering of people's relationship to the means of production and consumption, may be capitalist, feudal or communist in its specific content.

Likewise, a gender order could be egalitarian or even matriarchal, rather than patriarchal. For Matthews, the concept of the gender order, unlike the concept of patriarchy, enables a distinction to be made between the general *form* of gender relations and their specific *content*. This approach counters tendencies to universalism: the existence of patriarchy cannot be assumed but must be proven for each specific society (1984: 14). Rather than portraying women and men as puppets of a patriarchal system, the approach also recognises the active part played by individuals in the creation and recreation of gender relations, and thereby allows for the possibility of social change. As Matthews writes:

> the specific nature or content of any gender order is constantly in process, being formed and changed. It is fashioned by actions of individuals who are themselves formed in that interaction. It is created in the struggles and power strategies and contradictions and unintended consequences of a multitude of social groups and individuals and interests . . . The femininity and masculinity that are forged of these countervailing forces are never constant but always changing and, more often than not, internally inconsistent if not contradictory. (1984: 14–15)

Connell (1987; 1995) has integrated the concept of the gender order into his social theory of gender, and for this reason, the concept has become more closely associated with Connell than with Matthews. For Connell, the relationship between the body and gender is a central issue for gender theory. He argues that gender is the outcome of recurrent interpretations of, and definitions placed upon, the reproductive and sexual capacities of the human body. Femininities and masculinities are the multiple effects of these ongoing interpretations and definitions, impacting upon bodies, influencing personalities and shaping culture and institutions. In Connell's analysis, gender is a reoccurring creation of human agency, which at an institutional and structural level also acts to constrain individual agency. For Connell, empirical research has uncovered three major structures of gender relations, or the major ways in which the agency or practice of women and men is constrained. The three structures, of labour, power and cathexis (concerned with emotional relationships, including sexuality) constantly interweave with each other creating the 'gender order', or the overall structure of gender relations in a particular society, at a particular time in history.

For Connell, as for Matthews (1984), gender relations are regarded as in process, the outcome of human practice or agency, subject to resistance as well as conformity, contestation as well as acceptance. All this means that gender relations are open to disruption and change. Connell argues that there are 'crisis tendencies' in the contemporary gender order of the industrialised world. For example, in family relationships, Connell says that state policies have disrupted the legitimacy of men's domination over women (via laws on divorce, domestic violence and rape within marriage, independent pensions and taxation for married women, for example). Connell also identifies a tendency towards a crisis of sexuality, where forms of heterosexuality which privilege men over women have come under pressure from women's more assertive sexuality and from gay sexuality. A further example of a tendency toward crisis in the gender order is the joining together of women and men in groups which challenge the current patriarchal gender order, such as women's liberation movements, gay liberation, and anti-sexist politics among heterosexual men. In Connell's view, it is through individuals and groups, collectively and on a mass scale, 'prising open' the crisis tendencies in the contemporary gender order that gender inequality, along with other forms of inequality, can be eradicated.

Marshall (1994) finds the concept of the gender order valuable for the analysis of gender, particularly for understanding the relationship between individual gendered subjectivities and gender as a social structure. For Marshall, the gender order provides 'the mode of interpretation' through which individuals construct an embodied subjective and social identity. For Marshall, though, a fuller account is needed of the formation of gendered subjectivities in the configuration of power relations, especially in relation to understanding why it is that knowledgeable, acting subjects may nonetheless tend to participate in the legitimation of conditions that reproduce their position (1994: 117).

In evaluating the concept of the gender order, critics point to its advantages over the concept of patriarchy. Pollert (1996), for example, describes Connell's theory of the gender order as open to more diversity than patriarchy, and through its emphasis on gender as an ongoing process, as more adequately registering human agency. Similarly, Marshall writes that the approach allows a description of a society as patriarchal, 'without lapsing into the trans-historical, agent-less conception of "patriarchy"' (1994: 116). For some critics, however, the concept of the gender order has not overcome the problem of how to theorise gender in relation to class and 'race'. For example, West argues that Connell's (1987) approach fails to include either race or ethnicity as key concepts, an omission that may lead some critics to 'dismiss his contribution as a "white social theory of gender"' (1989: 1489). Pollert criticises Connell's theory of the gender order for its 'dualist' conception of gender and class, arguing that it is based on a diffuse, Foucauldian conception of power relations as detached from class relations (1996: 650). Despite a lack of clarity around the interrelations between gender, class and 'race', other critics (Maharaj 1995; Pilcher 1999) feel that Connell's theory of the gender order goes some way toward satisfying the criteria of a postmodern gender theory (as set out by,

63

for example, Fraser and Nicolson 1989), in that it is explicitly historical and attuned to cultural specificity in terms of time, place and diversity.

**See also:** *femininities, masculinity/masculinities, patriarchy, power*

### FURTHER READING

Connell develops his ideas on crisis tendencies in the gender order in his (1995) examination of changing masculinities. Pilcher (1998) examines Connell's theory of the gender order in the context of other gender theories, while a collection edited by Messner and Sabo (1990) is illustrative of the influence Connell's treatment of the gender order has had, particularly in masculinity studies.

# gender segregation

Gender segregation occurs when women and men are located separately from one another, while otherwise participating in a broadly similar set of activities. For example, in some countries, while there may be educational provision for both boys and girls, rather than being educated together in the same institutional location, they are instead deliberately segregated on the grounds of gender and are educated separately, in 'single-sex' schools or universities. Gender segregation in education can also be said to occur in the way that boys and girls often study different subjects. This is a example of gender segregation which may arise, not as the result of deliberate, legal and/or traditional policies of segregation, but rather as the outcome of a complex number of factors, not least the 'choices' made by individuals themselves. In contemporary Britain, as in many other Western industrial societies, paid work is also segregated by gender. The separation is not complete, but a range of evidence shows that women and men tend to engage in different types of jobs, and/or at different levels within job hierarchies, with important consequences for pay, and for prospects for training and promotion, among other things. Given the importance of paid work for the material and other key benefits it brings, many writers have focused on gender segregation in paid work in their analyses of power inequalities between women and men.

In an article first published in 1976, Hartmann (1982) identifies job segregation as the 'primary mechanism in capitalist society that maintains the superiority of men over women' (1982: 448). In development of her theoretical explanation of the origins of job segregation, Hartmann highlights the interests and activities of men as a group. Hartmann argues that, before the development of capitalism, a patriarchal system was established in which men controlled the labour power of women and children in the family. Through this, men learned the techniques of hierarchical organisation and control. As societies developed and became more complex, it became more difficult for men to maintain their power over women. According to Hartmann, men's strategy was to draw on the techniques of hierarchical organisation and control, which had already established women's domestic role, to create a 'sex-ordered division of labour in the wage labour system' of capitalism (1982: 447). In Hartmann's account, there is a 'mutual accommodation' between patriarchy and capitalism, which results in a 'vicious circle' of disadvantage for women. Job segregation invariably means that it is men who hold the jobs with greater material rewards, not least relatively high wages, compared to women. The lower wages earned by women in their jobs 'keep women dependent on men because they encourage women to marry. Married women must perform domestic chores for their husbands . . . This domestic division of labour, in turn, acts to weaken women's position in the labour market. Thus, the hierarchical domestic division of labour is perpetuated by the labour market, and vice versa' (1982: 448).

Hartmann's emphasis on the interrelations between the gendered division of labour in the home and the gendered nature of paid work is shared by many writers. However, her argument that job segregation is the outcome of intentional patriarchal strategies against women has been criticised. Crompton (1997), for example, draws on the historical analyses of Humphries (1984) to suggest that the exclusion of women from paid work can also be seen as an aspect of class politics, part of a broader struggle in which the working class aimed to control the supply of labour, and its price, to capitalists. Crompton herself favours neither Hartmann's emphasis on men and patriarchy nor Humphries' emphasis on class and capitalism. Instead, she argues that explanations 'of the structuring of the gender division of labour' should be multi-stranded (1997: 14). A broader approach, giving recognition to the complex range of factors which contribute to gender segregation, is also favoured by MacEwen Scott (1994). In her overview of the findings of a major British research programme on gender segregation, she notes that 'the primacy of the male breadwinner role continues to structure the labour market in a variety of ways, mainly through the material and ideological differentiation of the labour supply. In many cases, this is translated into employment structures and payment systems, which further rigidifies segmentation (e.g. part-time work). However, gender segregation is not based solely on primary or secondary earner status. There is much evidence that naturalistic beliefs about gender . . . play a fundamental role in the sex-typing of jobs . . . Patterns of gender segregation are sustained by "tradition" as much as by the rational strategies of individual employers and employees' (1994: 35).

An important reference point in the discussion of gender segregation in paid work is Hakim's (1979) paper for the British government's Department of Employment. In it, Hakim defines 'occupational segregation' as that which exists when 'men and women do different kinds of work, so that one can speak of two separate labour forces, one male and one female, which are not in competition with each other for the same jobs' (1979: 1). Hakim identifies two dimensions of occupational segregation. First, horizontal segregation where women and men are found in different types of occupations. Horizontal segregation is illustrated by the concentration or 'crowding' of women and men in different occupations. For example, in Britain in 2001, 24 per cent of women of working age in employment worked in administrative and secretarial occupations, compared to just 5 per cent of men. Of men of working age in employment, 20 per cent worked in skilled trades, compared to just 2 per cent of women (Twomey 2002). The second form of segregation identified by Hakim is vertical segregation, whereby women and men hold different positions in occupational hierarchies, with men tending to be at the higher and women at the lower levels. For example, in the British Civil Service in 2000, 50 per cent of the permanent staff were women, but they represented 62 per cent of the lowest grade staff and only 20 per cent of staff at the Senior Civil Servant level (Cabinet Office 2001). In her paper, Hakim uses census and large-scale survey data to undertake a comparative study of occupational segregation in Britain, the United States and other countries. Her focus is on whether or not the increased labour force participation of women since the early twentieth century has also resulted in a decrease in occupational segregation. Her analyses show that, while there had been some reduction in horizontal segregation, this was offset by increases in vertical segregation. According to Hakim, therefore, there was no overall decrease in the level of occupational segregation for the period of her study (although see Walby 1997 for a critique).

MacEwen (1994) points to the difficulties of defining and measuring gender segregation in paid work (see also Walby 1997). She notes that segregation can be measured objectively or subjectively. An objective measurement uses census or survey data to calculate the ratio of women to men in an occupation (as in Hakim's study, above). While this allows for a precise measurement of the degree of segregation, the problem is that the unit of measurement is the occupation rather than the job. Segregation is at the most extreme at the level of jobs. Since occupations are clusters or aggregates of jobs, this grouping together of jobs may obscure the full extent of segregation. For example, the occupation of 'teacher' obscures the pattern that women predominate as teachers in primary schools and men in secondary schools. Similarly, the occupational classification 'cleaner' obscures the predominance of men as 'street cleaners' and women as 'office cleaners' (MacEwen 1994: 5). In contrast, subjective measures of segregation ask about job segregation directly. Thus, interviewees in one major survey were asked the following question: 'In general, is your type of job done almost exclusively by men, mainly by men, by a fairly equal mixture of men and women, mainly by women, or almost exclusively by women?' (MacEwen 1994: 6). Although this measure also has its problems, it is argued that it gives a more accurate measure of segregation because the focus is on the more direct level of a person's job. Crompton (1997) also notes the difficulties of measuring segregation in paid work. For example, she suggests that the apparently simple distinction between horizontal and vertical segregation is in practice quite problematic. Crompton uses the example of clerks and managers. These are classed as different occupations (horizontally segregated) but since clerks are also subordinate to managers, they are also vertically segregated. Given that the majority of those in clerical occupations are women, Crompton asks, is this a reflection of horizontal or vertical segregation? Her suggestion is that in order to answer this question, it would be necessary to establish whether or not clerical jobs were linked to managerial jobs in a promotional hierarchy (1997: 44). Crompton also points to the difficulties of undertaking international comparisons of segregation in paid work. In Scandinavian countries, as in Britain, women are concentrated in the caring professions associated with welfare-state provision. However, unlike in Britain, these 'women's' jobs are relatively well paid and so the 'pay gap' between women and men in Scandinavian countries is lower than in Britain. 'In short, as far as women's equality is concerned, for practical purposes the problem is not so much occupational segregation as such, but the fact that women are poorly paid for what they do' (1997: 44).

**See also:** *domestic division of labour*

**FURTHER READING**

Cole (1998) undertakes a comparative analysis of gender segregation in Polish and American higher education. She shows that levels of gender segregation have changed and that this is a reflection of the shifts in gendered power relations within each country. Walby (1997) looks at sex segregation in local labour markets, in a critique of Hakim's argument that there have been no significant changes in occupational segregation during the twentieth century. For general statistics on gender segregation in Britain, see the web page of the Equal Opportunities Commission, www.eoc.org.uk.

# heterosexism

The word 'heterosexism' derives directly from the feminist creation of the term 'sexism' during the late 1960s. The first usage of the term heterosexism is given as 1979 by the Oxford English Dictionary and it is defined as 'prejudice and antagonism shown by heterosexual persons towards homosexuals; discrimination against homosexuals' (*OED* online). The felt necessity for the addition 'hetero' to sexism indicated the increasing tendency within feminism to see gendered inequalities in society as equally informed by the oppressive structures of racism and homophobia. It also indicates that lesbian feminists in particular still felt that much of feminist discourse accepted the centrality of 'heteroreality'. Gay and lesbian groups within and outside feminism began to feel the need to distinguish between sexism – directed at all women – and heterosexism, which indicates the prejudicial treatment of gay and lesbian individuals and the assumption that heterosexuality is the sexual choice of all people. The latter point, which takes us beyond the basic *OED* definition, is crucial to understanding why heterosexism is such an important concept. The concern, particularly from gay and lesbian groups, was that even if a patriarchal ideology could be successfully challenged, such a revolution in consciousness would not necessarily alter deeply entrenched homophobic prejudices.

As Diane Richardson states, 'heterosexuality infuses the social realm; it represents the idea of normal behaviour which is central to the concept of the social and the process of socialisation into the social realm' (1996: 13).

She goes on to acknowledge that heterosexuality is gendered and also acts principally to socialise women into acceptance of monogamous nuclear family life. In other words, the social institutions that endorse heterosexuality – marriage and family – come to define it. This is in contrast to the way 'homosexuality' is generally defined, which is primarily in terms of sexual identification – sexual practices, age of consent (for gay men) and intimate relationships. From this it is clear that heterosexuality, rather than being regarded as a set of sexual practices or preferences expressed by a clearly defined group, is simply related to 'normality', whereas homosexuality is expressed in terms of deviance, as if an individual's life is defined by their sexuality. This demonstrates that the opposite sides of this binary are perceived in entirely different ways – one where sexuality is incidental, a part of the wider picture, the other where it comes to define everything and informs negative discourses about gays and lesbians.

One of the most controversial essays on this theme is Adrienne Rich's (1980) 'Compulsory Heterosexuality and Lesbian Existence'. The intention behind the essay was, as she says in her preface, 'for feminists to find it less possible to read, write, or teach from a perspective of unexamined heterocentricity' (Rich 1986: 24) At the heart of Rich's argument lies the desire to show that heterosexuality or lesbianism are not 'choices' made equally available but that heterosexuality carries with it the assurance of normality. Unless an individual 'comes out' and asserts their homosexuality, they are assumed to be heterosexual. In this way Rich shows the extent to which heterosexuality acts as an institution rather than a sexual choice or practice. For women in particular Rich asserts that heterosexuality is an instrument of patriarchal power, which shapes their lives in ways that are perhaps yet to be analysed and means that heterosexuality is seen not only as the most desirable, but the inevitable journey in a woman's life.

In this way Rich implies that practices that entail or have historically entailed physical force, such as rape, beating, clitorodectomy, and those which rely on the shaping and control of consciousness of the self – such as the perpetuation of romance narratives in literature, art and film – shore up the institution of heterosexuality, either by the promise of happiness or implied threat of punishment. The popular portrayal of the male sex drive as all-consuming and in need of satisfaction once triggered is, Rich asserts, a contributory factor in the ways women are led to accept different sexual identities and controls for themselves than for men. For Rich, 'the failure to examine heterosexuality as an institution is like failing to admit that the economic system called capitalism or the caste system of racism is maintained by a variety of forces, including both physical violence and false consciousness' (1986: 51).

Crucially Rich implies that compulsory heterosexuality infects feminist scholarship and that, until it is subjected to further critical scrutiny, feminist discourse remains predominantly heterosexist. At key points and most controversially she seems to suggest that becoming a lesbian is politically superior to remaining heterosexual because there is 'a *nascent* feminist political content in the act of choosing a woman lover or life partner in the face of institutionalised heterosexuality' (Rich 1986: 66).

For some radical feminists it is implied that heterosexism delegitimates heterosexual intercourse altogether. Writers such as Andrea Dworkin and Sheila Jeffreys see all acts of penile penetration of the vagina as re-enactments of men's power, because they regard the act as ineluctably imbued with the symbolic meanings it has taken on in the past. Jeffreys finds it 'difficult to imagine what shape a woman's desire for a man would take in the absence of eroticised power difference since it is precisely this which provides the excitement of heterosexuality today' (Jeffreys 1990: 316). However, to suggest that heterosexual women can only enjoy penetrative sex by eroticisation of their subordination is to affirm that it is not possible to resist or subvert these dominant meanings and establish more egalitarian principles to sexual practices.

Of course the lack of definition of heterosexual practices allows heterosexuality's unquestioned dominance as an institution since it encompasses the very fabric of life. As Carol Smart suggests, '[h]eterosexual identity is therefore akin to a white colonial identity. It entails an effortless superiority, a moral rectitude, a defeat of the emotional and the neurotic by the power of the unconscious struggle and, of course, the certain knowledge of masculine superiority' (Smart in Richardson 1996: 173).

As the above discussion demonstrates, it is impossible to define heterosexism without looking at some of the debates around heterosexuality within feminism. Rich's pathbreaking essay prompted straight feminists to analyse what heterosexual identity for women means and Kitzinger and Wilkinson's collection tried to get straight women to articulate exactly what 'being' heterosexual was like. From this perspective, combating heterosexism wasn't just about acknowledging its hegemony, but was about being honest about the possible tensions between heterosexuality and feminism. As Fuss says, '[f]or heterosexuality to achieve the status of the "compulsory", it must present itself as a practice governed by some internal necessity. The language and law that regulate the establishment of heterosexuality as both an identity and an institution, both a practice and a system, are the language and law of defense and protection' (1991: 2). As Fuss implies, the 'homo' is always exterior and marginal to the 'hetero', but yet necessary to its very definition and existence. Looking at lesbian identity, Judith Butler reflects that 'compulsory heterosexuality sets itself up as the original, the true, the authentic; the norm that determines the real implies that "being" lesbian is always a kind of miming, a vain effort to participate in the phantasmatic plenitude of naturalised heterosexuality which will always and only fail' (Butler in Fuss 1991: 20–1). So nervous were early radical lesbian feminists of 'miming' heterosexuality in any way, there was a virtual taboo until the late 1980s on the discussion of practices or identities which reflected back to heterosexuality – for example, butch and femme or SM (sadomasochism).

Heterosexism is a term that is now used more broadly to show how the discourses of public life assume the norm of a certain kind of life-style and endorse it morally and materially. More and more in opposition to this, lesbian, gay, bisexual and transgendered groups are fighting for equal rights 'in relation to age of consent laws, to healthcare, rights associated with legal recognition of domestic partnerships, including the right to marry, immigration rights, parenting rights and so on' (Richardson 2000: 9).

It is also likely to be the case that a large number of heterosexuals themselves do not actively subscribe or profit from the institutions which support heterosexuality and may actually feel suffocated by the normative behaviours and values it assumes.

**See also:** *sexuality*

### FURTHER READING

Much discussion of heterosexism emerges in the work of gay and lesbian theorists, and Fuss (1991) is a good collection to start with. Rich's essay 'Compulsory Heterosexuality and Lesbian Existence' (Rich [1980] 1986) is essential reading to understand how contemporary debates on heterosexuality and heterosexism have been shaped. Richardson (2000) provides an update on contemporary debates on sexuality in general.

71

# identity politics/the politics of identity

The utopian vision of 'sisterhood' – the collecting together of all women under the same political banner – was in part responsible for the burgeoning interest in feminism and the emergent Women's Liberation Movement. It was inevitably going to come under fire once more women who weren't white, middle class, heterosexual and university-educated became involved, and the differences *between* women came to be seen as of equal importance as their similarities. Identity politics was the term used to describe, at times, bitter disputes between different feminist groups:

> The rage, the sensitivity, and the overwhelming, omnipresent nature of 'the enemy' drove parts of the women's movement into ideological rigidities, and the movement splintered as it grew. Who could say what was *the* central issue: equal pay? abortion? the nuclear family? lesbianism? welfare policies? capitalism? Groups formed around particular issues, constituencies and political styles, many sure that they had found the key to women's liberation. After 1970, women's liberation groups in all parts of the country suffered painful splits variously defined as politico-feminist, gay/straight, anti-imperialist/radical feminist. (Evans 1979: 225)

As Evans implies, it wasn't just the individual identity and background of participants that could split the groups and eventually the movement: conflicts about what a feminist identity *should* mean became just as important, as well as the question of who had the right to decide. At its worst this could lead to some fairly prescriptive opinions, which served to undermine the image of feminism as a broad-based movement.

It could be argued that identity politics is inscribed in the very terms of the emergent Women's Liberation Movement. If everyone's opinion is equally valid, who is to mediate between them to form a shared agenda? This open-house policy is aired in the influential British feminist magazine, *Shrew*:

> Everyone is encouraged to have their own ideas about how the movement should be run, and what it is to fight for. Indeed, those without ideas leave, since you cannot survive in W.L. [Women's Liberation] if you like to be fed your ideas. Argument with others is one good way of strengthening one's views, and so the ideological battles of W.L. are a reasonably effective alternative to the doctrinaire methods used by

72

many liberation movements for building up adherence to the ideology. The disadvantage of the W.L. method is that opposing ideas are strengthened as a result of the battles and that a coming together is made more unlikely the more the process snowballs. (Anon 1971: 10)

This is an early defence of the power of forceful debate, although one can imagine that some would retreat, not because they lacked their own ideas, but because those more accomplished at arguing were likely to win the round.

For some groups the politics of identity is about making a direct challenge to the dominance of other interest groups within feminism. So the Combahee River Collective state that '[t]his focus upon our own oppression is embodied in the concept of identity politics. We believe that the most profound and potentially the most radical politics come directly out of our own identity, as opposed to working to end somebody else's oppression' (in Nicholson 1997: 65). bell hooks agrees that 'sisterhood' as a concept was dominated by the definitions of bourgeois white women and based erroneously on the idea of common oppression – 'the emphasis on Sisterhood was often seen as the emotional appeal masking the opportunism of manipulative bourgeois white women. It was seen as a cover-up hiding the fact that many women exploit and oppress other women' (hooks 1986: 127–8). She felt that the inevitable result of identity politics was the configuration of women's groups whose members had similar backgrounds, so that there would be even less opportunity to frame a realistic challenge to oppression. For hooks and a number of black feminists, racism was intertwined with sexist oppression and if white women weren't struggling against racism they were denying the terms of their own privileges. Therefore, it is the racist socialisation of white women that needs further scrutiny, in that they otherwise assume they make better leaders and spokespeople for the movement. Lesbian feminists also had to juggle between two oppressed identities and also between a vying sexual identity framed by the discourse of social constructionism versus a 'biological' one which suggests a transhistorical lesbian 'essence' and underpins the idea of 'gay pride' or 'gay culture' (see Fuss 1989: 97–112). Not only are they constantly challenging their marginalisation in the women's movement (since the days when Betty Friedan, founder of the US National Organisation for Women (NOW), dubbed them the 'Lavender Menace'), their sense of sexual identity is fraught with difficulty.

It does not seem to be the case that there was ever a time when feminism was marked by a consensus, even though it was, and is, common to preface a remark with 'as a feminist . . .' (see Delmar in Mitchell and Oakley 1986: 8–33), but the effects of difference have been interpreted in more or less negative terms as the movement has matured. By the 1980s many felt that identity politics was stifling feminism with people feeling obliged to announce their own identity before making any statement and risking someone more 'oppressed' than them denying them the right to speak. Rather than celebrating heterogeneity in the way that the anonymous contributor to *Shrew* magazine suggests, feminists were more inclined to see the positing of differences as the stumbling blocks to feminism's future. The worst examples of identity politics were manifested in the fierce fighting and name-calling between the anti-porn and the libertarian anti-censorship lobbies. For Segal it was the increasingly torturous debates around heterosexuality that 'produced the final and fundamental rift between feminists at the end of the 1970s and which shattered any potential unity about the nature, direction and goal of feminism' (Segal 1987: 65).

It wasn't just the fact of differences between women, but how they were interpreted, used, and how it made people feel that there was a hierarchy of authenticity – a competition whereby some people were seen as more legitimately oppressed than others. What some, like Segal, saw as the closing down of the range of feminist debates also prompted feelings of alienation, that the women's movement had taken a wrong turning.

Postmodern and post-structuralist theories offer some relief from the endless cycle of identity politics since the idea of an essential identity is regarded as belonging to a past wedded to 'grand narratives' of truth and progress. During the 1980s the term 'woman' itself came to be seen as part of the problem. From a post-structuralist point of view, diverse women were trying to lay claim to an identity which is never stable in its range of meanings, but always slippery and culturally and historically diverse. For Monique Wittig the radicalism of the lesbian social position is that they can refuse to be a 'woman': '"Woman" is there to confuse us, to hide the reality, "women". In order to be aware of being a class and to become a class we first have to kill the myth of "woman" including its most seductive aspects' (Wittig 1992: 16). Others would argue that heterosexual feminists had much to learn from this perspective – that to refuse to be a 'woman' is to deny the dominant discourses that attempt to frame our selves in the interest of a hostile culture. Moreover denying the 'woman', as Wittig suggests, involves acknowledging the existence of 'women' in all their plurality (many critics would still want 'woman' to remain the organising feminist political principle – see also further discussions under 'Difference' and 'Essentialism'). For Judith Butler,

74

establishing a foundational identity to mobilise feminist politics is actually to restrict the possibilities of new unthought-of identities that feminism might make realities (Butler 1990: 147). In the 1990s, queer theory further challenged the politics of identity by denying the need for fixed sexual identities, identifying 'queer' as the badge of the sexual radical. Queer is a way of denying the normalcy of heterosexuality by blurring the gay/straight binary opposition and celebrating the plurality of responses that are made available. It's playfully disruptive of the old boundaries, yet some feminists remain sceptical of its political reach.

For hooks, as for many other veteran feminists, the perception of identity politics as either avoidable or necessarily negative was second wave feminism's first mistake: '[w]omen do not need to eradicate difference to feel solidarity. We do not need to share common oppression to fight equally to end oppression' (hooks 1986: 138).

**See also:** *difference, essentialism, queer theory*

### FURTHER READING

Either Evans (1979) or Echols (1989) gives a flavour of tensions in the early US Women's Liberation Movement; Segal (1987) at times controversially covers some of these issues from a largely British perspective. Hooks's (1986) essay is passionately argued and extremely accessible, whereas Butler (1990) and Wittig (1992) cover some of the theoretical ground.

# ideology

Ideology was a term used in Marxist theory to show how the worker under capitalism might be living in a state of false consciousness or distorted reality about their relations to capital. The argument went that once they began to see these relations as they really are – ones of oppression and exploitation – then a class-based revolution could overthrow capitalism by seizing the means of production. Louis Althusser's theoretical perspectives on ideology attributed to it a more complex role, so that it moves from 'false consciousness' to a means of representing reality where the act of representing is obscured. The emphasis is on the relationship of ideology to lived experience, and in this light ideology could be defined as the representation of the imaginary relationship of individuals to the real conditions of their existence. This imaginary relationship is portrayed by the effects of ideology as if it were the only possible reality – the idea being that ideology seeks to justify present conditions of existence by portraying them as entirely natural, as unable to safely be otherwise, while also educating children into 'seeing' things this way. The success of ideological processes, therefore, lies in the ways in which they conceal their own unstable cultural/historical specificity under the guise of universal, transhistorical, natural forms of behaviour.

The above characteristics primarily represent so-called 'dominant' ideology – that system of beliefs which holds sway and determines most people's view of the social order, but there are also oppositional ideologies (e.g. Marxism, feminism) which seek to change people's consciousness, by replacing the dominant version of the 'real' conditions of existence with their own. In this sense all representations of reality are mediated through ideology, and this viewpoint would hold up to question the claim that any expressed viewpoint could take up a position of ideological neutrality.

Althusser problematised the Marxist theory of the maintenance of relations of production under capitalism. In his essay 'Ideology and the Ideological State Apparatuses' he attempts to modify the classic Marxian account of the status of superstructure (law and the state/ideology) as subordinate to the infrastructure (economic base). Althusser argues that capital depends on the reproduction of raw material such as labour power to reproduce the conditions of production. In the case of the labourer:

76

> [the] raw materials needed to reproduce them include not only sufficient wages for food, clothing, housing and childrearing, but also an appropriate form of education to prepare them for the work they will end up doing. Not only must education provide the fundamental skills appropriate for labour power to reproduce itself, it must also pass on the skills of citizenship appropriate to their class – rules of morality, civic and professional conscience . . . and ultimately rules of order established by class domination. (Althusser 1984: 6)

In other words 'reproduction' of the labourer includes submission to a code of behaviour which serves the interests of capital but also naturalises the division of labour in its present form. So for Althusser, the material conditions of production are reinforced actively and coercively by a dominant ideology which simultaneously reproduces its own ideological framework as inevitable and immutable.

For Althusser, Ideological State Apparatuses are diverse, plural and operate as 'a certain number of realities which present themselves to the immediate observer in the form of distinct and specialised institutions' (Althusser 1984: 17) as opposed to Repressive State Apparatuses – instruments of actual coercion – which include the law, the police and the army. Althusser's list of Ideological State Apparatuses (ISAs) includes education, the family, the law, politics, trade unions, communications and culture – it is clear that some of these are sites of struggle against a dominant ideological perspective. He implies that ideology has a direct interventional relationship with the material conditions of people's existence and shows how the effects of these ISAs are felt in the private sphere of the home and family – in particular he cites the family and education ISAs as the most effective dominant ideological apparatuses in a mature capitalist formation. He asserts it is in the 'natural' 'apolitical' site of the family that ideology most successfully effaces its own effects. Clearly this model of the effects of the ISAs has application to the key concerns of feminist thought, not least in the way it shows how the public and private spheres come to be separated, and that division (as well as the notion of the private sphere as fenced off from public scrutiny) is presented as natural.

We can see that without a worked-out theory of ideology, early radical feminist perspectives on patriarchy seem crude: 'All men are our policemen, and no organised police force is necessary at this time to keep us in our places. All men enjoy supremacy and take advantage of it to a greater or lesser degree depending on their position in the masculine hierarchy of power' (Dunbar in Morgan 1970: 536). Clearly theories of ideology offer a more nuanced reading of this statement, examining the ways in which 'all' men don't have to actively keep women in their 'place' for most of them to remain there. The process of the ideology of gender that makes appeal to the essential differences of biological sex and builds up a knowledge of acceptable and unacceptable feminine behaviour, which has already been communicated to women through the process of education and gender socialisation within the family, does this most effectively. This representation is, furthermore, replayed by various means in the public domain – through codes of dress, film and TV representations of women, the way 'unfeminine' behaviour by actual women is treated by the press or in the law courts – so that it is constantly reinforced while allowing for subtle shifts by which ideology can also contain contradictions and maintain stability – for example the idea of the 'career woman'.

Theorising about ideology is particularly central to the work of socialist feminists, and Marxism is one male theoretical perspective which has proved attractive to a wide range of feminists because its analysis of the capitalist social formation as predicated upon class conflict appeared amenable to the inclusion of a consideration of gender inequality. Socialist feminists were seeking to find a model of patriarchy which accounted for both its tenacity over the ages set against its adaptability to historical and social change. Feminists have therefore asserted that there is such a thing as a 'patriarchal ideology', which encourages men and women to act in conformity with certain types of behaviour and to have certain life expectations which they act upon in their material lives. Kate Millett's view of socialisation itself anticipates such a view of ideology:

> Sexual politics obtains consent through the 'socialisation' of both sexes to basic patriarchal polities with regard to temperament, role and status. As to status, a pervasive assent to the prejudice of male superiority guarantees superior status in the male, inferior in the female. The first item, temperament, involves the formation of human personality along stereotyped lines of sex category ('masculine' and 'feminine'), based on the needs and values of the dominant group and dictated by what its members cherish in themselves and find convenient in subordinates: aggression, intelligence, force, and efficacy in the male: passivity, ignorance, docility, 'virtue' and ineffectuality in the female. This is complemented by a second factor, sex role, which decrees a consonant and highly elaborate code of conduct, gesture and attitude for each sex. (Millett 1977: 26)

Althusser's concept of subjectivity again seemed to have application for feminists in his view that ideology interpellates individuals as subjects in ways that profoundly affect our material existence – we are 'hailed' as individuals in that we are identified as subjects in the social formation; in this way 'individuality'is regarded by Althusser as an effect of ideology. Althusser maintains that 'the "obviousness" that you and I are subjects – and that that does not cause any problems – is an ideological effect' (1984: 46). In this he is moving away from the humanist view of the individual's essence preceding the subject and questioning the extent to which people are able to 'choose' their subject position in relation to the social order.

Although the concept of subjectivity and notions of interpellation have formed useful tools for feminists, Barrett foresees the 'the concept of ideology being replaced by the terms "discourse" and "subjectivity"' (Barrett 1988: xviii). Foucault's analysis of discursive formations conceives of discourse as an effect of power inscribed in all social relations. He sees relations of power between dominated and dominant as much more unstable and vulnerable than Marx did, but suggests instead that it is these networks of power, which pervade the entire social fabric, that are tenacious and resistant to transformation. Moira Gatens refers to a 'social imaginary' which she asserts can 'refer to those images, symbols, metaphors and representations which help construct various forms of subjectivity' (Gatens 1996: viii), although she states that this view of the social imaginary cannot be used as a substitute for the theory of ideology.

Regardless of whether any of these concepts directly replaces ideology, one problem identified about its use was that it projected a latent 'truth' that the process of ideology was always obliterating. In a period where postmodern perspectives on identity are part of the fabric of modern feminism, this reference back, if only in theory, to an essential truth is troublesome. Michèle Barrett, looking back on the uses of ideology, attempts to rescue a useful set of meanings: 'the retrievable core of meaning of the term ideology is precisely this: discursive and significatory mechanisms that may occlude, legitimate, naturalise or universalise in a variety of different ways but can all be said to mystify' (Barrett 1991: 166–7). In this way Barrett suggests that ideology always actually refers to the process of misrepresentation and therefore still has wider application than its notional appeal to a 'truth' would seem to suggest.

**See also:** *post-structuralism, power*

### FURTHER READING

Althusser's work on ideology (1984) gives the best possible introduction to the subject and Barrett's classic text on Marxist feminism (1988) helps to put this into a feminist context. Barrett, writing later (1991), reconsiders the use of the term in relation to Foucauldian theory.

79

# lesbian continuum

The 'lesbian continuum' was a phrase coined by Adrienne Rich in her pathfinding essay 'Compulsory Heterosexuality and Lesbian Existence' (1980, reprinted in Rich 1986).

Rich's notion of 'compulsory heterosexuality' here extends the definition of lesbian beyond that of sexual identity to encompass the homosocial bonds between women. In order to counter the numerous ways in which lesbian experiences and existence have been made invisible, and because of the difficulty of unearthing distinctly 'lesbian' experiences and events from the past in the wake of 'heteroreality', Rich proposes that a 'lesbian continuum' could include all women-identified experiences that women encounter in their lives.

This notion became an important one in lesbian feminism, even as it was highly controversial: it provides a way of envisaging a lesbian history without putting sexual encounters at the heart of sexual identity. The main criticism of it is the possibility that it effectively serves to desexualise lesbianism and therefore appears as just one more form of political lesbianism; additionally, it might be seen as allowing other feminists to claim to be a part of the 'lesbian continuum' without perhaps examining their own heterosexism. Since feminism provided such a homosocial space for women, might the idea of a lesbian continuum simply be used rhetorically in ways that serve no political purpose for a lesbian critique of the hegemony of straight feminism? In an Afterword to her original essay Rich defends the concept of a lesbian continuum, even though she agrees it can be misused to suggest that lesbianism as a sexual choice is inseparable from female friendship and that heterosexual relationships are inseparable from rape. She also recognises the ways in which it might conveniently be hijacked by heterosexual feminists

> who have not yet begun to examine the privileges and solipsisms of heterosexuality, as a safe way to describe their felt connections with women, without having to share in the risks and threats of lesbian existence. What I had thought to delineate rather complexly as a continuum has begun to sound more like 'life-style shopping.' *Lesbian continuum* – the phrase – came from a desire to allow for the greatest possible variation of female-identified experience, while paying a different kind of respect to *lesbian existence* – the traces and knowledge of women who have made their primary and erotic and emotional choices for women. (Rich 1986: 73-4)

Rich's term was not produced in a vacuum and owes much to Radicalesbians' early manifesto, 'The Woman Identified Woman' (1970). A lesbian is defined as the 'rage of all women condensed to the point of explosion' (in Koedt et al. 1973: 240); they explore the ways 'lesbian' as a word has been used as a term of abuse and held as a threat over women and an admonition to behave or face the consequences. They use this image to argue that unless women divert all their energies towards other women there can be no shift in current relations between the sexes. Where this manifesto differs is that it seems to offer a starker 'political lesbian' solution, arguing that '[u]ntil women see in each other the possibility of a primal commitment which includes sexual love, they will be denying themselves the love and value they readily accord to men, thus affirming their second-class status' (in Koedt et al. 1973: 243), even though it looks forward to a future where 'the categories of homosexuality and heterosexuality would disappear' (Koedt et al. 1973: 241).

From the beginnings of the Women's Movement, lesbians felt torn between a feminist politics and that of Gay Liberation – neither of which seemed to offer them the space to deal with their felt oppression as a woman and as a lesbian. For many, their experiences in feminism became more and more conflictual, not least because of the fear by some in the movement that 'ordinary' women would believe feminism to be overrun with lesbians; Betty Friedan, author of the classic *The Feminine Mystique* (1963) and founder of the National Organisation for Women (NOW) dubbed them the 'lavender menace'. Much of the substance of the ideas behind the Radicalesbians' manifesto and Adrienne Rich's essay were therefore profoundly challenging in an atmosphere of sometimes covert hostility. Writing in 1973, Jill Johnston is clearly grasping a notion similar to the lesbian continuum, which is also a concept that might release lesbians from the taint of being only to do with sexuality:

> The word lesbian has expanded so much through political definition that it should no longer refer exclusively to a woman simply in a sexual relation to another woman. The word has in fact had pornographic implications as though lesbian was a woman who did nothing but enjoy sex, an implication employed as a tool of discrimination. The word is now a generic term signifying activism and resistance and the envisioned goal of a woman committed state. (Johnston 1973: 278)

Rich's essay emerged in the mid-1980s, a time of much more intensive conflict in feminism. Rich might have also intended to provide a point of connection, a shared history, in a movement riven by identity politics. The lesbian 'continuum', much as it desexualises feminism, also, conveniently takes the attention away from heterosexuality too. Ultimately the idea of the lesbian continuum is about re-establishing the importance of all women's women-identified experiences in life, regardless of their stated sexual orientation. In common with Radicalesbians, Rich prioritises all communication with women, implying that men are incapable of being nurturant or supportive or able to sustain close friendships with men. Her model of male power accords completely with a traditional radical feminist definition of patriarchy and perhaps in this context slips into cultural feminism. This is a period during which, as Segal observes 'lesbians also fell silent about sex and sexuality, except in their forceful critique of women "sleeping with the enemy"' (Segal 1994: 172), but the next conflict was to emerge from within lesbian ranks.

During the late 1980s debates about the politics of sexual role-play within lesbianism were debated hotly. Some, like Sheila Jeffreys, averred that any engagement with butch/femme posturing was a fetishisation and re-enactment of patriarchal power. This can be set against the passionate fiction and essays of Joan Nestle who became the key champion of the eroticisation of difference asserting that 'Butch-femme relationships, as I experienced them, were complex erotic statements, not phony heterosexual replicas' (Nestle 1987: 100). Her view of sexual role-play in the 1950s is of showy resistance, the denial of invisibility, and her work, like that of queer theorist Judith Butler, honours the performativity involved in playing with gender.

Vestiges of the idea of a 'lesbian continuum' remain in the work of radical and cultural feminists, and in the politics of total separatism; yet many a younger lesbian/straight woman becoming accustomed to the colourful if commodified representations of 'queer' sex, finds the idea of sexual radicalism, the 'queer' way, more attractive.

**See also:** *heterosexism, queer theory, separatism*

### FURTHER READING

The Radicalesbians' manifesto is available in Koedt et al. (1973) or reprinted in Nicholson (1997) and, along with other essays in the Koedt collection, helps explain how lesbians perceived themselves in the movement, even as they were popularly perceived as taking over. This lays the ground for Rich (1986), whereas both Jeffreys (1994) and Nestle (1987) offer totally different visions of a lesbian politics beyond the lesbian continuum. Butler (1990) or Fuss (1991) provide the queer inflection on lesbian politics.

# masculinity/ masculinities

Masculinity is the set of social practices and cultural representations associated with being a man. The plural 'masculinities' is also used in recognition that ways of being a man and cultural representations of/about men vary, both historically and culturally, between societies and between different groupings of men within any one society.

The feminist critique of masculinity as that against which women are defined as 'the Other' has a long history, but writing on masculinities grew enormously from the 1980s onwards. In the words of one contributor, 'it seems as if every man and his dog is writing a book on masculinities' (MacInnes 1998: 1). In the literature on masculinities, evaluations of masculinity and explanations of the links between masculinity/ masculinities and those people defined as 'men' vary according to theoretical perspective. For example, in accounts drawing on the natural sciences, masculinity/masculinities are the result of physiological factors, such as hormones or chromosomes. Goldberg (1979), for example, identifies the 'neuro-endocrine system' (the interaction of the nervous system with the hormone system) as the biological basis of masculinity/masculinities. Such essentialism is also characteristic of populist 'celebratory' writing about masculinity, in which men are urged to reinvigorate their 'natural' masculinity. Robert Bly (1991), for example, sees masculinity as being damaged by the conditions of modern society, and prescribes a remedy in the form of men-only retreats and bonding rituals. In contrast, from the more critical, academic perspective of the social sciences, masculinities are understood as a form of power relation, both among men themselves and between men and women. In place of essentialism, masculinities are argued to arise from the social contexts in which men live, for example, from their positions in the various institutions and organisations of their society and/or in the context of the socially available discourses about gender.

Connell (1995; 2000) has developed a social scientific analysis of masculinities as part of his broader, relational theory of gender. For Connell, gender is the end-product of ongoing interpretations of and definitions placed upon the reproductive and sexual capacities of the human body. Masculinities (and femininities) can be understood, therefore, as the effects of these interpretations and definitions: on bodies, on personalities and on a society's culture and institutions. In Connell's account, masculinities occupy a higher ranking than femininity in the 'gender hierarchy' characteristic of modern Western societies. At the top of the gender hierarchy is 'hegemonic masculinity', the culturally dominant ideal of masculinity centred around authority, physical toughness and strength, heterosexuality and paid work. This is an ideal of masculinity that few actual men live up to, but from which most gain advantage and so Connell calls the next level 'complicit masculinity'. Below this in the hierarchy are 'subordinated

83

masculinities', the most important of which is homosexual masculinity. More generally, this form of masculinity includes a range of masculine behaviour which does not fully match up to the macho ideals of hegemonic masculinity. At the bottom of the gender hierarchy are femininities. (Although these may take a variety of forms, for example emphasised or compliant femininity and 'resistant' femininity, femininity is always subordinated to masculinity.) In Connell's analysis, the social changes of the twentieth century (in the industrialised West) have undermined the gender hierarchy, and the position of hegemonic masculinity within it. In this context, masculinity politics have developed: 'those mobilizations and struggles where the meaning of masculine gender is at issue, and with it, men's position in gender relations' (1995: 205). Connell goes on to identify the main forms taken by masculinity politics in Western industrialised societies, including masculinity therapy, such as called for by Bly (1991), gay liberation, and 'exit politics', in which heterosexual men actively oppose hegemonic masculinity.

The theorising of multiple masculinities by writers like Connell (1990) has led others to raise questions about the meaning of masculinity as a concept. MacInnes (1998) for example, points to the vague, confused and contradictory definitions of the concept present within much of the masculinities literature. If masculinities are so varied and fluid, then what is it that makes them recognisibly masculine? MacInnes suggests that, in fact, many writers on masculinities 'smuggle in' to their otherwise social constructionist accounts an assumption that it is only biological men who possess masculinity. MacInnes himself argues that masculinity does not exist as the property, character trait or aspect of individuals but should instead be understood as an ideology about what men should be like, and this is developed by men and women in order to make sense of their lives (1998: 2). Indeed, discursive approaches to masculinities, influenced by postmodernist/post-structuralist perspectives, have become increasingly prominent within gender studies. One example is the work of Speer (2001) which shows how, in talking about sport and leisure, young men draw on a range of particular cultural models of masculinities and in the process give shifting, gendered, accounts of themselves.

In his more recent work, Connell (2000) emphasises that masculinities are not simply equivalent to biological men. In other words, 'masculine' bodies, behaviour or attitudes can be the social practices of people who are otherwise defined as 'women'. For Connell, then, masculinities is a concept that 'names patterns of gender practice, not just

**84**

groups of people' (2000: 17). Elsewhere, he insists that masculinities cannot be understood only as discourses, since 'gender relations are also constituted in, and shape, non-discursive practices such as labour, violence, sexuality, childcare and so on' (2001: 7).

**See also:** *body, gender, gender order, men's movements/men's studies*

### FURTHER READING

Edley and Wetherall (1995) provide overviews of the various theories of masculinities, and identify key questions to assess the adequacy of each. Whitehead's (2002) *Men and Masculinities* is one of the more recent contributions to the topic. A special issue of *Feminism and Psychology* (volume 11, no. 1) is devoted to research on discursive constructions of masculinities and includes an introduction, overview and critique by Connell.

# men's movements/ men's studies

Men's movements emerged at the time of the Women's Liberation Movement, and the groupings gathered together under this umbrella title were as heterogeneous as early radical feminist groups. In a sense they all seemed to be a reaction to feminism, but that could be either a positive or a negative one. Men's consciousness raising (CR) groups, emerging during the early 1970s, generally had a benign relationship with feminism and women in general. There was an acknowledgement that all men had at least the potential to be the oppressor and had greater opportunities for power, and therefore it was important that men got together in their own separatist groups to discuss the effects this knowledge had upon them as individuals. Just as women in CR learnt a great deal about the processes of their own socialisation, so men came to understand the ways in which they were educated to be 'men' and what that meant.

In the USA and the UK there were a scattering of Men's Liberation Groups or smaller CR groups. Some felt that gender oppresses all

85

individuals and that men need liberation from masculinity, just as much as women need to be liberated from the thrall of patriarchy. However, more recent commentators (e.g. Pease 2000: 40–55) were sceptical about calls for 'liberation' from men's groups. It was felt that unless those groups exercised some consciousness about the social and ideological advantages they held over women, their call for liberation would be an empty politically naïve gesture – 'to assume that men can, unproblematically, experience "men's liberation" – that there are any analogies with gay or feminist politics – is, in the end, an illusion' (Tolson 1987: 144).

Given that this movement had a direct relationship to feminism, it is worth pausing to consider feminism's relationship to men. From the outset, modern feminism has concerned itself with thinking about men. The crucial use of the concept of gender, which identified masculinity and femininity as meanings culturally ascribed to men and women, had opened up ways of thinking about their arbitrariness and changeability. For example, women's striving for greater recognition in the public sphere of work and politics was generally regarded as 'masculine'; and in this way gendered ascriptions of such behaviour have in the past been used as a way of discouraging career aspirations among females. Feminism's scrutiny of gender binaries, therefore, potentially provided a radical point of departure for all men and women who didn't feel they conformed to such norms and could, through solidarity, break out of them. Early second wave feminism, although established in part as a reaction against men on the left, did not emerge as separatist from the start. Men were present at early conferences and socials (sometimes in a 'servicing' role, such as helping with the childcare) and it was only later that they were banned because their presence was considered disruptive or inappropriate.

Nonetheless as Rowbotham observed early in the 1970s, 'the creation of a new woman of necessity demands the creation of a new man' (Rowbotham in Wandor 1972: 3). If one subscribed to the social constructionist view of gender, then men could only be the enemy for a finite period; but in the meantime, given the commitment to separatism, it was difficult to establish where their place was. Men's movements, where that meant CR or other kinds of groups, were a logical step forward for anti-sexist men, providing a platform to discuss how men and women might be reunited across the gulf of gender politics. In any case, many feminist groups, particularly black feminists, lesbian feminists and socialist feminists, felt that they needed their continuing alliances with men fighting the same battles against the oppressive forces of racism, homophobia and advanced capitalism.

*men's movements/men's studies*

Some early anti-sexist men's groups wanted a space where they could recognise their privileges as potential oppressors as well as their responses to this, to confront 'both their internalized domination and their dominant position' (Pease 2000: 3). They seemed to celebrate male separatism as a demonstration of solidarity with women, which also left women space to take their own debates further. In an early men's movement paper from the UK called *Brothers*, one contributor argues that '[f]or me, personal politics must be fitted into a greater struggle. I know that if I am screwed up my politics will be; if I am sexist so too will be my revolution. But I cannot experience women's oppression. I can perceive it and learn from it. I can only experience my own (men's) oppression. I will and do support every demand women make. But I do not have the right to take over those demands' (Anon 1974: 3). In the UK the first conference of men against sexism was held in London on 10 June 1973; a year later there was a men's conference in Birmingham – a city which according to *Brothers* had its own men's liberation group.

At this time there seemed to be a consensus that the term 'feminist' applied to women alone and that men could call themselves either anti-sexist or pro-feminist in support of women's aims. During the 1970s as a whole there continued to be a groundswell of male support for feminism; in addition, many of these men's groups had quite clear socialist leanings. In fact the UK men's journal *Achilles Heel* was very much a socialist men's journal and is one of the most successful, having been founded in 1978 with its last issue appearing in 1999. Most of these men's groups comprised a majority of heterosexual men, perhaps because many gay men had found their political voice through the gay liberation movement. This heterosexual focus could, however, be seen as a strength of such groups since heterosexuality was so rarely interrogated by men – in terms of straight men's relationship to both women and gay men. Tolson, talking of his experiences with the Birmingham group, notes that '[f]or everyone, an immediate reason for his joining the group was the feminist challenge to male sexuality' (Tolson 1987: 138), and the result was movement towards understanding masculinity as a social problem. Victor Seidler, a founder of *Achilles Heel*, draws attention to the token essentialism of masculinity, where personally and because of social censure it is much more difficult for men to cross gender boundaries than it is for women. Nonetheless, the development of a body of knowledge about masculinity produced by men suggests importantly that sexism is not just women's problem, just as racism is as much a problem for whites.

Having said that these publications dealing with masculinity have been largely welcomed by feminists, there have been other forays into 'high' feminist theory which have been greeted with more suspicion. These volumes, the earliest of which to cause a stir was *Men in Feminism* (1987), often feature both male and female contributors, and in some cases debated men's role within feminism. A commonly expressed wish by some men to be called feminist pushed the debate in a more controversial direction, with feminists questioning the motives of men so keen to attach the moniker to themselves. For many of these men it seems they wanted to be able to freely use the feminist discourse which had framed their own thinking (many of them having been tutored by feminists) without constantly feeling they were outsiders. In a perfect world the dissemination of feminist perspectives over a wider constituency could only be positive; but it could also mean the co-optation of feminist ideas to anti-feminist ends or the cynical jumping onto the bandwagon of feminism's flurry of academic success at a time, in the 1980s, when feminist texts were jumping from the bookshelves. Some feminists felt obliged to welcome the newcomers – a veritable 'men's movement' within academia – partly because they were aware that feminism's lack of toleration of other constituencies had come to seem tyrannical in the popular consciousness. What concerned women most about this flurry of interest of men in feminism was the possible motivations behind wanting to lay claim to the identity feminist when, tacitly at least, since the late 1960s it had been the preserve of women alone. Why could not 'pro-feminist' or 'anti-sexist' suffice?

As these academic disputes settled down and moved on to other territories such as queer theory and postmodernism, the 1990s was primarily characterised by a renewed media onslaught on feminism by men who claimed that they were the new victims in a reverse sex war. In the UK the publication of Neil Lyndon's *No More Sex War* (1992) and David Thomas's *Not Guilty* (1993) aimed to spread this image of male victimhood into the broadsheets. Interestingly, at about the same time Naomi Wolf (1993) was asserting that women should deny victimhood and recognise that they are about to profit from a massive 'genderquake' – a shift in the relations of power.

The so-called 'mythopoetic' movement, which included Robert Bly's Iron John movement, was also a clarion call for men to retreat from contemporary masculinity and into their primitive selves. In *Iron John* (1991) Bly implies that feminism has softened men, and while he 'disclaim[s] hostility to feminism, his movement places no emphasis on helping the struggle against women's oppression, and seems to be part of a series of inward-looking "men's liberation" activities which . . . may even be part of the anti-feminist backlash' (Christian 1994: 11). This emphasis on spiritual growth seems to anticipate increasing media descriptions of 'men in crisis', supported by statistics about the increase in young male suicides, attributed to their loss of traditionally 'masculine' rights and identities and changing employment patterns. Of course much of this could equally be due to an increasingly unstable global workforce constantly shifting and relocating to meet the demands of the market, but feminism is, by and large, held squarely to blame. Even feminists such as Rosalind Coward and journalists such as Susan Faludi write with passion about this crisis in *Sacred Cows* (1999) and *Stiffed* (1999) respectively, raising the same concern about young men and their future and arguing that the mass media is replete with images of men as incompetent and disenfranchised (see Coward 1999: 90).

Even though there is more discussion about masculinity now, there seems to be less evidence of men's movements continuing, much less those which bear strong links to feminist movements. Just as feminism is better known these days for being located within women's and gender studies in the academy, so masculinity becomes more of a theoretical site of struggle than anything else. Media-hyped debates about the 'new man' in the 1980s and the 'new lad' in the 1990s do suggest that men are going through a period of transition, but whether this leaves us simply with men in crisis or an exciting new chapter in the history of masculinity is yet to be discovered. As Beynon remarks, 'the fact remains that in spite of the huge amount written about masculinity, we still need to know how men perceive masculinity today; whether or how they experience masculinity-in-crisis, how they enact "masculinities" and how they relate to other men and women' (2002: 143).

**See also:** *consciousness raising, gender, masculinity/masculinities*

### FURTHER READING

Both Pease (2000) and Beynon (2002) offer useful commentaries on studies of masculinity today, Beynon's being intended as introductory and covering popular culture. Seidler's many books (e.g. 1989) offer a useful background to the field. Faludi (1999) and Coward (1999) show how some women have responded to the notion of men in crisis and Whelehan (2000) is slightly more sceptical, relating it to a new era of 'retrosexism'.

89

# (the) Other

As used by the French writer Simone de Beauvoir, the concept of 'the Other' describes women's status in patriarchal, androcentric cultures. While men are 'the One' (in other words, beings in and of themselves), women are 'the Other', beings defined only in relation to men. A woman, de Beauvoir wrote, is 'defined and differentiated with reference to man and not he with reference to her; she is the incidental, the inessential as opposed to the essential. He is the Subject, he is the Absolute – she is the Other' (1997 [1953]: 16).

De Beauvoir's ideas on women as the Other were set out in *The Second Sex* (first published in English in 1953). Drawing on the philosophical arguments of Hegel and Sartre, de Beauvoir saw that relationships between individuals were marked by a fundamental contradiction. Each individual self seeks to act freely and autonomously, but simultaneously requires interaction with others in order to define that self. In de Beauvoir's words, 'the subject can be posed only in being opposed' (1997: 16). Generally, individuals are forced to recognise the reciprocity of Otherness. Through our encounters with other individuals, it becomes evident that, just as we see them as 'the Other', we ourselves are seen by them as 'the Other'. However, in the case of women and men, this reciprocity of Otherness is not recognised. Instead, 'one of the contrasting terms [men] is set up as the sole essential, denying any relativity in regard to its correlate and defining the latter [women] as pure otherness' (1997: 17–18). De Beauvoir offers a range of reasons for women's status as the Other, including the role played by women's reproductive capacities in limiting their autonomy in the eyes of men. An important aspect of her argument, though, lies in identifying women's complicity in their subordination. Men, in defining themselves as 'the One', position women as 'the Other'. Women do not regain the status of being 'the One', according to de Beauvoir, because they largely accept this state of affairs. 'Thus, woman may fail to claim the status of subject because she lacks definite resources, because she feels the necessary bond that ties her to man regardless of reciprocity and because she is often very well pleased with her role as the Other' (1997: 21). Therefore, it is suggested that women identify with the patriarchal, androcentric image of themselves (particularly as reproductive and sexual beings) and so regard themselves as the Other. They have 'chosen' to remain 'beings in themselves' rather

**90**

key concepts

than become 'beings for themselves' (Okely 1986: 59), because this status offers them benefits, including the evasion of full, adult moral responsibility and autonomy (Evans 1985: 61).

*The Second Sex*, widely recognised as a landmark text in the development of critiques of women's status, is also regarded as flawed in its argument and use of evidence (see Evans 1985). Nevertheless, de Beauvoir's development within *The Second Sex* of the concept of the Other has been lauded as a 'strikingly original theory of female subjectivity under patriarchy' (Moi 1994: 164; see also Evans 1985). Its influence is evident in a number of areas of gender studies. Paechter's (1998) analysis of the subordinate status of girls in the education system is one example. For Paechter, the positioning of girls and women in education is 'an exemplar' of the ways in which femininity has been constructed as Other throughout Western society. Paechter draws together a range of research evidence to show that boys/men have been regarded as the normal Subject of education, while girls/women have been positioned as the Other. For example, the history of the development of education in Britain shows that, until the middle decades of the twentieth century, the education of girls was seen as of secondary importance to that of boys. Moreover, educational provision for girls developed in specific ways, in that they were educated for domesticity (as future wives and mothers) and so were excluded from other forms of ('higher') knowledge routinely experienced by boys. In more recent years, although girls have been granted equal access to the formal curriculum, the problem of their 'underperformance' in science subjects has been located in girls themselves, rather than in the androcentric construction of scientific knowledge and pedagogy. In addition to showing how the education curriculum positions girls as Other, Paechter's analysis points to the role played by masculine behaviour and attitudes in school settings. Boys dominate in classroom talk, and in school space, whether in the classroom or in the playground. An important aspect of this, argues Paechter, is the way adolescent girls are subject to a 'disciplinary gaze'. The sexuality of girls is surveyed and consequently controlled by the attitude, language and behaviour of boys (and, often, male teachers) whose authority derives from the masculine-dominated rules of heterosexual culture. Paechter concludes that the Othering of girls within the education system is of particular importance, because it sets girls up for a lifetime of subordination, whereby femininity is that against which masculinity defines itself and asserts its superiority (1998: 115).

A rather different use of the Other can be found in the work of some postmodern or post-structualist feminist writers. In the work of Cixous,

Irigaray and Kristeva, for example, the concept of women as the Other has been developed through engaging with the ideas of Lacan and Derrida. According to Tong (1998), Cixous, Irigaray and Kristeva each follow de Beauvoir in focusing on women's Otherness but interpret this condition fundamentally differently. 'Woman is still the Other, but rather than interpreting this condition as something to be transcended, postmodern feminists proclaim its advantages' (Tong 1998: 195). In this understanding of Otherness, it is something of an advantaged, privileged viewpoint, enabling a critique of the dominant patriarchal culture through the celebration of feminine cultures, bodies and sexuality.

The critical evaluation of the concept of the Other centres around the issue of 'difference'. Commentators on *The Second Sex* point to its tendency toward universalism, in that de Beauvoir conveys the view that the Other is the experience of all women, at all times (Okely 1986). Contemporary perspectives, influenced by multicultural and postmodern feminism, emphasise the heterogeneity of women's experiences. For example, in analysing the experiences of African-American women, Hill Collins (1990) identifies the important role of 'controlling images' through which they are stereotyped, as 'Mammy', 'matriarch', 'welfare recipient' or 'hot mamma'. Hill Collins therefore points to the particular form of the Other experienced by African-American women. Similarly, Anthias and Yuval-Davies (1992) are critical of the tendency to position 'women' as Other in a dichotomous relationship to 'men'. They argue for a deconstruction of such binary categories, to encourage the analysis of diversity and commonality in a range of historically specific ethnic and class contexts. From the perspective of postmodernist and post-structuralist feminist analyses, the use of dichotomous distinctions (between 'the One' and 'the Other' or between 'Subject' and 'Object') uncritically reproduces the binarism in Western philosophical thought, a tendency so deeply implicated in the valuing of masculinity over femininity. Feminist writers such as Cixous, Irigaray and Kristeva aim to avoid both patriarchal conceptualisations and universalistic explanatory theories, instead emphasising difference, plurality and diversity. In her work, Paechter recognises the inadequacies of universalism and the way the concept of 'the Other' both encourages dualistic thinking and underemphasises difference. There are, Paechter acknowledges, innumerable Others arising from a range of sets of power relations between groups. Nevertheless, she argues, it is women who have most consistently and most particularly been positioned as Other and it is feminist writings that have been important in developing the analysis of Otherness. Paechter suggests that the importance of the concept of the

*(the) Other*

Other ultimately lies in the way it draws attention to the particular forms of masculinity forceful in creating other masculinities as subordinate, as well as femininities (1998: 115).

**See also:** *androcentrism, double standard, post-structuralism*

### FURTHER READING

De Beauvoir's *The Second Sex* is critically evaluated in Fallaize (1998, ed.), a reader that draws together some classic commentaries on de Beauvoir and her work. For an analysis of the way modern Western art has regarded women as 'the Other', see Pollock (1988). Gilligan's *In a Different Voice* (1982) is a classic text identifying the positioning of women as Other in psychological theories of moral development.

# patriarchy

Literally, patriarchy means rule by the male head of a social unit (a family or tribe, for example). The patriarch, typically a societal elder, has legitimate power over others in the social unit, including other (especially, younger) men, all women and children. However, since the early twentieth century, feminist writers have used the concept to refer to the social system of masculine domination over women. Patriarchy has been a fundamentally important concept in gender studies, leading to the development of a number of theories that aim to identify the bases of women's subordination to men.

Three of the most important theories in which patriarchy is a central concept are those commonly labelled as 'radical feminist', 'Marxist feminist' and 'dual systems theory'. In 'radical feminist' analyses, patriarchy is regarded as the primary and fundamental social division in society. In some radical feminist analyses, the institution of the family is identified as a key means through which men's domination is achieved (Millet 1977). In other radical feminist accounts of patriarchy, the control men have over women's bodies is regarded as important. For Firestone (1971), inequalities between women and men are biologically based, with the different reproductive capacities of women and men being especially important. In other radical feminist analyses, it is masculine control over

93

women's bodies through sexuality or male violence in the form of rape that is regarded as being of central importance (Rich 1980; Brownmiller 1976). In a further grouping of feminist analyses, often labelled as 'Marxist feminism', patriarchy is argued to arise from the workings of the capitalist economic system: it requires, and benefits from, women's unpaid labour in the home. The subordination of women to men in society therefore tends to be regarded as a by-product of capital's subordination of labour. Class inequality is argued to be the central feature of society and is seen to determine gender inequality (Barrett 1988). A third grouping of feminist perspectives gives theoretical priority to two systems – capitalism and patriarchy – in the explanation of patriarchy. Often referred to as 'dual systems theory', this perspective in many ways represents a synthesis of Marxist and radical feminist accounts of gender relations. Indeed, the dual systems approach can be seen to have emerged out of the critiques levelled at Marxist theories, which may over-emphasise class and capitalism, and the critiques levelled at radical feminist theories, which may over-emphasise patriarchy and/or biology. In some versions of dual systems theory, capitalism and patriarchy are understood as interdependent, mutually accommodating systems of oppression, whereby both systems structure and benefit from women's subordination (for example, Hartmann 1979).

While patriarchy has long been important in feminist analyses, it has also been the subject of considerable debate. There are a number of criticisms commonly levelled at interpretations of gender relations that make use of the concept of patriarchy. First, such interpretations have been said to display a tendency towards ahistoricism (in other words, a failure to acknowledge or account for historical variations in gender relations). Second, theories in which patriarchy is a central concept have been criticised for their reductionism (in other words, reducing the explanation of the basis of patriarchy to one (or two) factor(s), such as biology or capitalism or the family). Third, patriarchy encourages a rather limited conceptualisation of gender relations, as occurring only between women and men. Consequently, theories in which patriarchy is central tend to under-acknowledge the full extent of gender relations: involving relationships between men and men, women and women as well as between men and women. Fourth, and relatedly, theoretical accounts using the concept of patriarchy have been criticised for a tendency towards universalism (in other words, for failing to recognise cultural variations, in their assumption or suggestion that relations between women and men are the same the world over). In black feminist critiques, for example, it is argued that analyses of patriarchy that fail to fully examine and theorise racism are flawed and incomplete: women's subordination can only be eliminated if the system of racism is challenged, alongside those of patriarchy and capitalism. Fifth, theories employing the concept of patriarchy have been criticised for their abstract structuralism (in other words, a tendency to over-emphasise, or to reify, structures while failing to recognise fully the role individual agency plays, both in the ongoing creation of gender inequality and in resistance to it).

In her theory of patriarchy, Walby (1990) claims to have overcome the earlier problems of reductionism, ahistoricism, universalism and the tendency to lose agency in social and historical processes. For Walby, patriarchy is a system of social structures and practices in which men dominate, oppress and exploit women. Walby identifies six structures of patriarchy (household production, paid work, the state, male violence, sexuality, culture) that together are argued to capture the depth, pervasiveness and interconnectedness of women's subordination. Her theory of patriarchy also allows for change over historical time. Walby argues that, in Britain during the twentieth century, patriarchy changed from the 'private' form to the 'public' form. Private patriarchy is based around the family and the household and involves individual men exploiting the labour of individual women. Women are largely confined to the household sphere and have limited participation in public life. In public patriarchy, women are not excluded from public life but face inequality and discrimination within it, for example, in paid work. For Walby, the feminist movement was a key factor in bringing about the change from private to public patriarchy, via the struggle for the vote, for access to education and to the professions, to have legal rights of property ownership, rights in marriage and divorce and so on. However, patriarchy itself was and is not defeated. Walby says that it has merely changed its form so that now, as she puts it, rather than being restricted to the household, women have 'the whole of society in which to roam and be exploited' (1990: 201).

Although an improvement on earlier theories, Walby's reformulation of patriarchy has itself been subject to criticism. Anthias and Yuval-Davies (1992), for example, criticise Walby for her treatment of the relationship between gender and other forms of social inequality, especially class and 'race'. They argue that Walby's theory portrays capitalism, patriarchy and racism as systems that are, to a large extent, separate and independent of one another. The implication is that class and race are merely extra layers of oppression faced by some women. For Anthias and Yuval-Davies (1992), this does not adequately account for the fully fused nature of the relationships between patriarchy, capitalism and racism, nor for the way that class and 'race' make for a qualitatively different kind of gender inequality. Pollert (1996) argues that (as in earlier formations of patriarchy) Walby's theory of patriarchy conflates explanation and description. In other words, instead of identifying the origins of patriarchy or the root of its perpetuation, Walby's theory tends toward a circular argument where the *explanation* for the system of patriarchy are the *features* of patriarchy itself. To this extent, then, Walby's attempt to overcome the weaknesses of patriarchy as an explanatory concept is unsuccessful. At most, Walby can be said to have developed a more elaborate description of patriarchy, but not an explanation of why it exists or how it is perpetuated.

For these reasons, there is a growing consensus that patriarchy should be abandoned as an explanatory concept or theory and that it should only be used as an adjective, to *describe* relationships or institutions where men dominate women. Rather than attempting to reformulate patriarchy as an explanatory concept, various writers have advocated an alternative approach to gender theorising, one which 'encourages a focus on the specifics of social relations, rather than on homogeneous social systems' (Maynard 1995: 276. See also Connell 1987; 1995; Bottero 1998; Fraser and Nicholson 1989; Gottfried 1998; Marshall 1994; Pollert 1996).

**See also:** *gender order, postmodernism*

### FURTHER READING

An early and still relevant critique of the concept of patriarchy was made by Beechey (1979). Walby (1990) criticises patriarchy in terms of how the concept has been applied in the analyses of particular forms of men's domination over women, including paid work, sexuality and the state. Connell (1987) both critiques theories that rely on patriarchy and develops an alternative approach to theorising gender inequality in which the 'gender order' is a central concept. Importantly, Connell also pays attention to the full range of gender, analysing masculinities in relation to each other, as well as to femininities.

## pornography

It is very difficult to provide a clear definition of what constitutes 'pornography', as opposed to erotica or suggestive and titillating imagery.

Often the boundary between 'erotica' and 'pornography' seems to run along the lines of art versus tacky commercialism. This problem over exact definitions is a telling one, and helps explain the chequered history of pornography debates within modern feminism, because what constitutes pornography and whether pornography contains qualities specific only to this area or qualities found in other aspects of cultural production were key topics for discussion. Because of its subject matter, and the often sharp visceral reactions pornography summoned in women, the arguments and subsequent rifts over what feminists' position on porn should be were emotional and vituperative.

The word pornography today is used to describe sexualised depictions of women and men intended to provoke arousal in the spectator, often posed in scenes suggestive of sexual congress or anticipating a sexual act. Pornography, and all forms of sexualised representations of women, from beauty pageants to advertisements, were the targets of women's concern in the early days of second wave feminism. The crux of the argument was that these images affect men's behaviour towards women, so that they are likely to treat them as merely decorative objects, things to be circulated as status symbols without concern for their individuality or humanity. Women supposedly respond to them by desiring to be like the object of desire, even when the representation may be impossible to emulate – often depicting improbably thin, post-adolescent, white women. While the subject of pornography was part of the whole 'images of women' debate, the point was to draw attention to the ways in which women were represented and challenge them on the basis that these images hurt all women by profoundly affecting the way they are treated in their daily lives as well as suggesting that women are primarily judged by their physical attributes and sexual attractiveness. Early on, a link was made between imagery and its material effects on real people; not only did early feminists sticker and add graffiti to offending images on display, they also looked to produce more positive images of women which portrayed a range of bodies, ages, ethnicities and abilities.

'Images of women' criticism turned its attention to a wide range of static visual imagery as well as looking at literature and film. There was never absolute agreement about how harmful such images could be, only a consensus that women were adversely affected by them. However, during the early 1980s the anti-pornography wing became more of a pronounced 'movement' within second wave feminism, and some individuals, such as Andrea Dworkin and Catherine Mackinnon became focused on this single issue, taking it up as a quasi-moral crusade with an absolute mission to eradicate all porn. Sex for many feminists moved

97

away from being a question of pleasure and desire, to simply a means through which male power is enacted and this again affected the perception of pornography. Dworkin's language is deliberately provocative and her association of the image with violence to women is uncompromising: '[p]ornography is the propaganda of sexual fascism. Pornography is the propaganda of sexual terrorism. Images of women bound, bruised and maimed on virtually every street corner, on every magazine rack, in every drug store, in movie house after movie house, on billboards, on posters pasted on walls, are death threats to a female population in rebellion' (Dworkin 1988: 201).

As Susan Brownmiller observed, '[b]y a miserable coincidence of historic timing, an above ground, billion-dollar industry of hard- and soft-core porn began to flourish during the seventies simultaneously with the rise of Women's Liberation' (2000: 295), and activists such as Dworkin were responding to a massive growth in the porn industry as well as growing splits in the women's movement itself where 'the anti-porn initiative constituted the last gasp of radical feminism' (Brownmiller 2000: 325). Anti-porn feminists were particularly exercised by hard-core porn which they claimed depended on violent imagery, and by rumours of the existence of so-called 'snuff' movies (supposedly depicting the actual torture and death of a woman on-screen), and they perhaps misleadingly used this as the model for how pornography could be defined. Their attempts to get pornography outlawed was what triggered anti-censorship feminists to come out in opposition to their more extreme claims. During the 1980s, then, the battle lines became drawn between those who felt pornography should be banned and those who feared that ever more stringent censorship laws would put a greater curb on people's freedoms and would first affect those already seen as marginal – such as gay men and lesbians.

The anti-porn movement in the USA had ready-made allies in the emerging New Right and Dworkin and Mackinnon were active participants in the Meese Commission on Pornography in 1985, and attempts to pass an ordinance in Minneapolis to restrict and make an offence the circulation of pornography in 1984: as many have pointed out this linked feminism 'with the rather surprising bedfellows of the American religious right and other elements not hitherto associated with support for women's equality' (McNair 1996: 28). Many felt that this unholy alliance was too heavy a price to pay even if they did feel that pornography was a problem that needed to be addressed separately from the wider issues of representation. For many in the movement who still felt ambiguous about porn or felt happier looking at the wider field of images of women, the vehemence of some aspects of anti-porn lobbying was confusing and counter-productive. While many women wanted to investigate further the ways in which images of women may or may not directly influence the behaviour of both men and women, many feminists shied away from the proposition that male heterosexual consumers of pornography are always potential violent attackers of women. Again and again opposing positions return to the issue of censorship and the likelihood that in advocating harsher restrictions on heterosexual pornography you also risk bringing down harsher censorship on groups such as gays and lesbians where sexually explicit images were already subject to much tighter strictures, whether one could define them as 'porn' or not.

The 1982 Barnard Conference on Sexuality, which Vance helped to organise, was an attempt to address this increasing rift in feminism with the question 'how could feminism at the time reduce the sexual danger women faced and expand their sexual pleasure, without sacrificing women's accounts of either one?' (Vance 1992: xx). Some feminists felt that the anti-porn drive threatened to completely sweep away explorations of female desire and self-expression in a movement which was already having grave problems separating heterosexuality as a sexual orientation from heterosexuality as the enactment of men's power over women. This US conference was to become notorious because it intensified the gap between anti-porn and sex-positive feminists – not least because for some its deliberately provocative and uncensored pro-sexuality aim was more narrowly interpreted as anti-feminist. Consequently, the conference was picketed by Women Against Pornography and the porn debate became polarised between the anti-porn and pro-sex positions even though these poles are by no means opposite sides of the same argument. On the one hand anti-porn activists wished to control the circulation of pornography, and on the other hand pro-sex advocates wanted to explore the possibilities of a non-patriarchally defined female sexuality (which might involve the use of sexually explicit imagery). Anti-porn advocates were also concerned by what they regarded as the preponderance of anti-feminist sexual roles in feminism – such as sadomasochism, and butch/femme roles within lesbian relationships – which indicates how much of a minefield the whole issue of sexuality was becoming.

From Carole Vance's point of view, 'The fantasy that violence against women is located or originates in objectionable sex magazines or videos rather than being part of the deep cell structure of every institution in our culture struck some feminists as hopelessly naïve and wrong, as did the suggestion that the excision of the sexually explicit would solve the problem' (Vance 1992: xx). Anti-censorship feminists think that among other things, it is time that women were allowed to experience the breadth of their own sexual responses untrammelled by repression and guilt. Vance in particular feels that danger of sexuality for women has been overstated, which 'runs the risk of making speech about sexual pleasure taboo. Feminists are easily intimidated by the charge that their own pleasure is selfish, as in political rhetoric which suggests that no woman is entitled to talk about sexual pleasure while any woman remains in danger – that is – never' (Vance 1992: 7). Elizabeth Wilson concurs with Vance in her view that 'there has been a shift from the attempt to understand how we respond sexually as women and how we internalise oppressive notions of femininity and female sexual response, to a simpler position which lays the blame squarely on pornography for creating a climate of sexual violence and terrorizing women' (Wilson in Segal and McIntosh 1992: 18).

Perhaps into the 1990s the swing moved much more from anti-porn and towards pro-sex, and many commentators, dissecting the 'pro' and anti-porn debates have noted that the argument for making porn a special case in the area of representation is highly questionable. In addition, a renewed focus on heterosexuality has allowed for some more honest explorations of female sexual pleasure (see Segal 1994; Richardson 1996). The anti-porn movement became something of an anomaly because as Gayle Rubin points out, 'there were never groups called Women Against Film, Women Against Television, or Women Against the Novel, even though most film, television and fiction were demonstrably sexist' (Rubin in Assister and Carol 1993: 19). A more pluralist approach to the question of pornography does not rule out discussion of the real problem of the portrayal of violence, misogyny and abuse, but it allows room to consider the view that other media are sexist too. Such an approach opens up discussion about related matters which might be deemed more proactive, such as improving sex education, support for sex workers and affirming the right to sexual diversity

For Segal 'we have finally arrived at the crux of the problem which has fanned the pornography debate within feminism: *Is it, or is it not, possible for women to conceive of, and enjoy, an active pleasurable engagement in sex with men? Is it, or is it not, possible to see women as empowered agents of heterosexual desire?*' (Segal in Segal and McIntosh 1992: 79). The old liberal notion of freedom of expression still holds sway and most people are anxious not to see their rights eroded, especially as it seems to be women, straight and gay, and gay men who suffer most keenly. More and more women today feel that it is perhaps misguided to single out pornography and its production for special attention since it is only one way in which women are exploited among many – this does not imply necessary agreement that pornography offers any kind of radical sexual statement. There may well be a middle ground in all this and for Bryson 'the solution will lie with more open discussion, and with an insistence that men examine and justify their use of pornography. For some, this will include the development of erotic material for and by women' (Bryson 1999: 193).

**See also:** *heterosexism, sexuality*

### FURTHER READING

Vance's collection of essays from the Barnard conference (1992) give a flavour of the rifts within feminism at the time. For the 'other' side of the discussion any of Andrea Dworkin's writings make the position clear, but her collected prose (1988) is accessible and provocative; Griffin's (1981) arguments are in a similar vein. Segal and McIntosh (1992) and McNair (1996) – the latter having a more postmodern inflection – will yield many more pointers for discussion.

# post-colonial theory

101

The term 'post-colonial' was originally used in the 1970s to refer to nations who moved beyond imperialist rule after the Second World War and later came to be used to reflect on how all cultures had been affected by European imperialism up until the present day. The term 'post-colonial' has therefore gathered meanings over time so that now it has a multitude of applications across different historical periods, locations, political contexts and identities – 'it addresses all aspects of the colonial process from the beginning of colonial contact' (Ashcroft et al. 1995: 2). While there is no single definition of post-colonial cultures, and indeed they may have little in common, they can be said to be immersed in a heady mixture of indigenous practices and knowledges, and imperial power and cultural hierarchies – a product of both repression of local knowledges and resistance to imperial forms. These tensions between the 'authentic' identity of indigenous peoples and the imprint of colonialism which remains indelible result in a sense of cultural hybridity.

Post-colonial theory emerged in the late 1980s from the same theoretical roots as post-structuralism and postmodernism, but is particularly influenced by the work of Edward Said, Gayatri Spivak and Homi Bhabha. It also drew upon work undertaken in a primarily literary critical context – that of post-colonial criticism (which itself subsumed Commonwealth literary studies), 'bringing to the forefront of concern the interconnection of issues of race, nation, empire, migration and ethnicity with cultural production' (Moore-Gilbert 1997: 6). Post-colonial criticism was able to identify the attitudes to empire and colonisation expressed in literature from numerous historical periods as well as, later, looking at travel writing and journals. With regard to works of classic Western literature this often involved a radical reinterpretation of the texts and a consideration of the links between artistic expression and colonial political endeavour.

The critical influences of post-colonial theory clearly extend far beyond the period when the term came into usage and beyond the scope of the Anglo-American universities; additionally the field of study has been profoundly influenced by writers such as Frantz Fanon and his classic text *The Wretched of the Earth* (1968). Moving away from the central interest in literature in post-colonial criticism, post-colonial theory is interested in the discourse of post-colonialism and how it is inscribed by a Eurocentrist belief in the intrinsic value of Western knowledges and civilisation. Post-colonial theory also aims to bring to visibility voices from the 'margins', whether it be from other previously colonised nations or from the wider diaspora. Edward Said's *Orientalism* (1978) is a key text for its insistence on the ways in which Western modes of representation and theories of knowledge are linked to the meanings of Western economic and political discourse, including the Eurocentrism of other 'high' theories such as postmodernism. Such a position facilitates the analysis of the ways in which the colonial legacies of Europe still shape dominant perceptions of both colonisers and colonised. The central thrust of these perspectives is in showing the way that society's cultural formations are imbued with this legacy of colonisation which still demarcates the 'centre' and 'margins' of cultural visibility.

For some feminists, post-colonial theory never gives enough space to gender difference; yet post-colonial theory was also a way of moving from the ethnocentrism of what might be thought as the 'mainstream' or dominant voice in feminism. Mainstream post-colonial theory has tended to assume that the prime movers of colonisation were men and that colonisation becomes a kind of masculine metaphor, but feminist post-colonial theorists have unearthed the ways in which women were involved in colonialism – both positively and negatively. A feminist perspective not only facilitates a re-evaluation of the way 'third world women' have been homogenised in post-colonial discourse, but also reviews the relationships of power between women as colonisers and colonised. Feminists' concern with issues such as sexuality and the body have yielded important analyses of the eroticisation of women's bodies and the projection of illicit desires into the space of the colonised. Women had an ideological role to play in colonialism as guardians of the 'race', in face of moral panics about miscegenation or compromising the perceived 'purity' of the European woman and these fears have also had an impact on the depiction of the non-European colonised woman (see Mills in Jackson and Jones 1998).

Feminist studies have shown the ways in which women function in post-colonial discourse – when associated with the colonisers they are neither 'other' nor holders of means to power, but they are implicated in and act as reinforcers of power relations as well as being appealed to as the moral centre of the colonising will. As Anne McClintock notes, 'white women were not the hapless onlookers of empire, but were ambiguously complicit both as colonizers and colonized, privileged and restricted, acted upon and acting' (1995: 6). White women might have seen how they were 'colonised' and rendered 'other' by the effects of partriarchy and have found their oppression within their own societies took on a new meaning under colonialism, even if gender divisions remained unchanged.

Some feminists perceive in post-colonial theory a danger that feminism becomes distracted by an organising principle where gender specificity is perceived as marginal. Yet writers such as Trinh T. Minh-Ha perceive a necessity in maintaining a feminist and post-colonial perspective and in denying their incompatibility, because otherwise the 'pitting of anti-racist and anti-sexist struggles against one another allows some vocal fighters to dismiss blatantly the existence of either racism or sexism within their lines of action, as if oppression only comes in separate monolithic forms' (Trinh in Ashcroft et al. 1995: 268). Post-colonial theory from a feminist perspective could in fact facilitate further analysis of difference as well as investigations into how women have historically wielded power over other women within the logic of colonialism. The language of borders, margins and spaces where the post-colonial critic denies her identity as marginal or encompassed by the mainstream speaks eloquently to the ways in which feminists have articulated female identity and resistance to male power.

103

There have been wider criticisms of post-colonial theory, for instance 'that the institutional location of post-colonial theory in the Western academy necessarily and automatically precludes it from being able to perform radical liberatory kinds of cultural analysis' (Moore-Gilbert 1997: 3). It is argued that post-colonial writers and thinkers from other cultures are 'exported', theorised and made palatable for the cultural elite and then sent back to these cultures in a more 'Westernised' form. Audre Lorde seems to make a similar point when she argues that the 'centre' thrives on getting the 'other' to explain its 'otherness' in just one more cycle of domination: '[w]henever the need for some pretence of communication arises, those who profit from our oppression call upon us to share our knowledge with them. In other words, it is the responsibility of the oppressed to teach the oppressors their mistakes . . . The oppressors maintain their position and evade responsibility for their own actions' (Lorde in Crowley and Himmelweit 1992: 47).

Further criticisms of post-colonial theory are similar to those directed at post-structuralism or postmodernism – that it has too oblique a reference to politics to be a radicalising perspective. This is as much to do with broader debates about the applicability of high theory to political analysis and any defence depends on one's belief or otherwise in a post-Foucauldian analysis of power and the construction of the subject through discourse. For others, 'the increasingly unfocused use of the term "post-colonial" over the last ten years to describe an astonishing variety of cultural, economic and political practices has meant that there is a danger of its losing its effective meaning altogether' (Ashcroft et al.1995: 2).

Theorists interested in the phenomenon of globalisation might argue that the term 'post-colonial' fails to account for the shaping of the identities and lives of men and women in contemporary society, where the effects of economic globalisation have intensified poverty and deprivation for some groups while empowering others. Gender remains an important category in the analysis of global power, and from an international relations perspective it has been argued that 'the failure to resolve global dilemmas of poverty, pollution, nuclear proliferation and so on, is in part, a result of the neglect of women's contributions to political-economic development and the lack of support of these contributions by international aid agencies and governments' (True in Burchill et al. 2001: 240). In this view, women are the greater casualties of global economic structures because the ways in which globalisation operates at an economic level affect the domestic sphere (family subsistence, male migration, etc.), even though the domestic remains unaccounted for in global economics.

See also: *postmodernism, post-structuralism*

### FURTHER READING

Ashcroft, Griffiths and Tiffin's anthology, *The Post-Colonial Studies Reader* (1995) is probably a good place to get a solid grounding in the range of post-colonial theoretical writings. Said's *Orientalism* (1978) and Gayatri Spivak's *In Other Worlds* (1988) help explain the emergence of post-colonial theory as distinct from post-structuralism. McClintock (1995) is another key text which looks at race, gender and sexuality. For those wanting to look further into issues raised by the final paragraph, Halliday (1994) is a good place to begin.

# post-feminism

It must first be stated that there is no agreement about how post-feminism can be defined and consequently definitions essentially contradict each other in what they say about the term. At its most straightforward, the prefix 'post' in this context appears to mean 'going beyond' or 'superseding': it could therefore be seen as a confident announcement that feminism has achieved its key aims and that there is full equality for all women and a blurring of the boundaries between traditional ascriptions of gender. Given that a brief scrutiny of our current social formation does not support this view, we might, however, imagine that a post-feminist position is one formulated due to dissatisfaction with existing feminist politics and is to be located in an entirely new area or set of propositions altogether. Part of this dissatisfaction might be an awareness that even in its heyday, second wave feminism did not achieve its aim of speaking to the majority of women.

Either of these definitions seems possible and the notion of superseding or going beyond has been widely utilised in popular culture, and to some extent in academic discourse. Given that 'feminism' remains within the term post-feminism, albeit problematised by the prefix of 'post', this illustrates that 'feminism is portrayed as a territory over which various women have to fight to gain their ground; it has become so unwieldy as a term that it threatens to implode under the weight of its own contradictions' (Whelehan 2000: 78). The 'post' is not the end of feminism: actually feminism is constantly to be picked over only to be rapidly set aside again or dismissed as old hat. For Myra Macdonald, 'post-feminism takes the sting out of feminism' (1995: 100); it removes the politics and claims the territory of self-empowerment.

There are some more complex and challenging definitions of the term and according to writers such as Sopia Phoca who co-produced an introductory guide to it, 'post-feminism is considered as a different manifestation of feminism – not as being anti-feminist' (quoted in Ashby 1999: 34) and as being associated with the development of post-Lacanian psychoanalysis, French feminism and post-structuralist theory, suggesting perhaps a permanent fracturation between second wave-style personal politics and 'high' theory. Ann Brooks (1997), however, would argue that it is not a question of depoliticising feminism, but of marking a conceptual shift between the 'old' and the 'new' – from a model based on equality, to debates around the revivified and theorised concept of difference. For Brooks the term 'post-feminism' 'is now understood as a useful conceptual frame of reference encompassing the intersection of feminism with a number of other anti-foundational movements including postmodernism, post-structuralism and post-colonialism' (Brooks 1997: 1).

Other critics would argue that the 'post' prefix added to modernism, structuralism or colonialism seems to unproblematically connote the 'going beyond' both spatially and chronologically that has occurred in modern theory; yet Brooks asserts that post-feminism used in this theoretical context signifies feminism's maturity. She reflects that rather than 'post' meaning going beyond or breaking with, in these contexts it means 'a process of ongoing transformation and change' (Brooks 1997: 1). Other kinds of 'rebranding' for feminism of course include the use of 'third wave' feminism where again the prefix is used to imply key shifts in the meaning of 'feminism' itself and in this theoretically-informed definition of post-feminism there might be seen to be common ground between third wave and post-feminism, although third wavers would certainly reject any suggestion that feminism is over. Brooks herself acknowledges the way post-feminism is associated with a negative portrayal of feminism in the mass media – particularly in the way the rhetoric of post-feminism is summoned in the backlash against feminism (see also Faludi 1992).

One of the reasons it is argued that the move to post-feminism is essential is because of the influence of postmodern thinking which refuses the 'grand narrative' of gender difference, so that it becomes increasingly impossible to lay claim to the identity 'woman', because of the impact of 'difference' theories and the contestation of knowledges about how 'woman' is constructed. Brooks's version of post-feminism puts 'woman' under erasure; of course one could argue that this denies any political agency to a feminist who cannot lay claim to that identity, 'modernist' as it is, suggesting as it does a retreat to the self and ultimately the individualist framing of identity so favoured by enlightenment liberalism. The category 'woman', no matter how unsatisfactory as a means to summon up the wealth and diversity of women's experiences and identities, allows at least a space to lay claim to a wealth of shared experiences (gendered pay differentials, the impact of sexual violence, the relationship of nation to gender for instance) which permits a collective oppositional response to injustices against women.

For critics who are still happy to call themselves 'feminist' without any prefixes, such a model of feminism does not readily allow for an acknowledgement of some highly productive shifts in feminism since the 1970s. Feminist politics has not remained static, and many of the central issues, so radical in the 1970s, are now accepted as part of mainstream politics. As Sylvia Walby notes, 'Who would now call someone who believes in equal pay feminist? Yet before 1975 this was not law and was controversial' (1997: 163). Rene Denfeld, in her critique of second wave feminism, *The New Victorians*, bears this out when she points out that while the next generation has problems with the epithet 'feminist', they have no problem supporting the principles of equal pay and educational opportunities (Denfeld 1995: 4). For Denfeld this change from broad support of feminism to scepticism and alienation is a response to a change in the terms of second wave feminism itself: 'It has become bogged down in an extremist moral and spiritual crusade that has little to do with women's lives. It has climbed out on a limb of academic theory that is all but inaccessible to the uninitiated . . . feminism has become as confining as what it pretends to combat' (Denfeld 1995: 5). Denfeld is pointing to widely aired anxieties that feminism has become just one more arcane theory – stemming from what she perceives to be a majority of cultural feminist writers creating and delivering women's studies curricula in American universities, containing an alleged anti-male agenda. It is as if she actually doesn't want to dismiss feminism but rather to take it 'back' from whoever she feels has stolen it. The irony is that 'post-feminism' from both Phoca and Wright's and Brooks's perspective is in many ways just such another 'inaccessible' theory for the uninitiated.

Tania Modleski is more concerned that while 'woman' is being put under erasure in the debates about difference, conceptual shifts such as the 'men in feminism' debate (a debate about whether men should call themselves feminists or be feminist critics independently of women) might make women disappear from feminism altogether. Talking about one particular anthology of 'male feminist' criticism she observes that '[i]n an unusually strong post-feminist irony, the final essay of this volume which banishes women from its list of contributors is a complaint about the way heterosexual men have become invisible within feminism!' (Modleski, 1991: 12). Modleski's dissection of post-feminism in the critical sphere in many ways anticipates Susan Faludi's arguments in *Backlash* where it is the appropriation of the language of feminism which is seen to be used against itself in popular culture. Modleski's combination of questioning theory and using examples of popular film, television and news, suggests that this appropriation goes much deeper and, she would argue, drives us straight back to male-centred discourse and critical authority.

There is still the accusation that second wave feminism failed to cede the hegemony of white middle-class heterosexual women to other groups of women, and there is clearly some truth in this claim. But nonetheless it is clear that many feminists (particularly at the level of grassroots politics) did acknowledge the common links between different sites of oppression; and the growth in political and critical perspectives by women of colour, working-class women and lesbians suggests that for them the struggle is not over. One can think of key voices in black American feminism, such as bell hooks and Patricia Hill Collins who emphatically lay claim to 'feminism' as a term which still has political resonance, and this suggests that not all proponents of feminist discourse are ready yet to cede the ground to post-feminism, but would rather address the gaps, in the belief that there might be some consensus about what feminism can do.

**See also:** *difference, feminisms, postmodernism, third wave feminism*

### FURTHER READING

Ann Brooks (1997) gives a fairly comprehensive account of what 'post-feminism' means in a theoretical context; for those still struggling with French feminism, post-structuralism and Lacan. Phoca and Wright (1999) offer a crisp and concise account, liberally using illustrations and graphic narrative. Modleski (1991) and Faludi (1992) offer challenges which provide illuminating comparison.

Postmodernism is a broad set of ideas and arguments relating to advanced industrialised societies of the late twentieth century onwards. It is concerned with the description and analysis of the distinctive features of these societies and with theorising the ramifications of these features for relations between social groupings, for individual selves and identities, and for the status and forms of knowledge, science and culture. Postmodernism as a concept is sometimes used interchangeably with that of post-structuralism. In this volume, however, the two concepts have separate entries in order to clarify the differences between them. We follow the view of writers like Marshall (1994) in regarding post-structuralism as primarily a theory of knowledge and language, and postmodernism as primarily a theory of society, culture and history.

It is hard to identify a single, concise illustration of postmodernism, partly due to variations in the meaning of the concept according to disciplinary perspective and partly due to the tenets of the concept itself: a key idea of postmodernism is that things are not certain, orderly and fixed, but are instead uncertain, disorderly and fluid. That being said, there is reasonably widespread agreement that the key authors of postmodernism include Lyotard, Baudrillard and Jameson; Foucault is also often labelled as a postmodernist writer. There is reasonably widespread agreement, too, that a shared feature of postmodernist perspectives is the critique of 'modernism' as a set of ideas, arguments and analyses. Briefly, modernist thinking is argued to encapsulate the Enlightenment belief in the practices and values of science as a way of understanding both the natural and the social world. Rational thinking and a belief in progress are seen to have underpinned the development of the key social, economic, political and cultural features of modern societies, from, say, the fifteenth and sixteenth centuries up until the mid to late twentieth century. Modernist thinking was reflected in, for example, the organisation of large-scale methods of production, in the development of mass party politics, trades unions, and the welfare state, and in large-scale, universalist social and political theories which explained or otherwise 'justified' modern societies, including Parsons' structural functionalism and Marxist historical materialism. In contrast to modernism, postmodernism encapsulates a turning away from the Enlightenment project, through a rejection of the authority of science and a questioning of the inevitability of, and benefits of, progress. In the

**109**

analyses of postmodernist authors like Lash and Urry (1987), Jameson (1991) and Baudrillard (1990), for example, advanced industrialised societies exhibit features such as disorganisation and fragmentation, insecurity, uncertainty and unpredictability (for example, in the rise of 'flexible working', the decline of class-based politics, and through the 'hyperreal'). For authors like Lyotard (1984), there has been a loss of faith in the powers of science and other universalist 'metanarratives' (or large-scale theories) as the route to improve the human condition. Instead, there is increasing plurality in cultural representations and knowledge forms, with greater recognition of the local and the specific and of minority social groupings, differences and diversity.

The impact of postmodernism has been significant across a wide range of academic disciplines. It is a concept which has proved impossible to ignore, although it remains a highly controversial one that has elicited a variety of responses, including within gender studies. For some writers, there is a strong affinity between feminism and postmodernism. Hekman (1990), for example, argues for a 'postmodern approach to feminism', in part based on the similarities between the two. Both feminism and postmodernism critique dominant knowledge forms, especially conceptions of science which privilege rationality, causal explanation and either/or dichotomies. Furthermore, Hekman sees feminism and postmodernism as 'complementary and mutually corrective'. A postmodern position can help resolve some of the key issues debated in feminism (for example, the existence of an essential female nature), while, in turn, feminism can contribute to postmodernism through bringing in gender, a focus which it otherwise often lacks (1990: 3–8). More broadly within gender studies, an important consequence of the postmodernist challenge to the legacy of Enlightenment thinking has been the destabilising of dichotomous gender categories and the increased recognition of differences within those grouped as 'women' and 'men' (age, class, ethnicity, sexuality, dis/ability, etc.). Relatedly, there has been a shift away from large-scale theories which seek to causally explain gender relations in a universalist sense (for example, patriarchy), to approaches which centre on the analysis of language and discourse in the construction of gender (for example, Butler 1990). For Brooks (1997), such intersections of feminism with postmodernism have produced 'post-feminism'. In other words, through an engagement with postmodernism, feminism has matured into 'a confident body of theory and politics, representing pluralism and difference and reflecting on its position in relation to other philosophical and political movements similarly demanding change' (1997: 1).

Responses to the development of 'postmodernist feminism' by some other writers have, however, been less positive. If, as postmodernist arguments propose, 'women' and 'men' are untenable unitary categories, then where does this leave feminism as a political project? Walby argues against postmodernist feminism, insisting that the 'signifiers of "woman" and "man" have sufficient historical and cross-cultural continuity, despite some variations, to warrant using such terms' (1994b: 229). Other critics, Walby included, emphasise the continued importance of empirical investigations into gender relations, and especially of focusing on material aspects, rather than merely examining representations and discourses (for example, Maynard 2001; Jackson 1998). As Oakley contends, 'if we took the admonitions of the postmodernist . . . theorists seriously, we would abandon altogether the interest a practical feminism must have in establishing how peoples' material resources, life chances, and experiences are affected by their gender' (1998: 143). A further set of responses to the influence of postmodernism within gender studies amounts neither to its wholesale acceptance or rejection. In a general sense, most writers within gender studies recognise that postmodernism has quite rightly focused attention on diversity and difference, and that its critiques of 'grand narratives' have at least some value (for example, Maynard 1995; Walby 1994b). Moreover, some contributors to the debate on postmodernism and gender studies have begun to question the very distinctions that have been drawn between the modern and the postmodern. Zalewski (2000) analyses modern and postmodern feminist perspectives on the issue of new reproductive technologies. She argues that, although different, their perspectives on new reproductive technologies are not necessarily contradictory and can even be seen as complementary. Similarly, in Felski's (2000) analysis, modernism and postmodernism are not antithetical concepts, partly because neither are unified, coherent or self-evident entities. Felski's argument is that feminist theory can help deconstruct the distinction drawn between modernism and postmodernism and reveal the 'leaky boundaries' between the two concepts. For Felski, feminism can benefit from an engagement with postmodernism as a concept, but also needs to retain some 'modernist' concerns. In other words, feminism should pay attention 'to diverse and often contradictory strands of cultural expression and affiliation without losing sight of broader determinants of inequality' (Felski 2000: 206). Feminist analyses also need to realise that 'power and inequality do not simply reside in language, even though we can only make sense of them through language' (2000: 206). In outlining these terms of feminism's engagement with postmodernism, Felski is in keeping with the broader reception given to the concept within gender studies.

111

**key concepts**

### FURTHER READING

The volume edited by Nicholson (1990) remains a key text in the debate on feminism and postmodernism, with chapters by Flax, Di Stefano and Bordo among others. Waugh (1998) gives a succinct assessment of the relationship between feminism and postmodernism. Gender is not the focus of Woods' (1999) *Beginning Postmodernism*, but it is a useful overview of the influence of the concept across a wide range of disciplines including architecture, the arts and popular cultures.

# post-structuralism

Post-structuralist thought is seen to emerge primarily from the work of Jacques Derrida, Jacques Lacan and Michel Foucault. It offers an antidote to liberal humanist ways of seeing the world, particularly in their theories of the 'self', which move from the liberal conception of a unified and rational self, to fragmentary and contradictory and constructed from the discourses around it. Given that post-structuralists reject the concept of the subject as a fixed entity, they deny any notion of essence at the heart of the self, but argue that we only come to know ourselves through the medium of language, and individual words themselves only gain meaning as part of a system. As it is, we can never get to the bottom of this system, find the origin of utterance: as Jonathan Culler remarks, 'however far back we try to push, even when we try to imagine the "birth" of language and describe an originary event that might have produced the first structure, we discover that we must assume prior organization, prior differentiation' (1983: 96). Derrida's notion of 'deconstruction' pursues this frustration with the elusiveness of originary meaning, and is the process by which the knowledge of the Enlightenment, the binary logic in Western thought of true/false, good/bad, rational/irrational and perhaps man/woman, are dismantled. Take for example the man/woman binary: 'man can proceed without the mention of woman because she is deemed to be automatically included as a special case; male pronouns exclude her without calling attention to her exclusion; and if she is considered separately she will still be defined in terms of man, as his other' (Culler 1983: 166).

Post-structuralism emphasises the importance of language in structuring our experience of the world – meanings are not inherent in the thing or action itself but are created by words and their relationship to other words. Meanings, it is argued, cannot be fixed or remain stable, but are endlessly remade through the process of reading/speaking and changes in social life. At the heart of the post-structuralist perspective lies the principle that language produces social reality, which varies across cultures and time.

Diane Elam in her book on feminism and deconstruction suggests that the two perspectives are on the face of it incompatible, one being political and the latter being philosophical (Elam 1994: 1). She expands on this by showing that feminism upsets our traditional definitions of politics just as deconstruction unseats some of the certainties, the casual binaries of philosophy. Post-structuralism, like feminism, remains ultimately difficult to define because of its pluralities and its denial of singular definition, yet Elam sees the common ground between feminism and deconstruction as that of subjectivity. Given that feminism is a political movement, identity politics remains crucial to feminists and (as discussed in the entry on Essentialism), one still needs to make use of the category 'woman', unstable as it might be: 'If one were to spend all of one's time worrying about deconstructing the subject while also attempting to run election campaigns, argue sexual harassment cases, or explain to students why sexist language is inappropriate, then not much would get accomplished from a feminist perspective' (Elam 1994: 72).

Chris Weedon makes the point that there is a tension between seeing individuals as agents of choice and change and looking at the means by which oppression is filtered through social institutions and practices. She argues that 'for many women, a feminist perspective results from the conflicts and contradictions between dominant institutionalized definitions of women's nature and social role, inherent in the sexual division of labour ... and our experience of these institutions in the context of the dominant liberal discourse of the free and self-determining individual' (Weedon 1987: 5). For this reason she avers that a theoretical perspective that challenges the naturalness of individualism will allow an examination of the means by which power is sustained and mediated through such institutions as well as reveal that the liberal appeal to female individuality attempts to obscure the way that women often feel unable to embrace the 'choices' offered to them.

A post-structuralist perspective, it is argued, allows us not just to evaluate the material possibilities available to women, but it also gives us a sophisticated account of how ideology (or discourse) makes these choices impossible or contradictory. For example, Weedon notes how feminists have traditionally responded to the family and illustrates some central tensions: 'the positions of wife and mother, though subject to male control, also offer forms of power – the power to socialize children, to run the house, and to be the power behind the throne' (Weedon 1987: 19). Althusser's theory of ideology was crucial to the development of post-structuralist thinking, particularly in the concept of interpellation, where subjectivity is perceived as constructed through ideology – the individual recognises herself but does not recognise the ways in which the subject position is constructed and 'assumes that she is the *author* of the ideology which constructs her subjectivity' (Weedon 1987: 31). This way of perceiving social reality is of course perfectly compatible with some earlier feminist views of female oppression, even though they lacked the theoretical language of subjectivity (see, for example, Tax in Koedt et al. 1973).

The concept of discourse, very much the product of Michel Foucault's theoretical work, is also central to post-structuralist perspectives. Discourse is not simple to define, but fundamentally refers to the organising principles of social institutions and how they shape the means by which we can come to 'know' anything. There is talk of discursive fields such as the law or the family or science; these aren't necessarily mutually exclusive, but contained within discursive formations that can be subject to what Foucault terms 'epistemic shifts'. Crudely speaking, an epistemic shift occurs when new discoveries or interpretations profoundly affect the way we come to know a field to the point where its entire basis is questioned – science is a good case in point. The shifting loci of discursive formations allow for the emergence of oppositional discourses which may operate as marginal to the dominant formations, but offer the possibility of challenge.

The key problem that those sceptical of the radical potentialities of post-structuralism will return to is how any challenge to the dominant discursive regimes may be undertaken. This problem remains: while the concern with language means that post-structuralism has been readily embraced in the study of literary texts, and while it is certainly compatible with exposing gaps and instabilities in modern Western thought, it is not clear how one militates for change rather than simply offering 'resistance' to the status quo. There is much political mileage in the activity of feminists resisting dominant subject positions and Weedon characterises this as 'the first stage in the production of alternative forms of knowledge or where such alternatives exist, of winning individuals over to these discourses and gradually increasing their social power' (Weedon 1987:

111). The means by which a post-structuralist analysis allows for a more nuanced interrogation of the relations of power has proved instructive and potentially transformative for feminists.

**See also:** *ideology, postmodernism, power*

### FURTHER READING

Both Elam (1994) and Weedon (1987) offer a useful gloss on the relationship of feminism to post-structuralism, though perhaps Weedon is the most accessible in the first instance. The work of Derrida, Lacan and Foucault, approached with this preparation, may yield more insights.

———————————— power ————————————

To define power is an enormously complex matter and we can only attempt a thumbnail sketch here in order to examine the way power has been used in the arena of feminist and gender studies. In the most general terms, to possess power is to have the ability to achieve whatever is desired regardless of any opposition. Power may be expressed through consent based on the perceived legitimacy of those who hold it (e.g. the state, run by an elected government). Power in its more overtly coercive form may be seen to be expressed by control with a lack of perceived legitimacy. Some cultures perhaps allow for the alignment of both models of power where coercion of individuals is legitimated by religious or ideological means – for example where archaic religious laws operate parallel to a modern legal system.

In modern democracies, there is a superficial limiting of power: first, the organisation of state power is supposed to encourage belief that corruption is difficult; second, liberal democracies affirm the public/private division within the state with a general policy of non-intervention in the home. This latter perspective has of course been of special interest to feminists over the past thirty years who embodied their notion of how patriarchal power operates in the slogan 'the personal is political' showing that the state policy of non-interference in the home can lead to a legitimation of male power in cases such as domestic violence. For Marxists the state wields power through both economic and ideological means in order to shore up the political and economic status quo (see Gatens 1996 for further discussion). The concept of ideology shows how power can be exercised through less tangible and direct means and has been central to feminist analysis, not least in the examination of state rhetoric of equality or equal opportunity.

All political movements must have a working definition of how power is defined and this will to some extent structure their vision of how to change current relations of power. Radical feminists were inclined to conceptualise power in terms of patriarchy, so that even the most disenfranchised man was seen to have more access to power and the privileges of our culture than any woman. This idea of power was interrogated by Marxist feminists who felt that it lacked any historical specificity or any sense of how power actually functioned; for these reasons they looked at what they called a 'patriarchal ideology' and the means by which, both economically and structurally, the state operated first and foremost in the interests of men.

The Women's Liberation Movement had, perhaps inadvisedly, given too little attention to the way power was structured within its own ranks. The 'official' view was that feminism rejected all hierarchies of power in a 'structureless' movement with no leaders and no spokespeople: everything was to be done on rotation and with the complete agreement of the entire group. This meant that less 'formal' networks of power were allowed to take hold and fester with the result that the 'politicos' tended to hold sway and that the dominant group of white, middle-class heterosexuals obscured the interests and perspectives of other members. Power for early second wave women was about the power for self-definition and the ending of male domination. As Lynne Segal put it, 'we wanted power to participate in the making of a new world which would be free from all forms of domination' (1987: 2), but this desire meant the rejection of the role of the dominant without a clear idea of what would take its place. When it came to debating power structures within the Women's Liberation Movement, both words 'power' and 'structure' were shunned as having patriarchal overtones of leadership and hierarchy, but after a few years of organisation along these lines, many felt that 'structurelessness' was itself tyrannical, leading to unofficial leaders, needless bureaucracy and 'stars' being able to take control without any recourse to objections from the rest of the group. 'Joreen' (Jo Freeman) in 'The Tyranny of Structurelessness' (1972) saw the need to formalise a group's structure, noting that the 'more unstructured a group is, the less control it has over the directions in which it develops and the political actions in which it engages' (Joreen in Koedt et al. 1973: 296). This turned out to be a very prescient view because radical feminist groups in the USA and the UK found it very difficult to organise so that they could communicate with each other or form some kind of federation that allowed ideas to spread effectively. Ultimately the liberal women's organisation in the USA, NOW (The National Organization for Women), would endure because it had no problem with taking the classic model of democratic organisation with leaders voted in and out.

Feminists did not anticipate the force of the power struggles that would be encountered as an effect of group dynamics and the rehearsing of identity politics, nor had they adequately thought through how a power struggle with patriarchy would end if one could only express it in terms akin to 'class struggle' where the dominated emerged now dominant from the fray. Feminists clearly didn't want that kind of victory because they wanted to dismantle the system of power which perpetuated such divisions; they had also realised that any goal of 'equality' itself implied a power relationship depending on which group of men one wanted to be equal with.

Some embraced Foucault's theoretical reflections on power because he moved away from the simple model of power being defined as an exchange between oppressors and oppressed to that which filters down through all social relations. This model suggests a form of self-governance in a 'panoptical' model where people police themselves on the assumption that at any time they might be under surveillance. Foucault's theory of discourse, as that which creates the conditions of knowledge at any given time, means that discourse itself acts as a kind of surveillance. In addition, this model of power challenges the monolithic notions of male power: instead it is inscribed in discourse where it is not always easy to identify actual agents, or perhaps it is simply the case that agency has become less important, subordinated to the network of power itself.

Foucault suggests a way of looking at power which is beyond that embodied by the state or class of people to that which is exercised at a microcosmic level. For feminist theorists such as Jana Sawicki, such a model allows us to think beyond a concept of power as a possession and to think about 'how subjects are constituted by power relations' (Sawicki 1991: 21). She goes on to assert that Foucault's conceptualisation of power moves beyond the idea of it being merely repressive to it also being productive. A useful example can be found in his account of how the discourse of psychoanalysis uses sexuality as the means by which we discover our true selves – of course just as these discourses promise to liberate, they set up strata of normalising forces which inevitably restrict. If Foucault offers a positive way to challenge power, it is through his suggestion that with power comes the possibility of resistance in a constant struggle, depending on the ways various discourses are utilised because '[d]iscourse transmits and produces power; it reinforces it, but also undermines and exposes it, renders it fragile and makes it possible to thwart it' (Foucault 1979: 101).

So-called 'new' feminists of the 1990s seem to have moved back to a more liberal perspective in their imagined future for feminism where they assume equality will be achieved through a classic 'male' model of competitive, meritocratic power. For them second wave feminism failed because it could not stomach the idea of power along the lines of hierarchies of privilege naturalised by the fact of democracy. In fact, as has been discussed above, it was positively eschewed, and instead the majority of women in the Women's Liberation Movement were committed to the principle of shared power and alternating of roles within political activism. In her book, *The New Feminism*, Natasha Walter muses that there have never been so many images of powerful women and gives as examples an actress playing the role of a strong career woman, the 100 Labour women MPs standing together for their first photo-shoot after the UK 1997 General Election, businesswomen and women working for causes as evidence of women's 'growing power' (Walter 1998: 168). For Walter the fact of women's increased presence in the public domain is evidence of power: looked at again one notes that these women's power is still mediated through those who act as figureheads to the real operations of power – the obvious examples being the women MPs subject to the strictures of their male Prime Minister and the masculinist culture of Parliament. She is dismissive of the 1970s' feminist desire to deny power to those who wield it rather than take it up themselves, missing a rather large political point about why feminists rejected that kind of power, even if she is right to observe that this rejection offered no substantial alternative.

Predictably perhaps, Walter favours Margaret Thatcher as a model of the new female power, and while acceding that she did not actively encourage the advancement of other women into political power, she asserts that 'she normalised female success' (Walter 1998: 175). This position may seem to have a rather questionable foundation, but the emergence of a Labour victory in 1997 and the return of more women to Parliament than ever before seem to have turned women's minds to Thatcher as some kind of meaningful figurehead. Helen Wilkinson muses on Thatcher's 'free market feminism' and while understanding the scepticism with which women regarded her in the past, Wilkinson defends her by arguing that she 'did not shy away from showing how much she loved power, and in turn she made it legitimate for us to love it too' (Wilkinson in Walter 1999: 31). One might also observe that ultimately what Thatcher legitimated was an individualist approach to power, and being herself the exception to the rule, she demonstrated everything there is to say about patriarchal privilege. For Elizabeth Wilson, commenting on Thatcher's election as leader of the Conservative Party in 1975, 'she is the Exceptional Woman in a well-worn mould, whereas we stand for all women who are struggling to break out of the mould altogether, and to smash those deadly, steely-saccharin images of success' (Wilson in Feminist Anthology Collective 1981: 14).

Thus, the new feminism seems to return women to a liberal image of power as monolithic, which if Foucault's model has any weight, is outmoded anyway. The feminist CR groups have gone and the debates about structurelessness seem to be long forgotten or outrageously misrepresented. These are replaced with Naomi Wolf's idea of 'power groups', a kind of women's club which acts solely as a means of transferring power among women –'[f]or women usually lack money, but they often have access to one thing that is increasingly valuable in today's economy: information' (Wolf 1993: 314). It seems that feminists have yet to find a model of power that accounts for the persistent ideological dominance of patriarchy and its subsequent material effects – or at least one which also offers the clear and practical possibilities of resistance.

**See also:** *ideology, patriarchy, second wave feminism*

### FURTHER READING

Joreen's infamous pamphlet (reprinted in Koedt et al. 1973) is worth trying, but failing that Echols' (1989) account of those years in the USA will give a good sense of the model of power feminists were trying to work with. Foucault (1979), though not purely on power, is one of his more accessible works and Gatens' (1996) commentary on modern power relations is useful. Walter (1998) and Wolf (1993) bear some comparison with each other.

# psychoanalytical feminism

Freud is the most famous 'father' of psychoanalysis who developed his methods after being involved as a neurologist treating patients for hysteria. His work with Josef Breuer in the 1880s allowed them to develop the method of the 'talking cure' – helping patients recover from the symptoms of hysteria by getting them to uncover the forgotten trauma at its source. The theory of the 'unconscious' was structured on this idea that there were parts of the mind's functioning that were inaccessible to the individual themselves, but which were manifested by other means – dreams, slips of the tongue and physical ailments.

Feminism's early relationship to psychoanalysis was largely a critical one. Kate Millett, considering the legacy of its founder, Sigmund Freud, in her best-selling *Sexual Politics*, contends that his understanding of the female is based upon his idea of penis envy, which results in the inevitable conceptualisation of woman as lack. For Millett this means that Freud's theories are essentially conservative, working in the interests of patriarchy and she argues that 'the Freudian position came to be pressed into the service of a strongly counterrevolutionary attitude' (Millett 1977: 178). It is Freud's theory of the Oedipus complex which provides a central problem for feminists, where the female is supposedly perceived by the male (and perceives herself) as castrated when she sees the male genitals and discovers her own lack of a penis.

It is probably useful to include Freud's explanation of the female version of the Oedipal complex:

> The little girl's clitoris behaves just like a penis to begin with; but, when she makes a comparison with a playfellow of the other sex, she perceives that she has 'come off badly' and she feels this as a wrong done to her and as a ground for inferiority. For a while she still consoles herself with the expectation that later on, when she grows older, she will acquire just as big an appendage as the boy's. Here the masculinity complex of women branches off. But a female child does not understand her lack of a penis as a sex character; she explains it by assuming that at some earlier date she had possessed an equally large organ and had then lost it by castration. (Freud, trans. Richards 1977: 320–1)

The healthy resolution of this complex, according to Freud, is the acceptance of her castration and the wish to take her mother's place in her father's affections and thus acquire a 'feminine attitude' towards men in general. Her lack of a penis, it is asserted, makes her long for a baby and '[t]he two wishes – to possess a penis and a child – remain strongly cathected in the unconscious and help to prepare the female creature for her later sexual role' (Freud, trans. Richards 1977: 321).

The image of women as 'castrated' men who must prepare themselves for a passive sexual role conveys the idea of their secondary status to men – that their lack of the penis is translated in social terms as lack of power, status and authority. Simone de Beauvoir critically picked up on this image of the castrated woman in *The Second Sex* and the title of Germaine Greer's *The Female Eunuch* (1971) clearly makes reference to it. While later psychoanalysts such as Melanie Klein were to argue for a shift in focus on to the mother's anatomy and generally emphasise the maternal as a more important theoretical precept, Freud's theories were largely seen as the perfect embodiment of using the male principle to explain normal 'humanity' and then tacking women on to the end of it. Read literally, Freud's perspectives on the development of female sexuality are perhaps too easy to deride and expose as unremittingly patriarchal. Juliet Mitchell's book, *Psychoanalysis and Feminism* (1975), was to overturn some knee-jerk prejudice by proposing that Freud's psychoanalytical model should be viewed as descriptive of the society in which he lived, rather than being prescriptive about the desired relationships between men and women. Cast in this light, the phallus becomes a symbol of patriarchal power rather than a reflection of how the world should be. Moreover, it has been pointed out that the areas of life focused on in psychoanalysis – the family, sexuality, childhood and the body – are those of primary concern to feminist thought.

Melanie Klein, practising child analysis in the 1940s and 1950s, felt that the child's formative years were governed by anxiety and emotions rather than sexuality and pleasure. The child is represented as suffering warring emotions of love and hate depending on whether its immediate needs have been satisfied by the mother. Generally her theoretical perspective uses the imagery of the maternal body, so for instance the breast is split into 'good' and 'bad' breast, coming to represent the split between the child and the mother. Rather than patriarchal power being sustained by penis envy and the fear of castration, she sees patriarchal power as motivated by 'womb envy' – experienced by children of both sexes – although girls may well grow up to have babies while boys have to seek to create through other means. However, Klein's work has been criticised because it is seen to base gender identity very heavily on biological determinism (see Minsky 1996: 103–7), a tendency in psychoanalytical thinking about which most feminists felt uncomfortable.

Mitchell's reappraisal of Freud was highly influential on feminist thinking and opened up psychoanalytical feminism as a fruitful area of study and her references to Jacques Lacan brought his work to a broader Anglo-American audience. Many feminists have found the unconscious to be a useful organising concept because, in Freudian theory, it assumes that there is a dimension to our identity beyond the reach of our conscious thoughts and actions that determines what we do and how we feel without us knowing it, and which comes through, via projection, in our behaviour to others. It can perhaps be best expressed as the site of repressed desires, compulsions, anxieties, phobias, obsessions and dreams and in Lacanian thought is the driving force behind language formation. The siting of the unconscious somewhere between language and desire offered a welcome extra dimension to the feminist study of female subjectivity, where resistances and conflicts could paint a broader picture of the female self under patriarchy.

It was Lacan who, importantly, stressed that the moment of the child's acquisition of language is the moment of entry into the social or phallic order. The process of the child's movement from total identification with the body of the mother through to language acquisition and entry into the world of sexual difference is described in terms of stages. Thus the mirror stage denotes the moment when the child recognises itself as separate from the mother (the formation of the ego) and the symbolic stage represents the child's entry into language and subjectivity as delineated by the social order. This entry into the symbolic is accompanied by a sense of loss of bond with the mother once the child recognises that it is actually separate from her – this 'imaginary' realm is for Lacan what constitutes the unconscious. This entry into language is seen as an entry into the phallic order – in general Lacan uses the term phallus rather than penis to signify the way power is symbolised in the symbolic order.

Under Lacan psychoanalysis becomes more focused on the study of the construction of the subject through language and Lacan adopts Saussure's structuralist concepts of sign/signifier, where the meaning of a word depends upon its relationship to the rest of the language system. It is not inherent, but rather arbitrary and relational. In this formulation the unconscious becomes a linguistic structure; and as a post-structuralist thinker Lacan does not frame the idea of the self as having a coherent identity. The phallus comes to symbolise sexual difference; it also symbolises the father (since acquisition of language means entry into the symbolic order and patriarchal power of the phallus), whereas the imaginary (pre-mirror stage) represents the fusion with the mother, so the unconscious plays out the anxieties of loss of the mother. It is asserted that the child becomes aware of sexual difference at about the time it acquires language which conveys the meanings by which we understand our culture and our selves, and yet is underpinned by our unconscious desires to return to the mother. For Minsky, '[i]n Lacan's world where no one has a genuine identity, women represents a double lack – her own lack of the valued phallus, and as a projection of male lack produced by his symbolic castration by his father. So women are doubly powerless' (Minsky 1996: 162). Women are constructed only with reference to the phallus, and therefore her femininity serves the function of a masquerade – a playing of the part determined by masculine phallic logic as lacking rather than as positively being woman.

Luce Irigaray's work on Freud, as well as Julia Kristeva's, picked up on a more maternal model of psychoanalytical thinking and their appropriations of Freud owe a debt to the work of Jacques Lacan. The work of French feminists Kristeva and Irigaray became influential from the mid-1980s in Britain and America when their work was more widely translated. They were drawn to Lacan's reworking of Freud and the possibilities for theorising identity within the sphere of language and challenging the phallic order. They suggest that one can be freed from the patriarchal stranglehold of the symbolic order through the use of poetic language, more associated with the unconscious, and therefore challenging to the male-identified symbolic. The reference to the 'feminine' principle of the unconscious at least suggests a space beyond the phallus and the possibilities of resistance, if not transformation of social realities based on the positioning of woman as other.

Kristeva's concept of the 'abject' represents that which is marginalised in society in the pre-Oedipal stage, which she calls the 'semiotic'. She sees the need for women to make language their own so that they can communicate feminine experience, and experiment with new ways of structuring that experience. Her emphasis on the maternal as against lesbian or other female identities has, however, led to some criticisms of her work (see Vice in Jackson and Jones 1998). Theorists such as Irigaray are especially interesting because of the way they attempt to destabilise the masculine imagery of the phallus by using imagery based on the female anatomy. Her model of two lips speaking together provides a feminised counter to phallocentricism as both an explicitly female sexualised image and a suggestion of the female appropriation of language. For Irigaray,

123

female sexuality is seen as hidden and multiple in the experience of *jouissance* of the whole body rather than genitally expressed.

In psychoanalytical feminism, we see different theorists grappling with ways to appropriate the theories put forward by men that facilitate analysis of the tenacious hold of a patriarchal order, but which also allow for the imagining of resistance and challenge to that order. Lacan's model of the symbolic does imply the unquestioned dominance of men, given that one has to recognise that 'outside the symbolic law, there is psychosis' (Brennan 1989: 2). Yet the notion of femininity as masquerade suggests a female potential for gender mobility which has been taken up in feminist film theory (particularly in theories of spectatorship) and in queer theory.

**See also:** *queer theory, sexuality*

### FURTHER READING

Minsky (1996) is a very clear and useful summary of the key ideas of Freud and the way his work has been taken up and transformed by Melanie Klein, Jacques Lacan, Julia Kristeva and Luce Irigaray. There are also readings from each of these theorists included in the volume. Freud in translation is surprisingly accessible and *On Sexuality: Three Essays on the Theory of Sexuality* (1977) is a very useful starting point.

# public/private

In its most basic liberal political formulation, the concept of the public and the private portrays social relations (especially in the modern Western context) as comprised of two, largely separate, realms. The public realm is characterised by activities individuals undertake in wider society and in common with a multitude of others, such as engaging in paid work, and exercising political, democratic rights, under the overall jurisdiction of government and the state. In contrast, the private realm is characterised by activities undertaken with particular others, relatively free from the jurisdiction of the state. It is the realm of the household, of home and of personal or family relationships. Within gender studies, interest in the public/private dichotomy arises from its gendered nature, from the association of masculinity and the public and of femininity and the private. Historically, it is men who have acted within the public realm and have moved freely between it and the private realm, while women (and children) have been mostly restricted to the private realm, and subjected to the authority of men within it. Within contemporary society, the public and the private remains a concept with 'powerful material and experiential consequences . . . a basic part of the way our whole social and psychic worlds are ordered' (Davidoff 1998: 165).

The liberal political origins of the public/private concept lie in the writings of the social contract theorists, such as Hobbes and Rousseau, and their attempts to explain the genesis of the legitimacy of government and the state. In such writings, the new social order that emerged from the social contract comprised two spheres: the one, public and political, and the other, private and removed from politics. Importantly, in classical social contract theory, these spheres were gendered spheres (Pateman 1989). Only men were deemed to possess the capacities for citizenship and thus the public realm was necessarily a masculine one. For the social contract writers, women were beings whose sexual embodiment prevented them from having the same political standing as men. Therefore women were incorporated into the new social order differently from men, via the private sphere. In the writings of the classic social contract theorists, then, we have a clear example of the ideological function of public/private concept. In other words, of the way in which ideas about gender, the public and the private have together formed a justifying rationale for the development and maintenance of social relations in which most men are privileged over most women.

Feminist writers have engaged with the public and the private in a variety of ways. Some have undertaken historical or anthropological analyses of the origin and development of the public/private dichotomy. For example, Davidoff (1998) focuses on the concept of the public and the private as it was understood in nineteenth-century England. She examines the gendered nature of various concepts directly related to the public and the private (including 'the individual' and 'rationality') and shows how these have structured, in particular, women's relation to the public sphere. Ortner's (1974) classic essay explains women's association with the private, domestic sphere in terms of the way, in societies across the world, femininity is constructed as being closer to (devalued) nature, whereas masculinity is constructed as closer to the more highly valued culture. The concept of the public and the private has also had a role in the development of theories of women's subordinated status. For example, some feminist writers have drawn on Marxism to account for

125

women's secondary status in the public sphere, in combination with theories of patriarchy to account for women's subordination within the private sphere (for example, Hartmann 1979). Similarly, Walby (1990) employs the concepts of the public and the private in her explanation of the changes in women's status in Britain. According to Walby, in private patriarchy, the oppression of women is based around the household and involves individual men exploiting individual women. Under this form of patriarchy, women are excluded from participation in wider society. In the public form of patriarchy, the formal barriers to women's participation in, say, paid work and politics, are removed. Women may no longer be excluded from participation in wider society, but patriarchal strategies of segregation (for example, in paid work) and subordination (for example, sexual harassment) mean that they face inequality and discrimination within it. As Walby puts it, 'Women are no longer restricted to the domestic hearth, but have the whole of society in which to roam and be exploited' (1990: 201).

In a range of studies, researchers have uncovered the myriad ways in which the ideology of the public and the private continues to construct the lived experiences of women and men as gendered beings. For example, in the field of criminology, research has revealed that notions of the public and the private are drawn upon by criminal justice professionals in the investigation and prosecution of domestic violence (Dobash and Dobash 1992). For example, studies by Grace (1995) and by Wright (1995) together suggest that, in the processing of cases of domestic violence by the police and the courts, notions of the privacy of marriage, home and the family mean that violent masculine behaviour is often neutralised and decriminalised. Cohen (2000) analyses legislation which imposes a 'duty of privacy' on gay and lesbian military personnel in the USA. This is a restriction on the expression of sexuality in the public sphere not required from heterosexuals. In studies of the labour market, researchers have shown how ideas about the public and the private act to structure the experiences and opportunities of women and men, whether in relation to forms of paid work (part-time or full-time), occupational groupings, training and promotion, or pay (see Crompton 1997 for an overview).

Such empirical studies on a range of issues have revealed that, rather than being separate realms, as suggested by their traditional depiction as binary opposites, the public and the private are mutually interdependent sets of social relations. For example, studies of gender, household work and paid work have shown that men's advantaged position in paid work cannot be understood separately from the fact that women continue to perform the bulk of housework and childcare. Much of the analysis of the effects that constructions of the public and the private have on women's and men's experiences and opportunities can be drawn together using the concept of citizenship. Lister (1997) examines how the ideology of the public and the private has effectively served to exclude women from the category of citizen, with consequences for their political participation (for example, representation in parliament and other formal political institutions), for their economic dependency (via their relationship to paid work and to the welfare state), and for their bodily integrity (for example, in cases of domestic violence, rape or sexual harassment).

In the light of evidence such as that cited above, most writers are critical of the role played by constructions of the public and the private in the perpetuation of gender inequalities. Moreover, the traditional liberal formulation of the public and the private itself has undergone critique. First, for its erroneous depiction of the two spheres as being separate and clearly bounded, rather than being mutually interdependent realms whose boundaries are fluid and changeable, drawn and redrawn in day-to-day social relations and through longer-term processes of political struggle. A second criticism of the traditional formulation arises from its narrow conception of politics as formal and institutional, and as taking place only in the public realm. This limited view simultaneously defines as irrelevant to politics all activities and relations of the private sphere (marriage, sexuality, motherhood, household labour, etc.), while also acting to conceal the gendered relations of power and domination that take place behind its 'closed doors'. As suggested in the slogan 'the personal is political', feminists have shown that the realm of the private is not insulated from politics. For example, laws and policy formulated through the formal, institutional political process of the public sphere directly impact on experiences in the private sphere. Furthermore, when the notion of politics is itself rearticulated, away from formal institutional processes, and incorporates relations of power, then the political nature of gender relations in the private realm is no longer obscured. A rather different articulation of the relationship between politics, gender, the public and the private is argued for by writers such as Ruddick and Elshtain, who suggest (among other things) that the masculine values of the public sphere need colonising by the feminine (caring, maternal) values of the private sphere (for references and critique, see Dietz 1998; Squires 1999).

Despite the powerful role played by conceptions of the public/private divide in reproducing gender inequalities, and the inadequacies of its traditional liberal formulation, most writers argue that what is required is a rearticulation of the concept, rather than its complete abandonment. Lister (1997) identifies three main elements to the reconstruction of the public and the private dichotomy, and of the relationship between them. First, it is necessary to deconstruct the gendered qualities and attributes associated with the public and the private, so that the terms no longer operate as euphemisms for masculinity and femininity, and relations of power between them. For example, as Sypnowich (2000: 103) argues, 'the patriarchal concept of the private as a domain of natural authority, immune to political scrutiny, can be given up without abandoning a concept of the private as a sphere of freedom important to all individuals, men and women'. Second, the multiple and complex interpenetrations of the public and the private must be fully acknowledged, along with the role their entangled relationship plays in structuring gender inequalities. Third, recognition must be given to the changing boundaries of the public/private divide and to the fact that the very act of classifying activities as one rather than the other is an exercise of power (Lister 1997: 120–1). In short, as Weintraub observes, the public/private distinction remains 'a powerful instrument of social analysis and moral reflection if approached with due caution and conceptual self-awareness' (cited in D'Entreves and Vogel 2000: 2).

**See also:** *dichotomy, domestic division of labour, sexual contract*

### FURTHER READING

A collection of readings edited by Landes (1998) draws together feminist work on the public and the private from a number of disciplines, and includes contributions by Seyla Benhabib, Carol Pateman, Anne Phillips and Iris Marion Young. A volume edited by D'Entreves and Vogel (2000) assesses the changing nature of the public/private divide, from the perspectives of law, politics and philosophy.

**128**

# queer theory

Queer theory developed in the humanities in the mid-1980s and grew in the wake of growing theoretical interests in sexuality, particularly through the work of Michel Foucault. This was coterminous with the adoption of the term 'queer' by gay and lesbian activist groups such as Queer Nation, ACTUP and OutRage in the USA and Europe. It was a deliberate appropriation of a term always used pejoratively and homophobically in the past in order to facilitate more radical declarations of gay and lesbian visibility. This strategy of visibility and rebellious assertion of 'deviance' was to characterise much of the political work conducted in the wake of the AIDS epidemic. Once cast as offensive, the term 'queer' is now used against the knowledge of its past meanings to 'offend' the general public and to anticipate their normal lexicon of abuse. To put it in Judith Butler's more complex terms, 'the subject who is "queered" into public discourse through homophobic interpellation of various kinds *takes up* or *cites* that very term as the discursive basis for an opposition' (in Phelan 1997: 18). 'Queer' has come to be associated with a new militancy in gay and lesbian politics – a determined push for visibility and a celebration of the transgressive.

In principle this is a stance that denies and interrogates the privileges of heterosexuality and tries to openly question dominant ideas of normalcy and appropriate behaviour. The adoption of the term 'queer' suggests a blurring of boundaries between straight and gay sex and validates those who would in the past have been considered sexual 'outlaws'. It is a deliberately provocative political and theoretical stance in that it foregrounds sexual identity, pleasure, and desire, and their part in the construction of our knowledge of self. Queer theory has been embraced by some as a means out of the gay/straight split (given that post-structuralist thought has encouraged the dismantling of such binaries) and a move beyond the politics of identity, in that 'queer' plays around with identity and refuses to be fixed or categorised.

Foucault's writings on sexuality and his notion that the body is immersed in discourse and given meaning by it have made a huge contribution to the development of queer theory. Adopting a 'queer' position amounts to a celebration of one's 'outlaw' status as well as actively denying the meanings attached to sexual identity: this is not a plea for the assimilation of 'gay' culture into 'straight', but rather a celebration of continuing marginality which then holds the 'centre' (heterosexuality) up for scrutiny. For some gays and lesbians the blurring of sexual identities ignores the fact that being known to be gay can have real material consequences on people's lives. In some senses an outlaw identity is already thrust upon gays and lesbians by a straight mainstream which will discriminate on the basis of these assumptions. In the UK, for example, Section 28 of the Local Government Act 1988 prevented the 'promotion of homosexuality' in schools, effectively a gag to teachers who

129

wanted to discuss homosexuality, which had a profound effect on the way children could learn about sexuality. At the time of writing, although it had been repealed in Scotland in 2000, England has yet been unable to push its repeal of Section 28 through the House of Lords. Cynics might therefore argue that 'queer' is a useful banner for those straight white middle-class individuals who felt themselves disenfranchised by identity politics, and who therefore wanted to display their radical credentials in an environment where identity was under erasure.

Queer theory in academia helped to bring together aspects of lesbian and gay studies with other postmodern theoretical writing; but even in this environment some are sceptical about the motives for wanting to take the label queer – as Caroline Gonda says, 'anyone who feels at odds with social or sexual convention can claim the label "queer", including, presumably, heterosexual men' (Gonda in Jackson and Jones, 1998: 124). Queer theory questions the usefulness of gendered binary distinctions and re-examines their role in the centralisation of heterosexuality. It has links with theories of embodiment and performativity in gender and draws much of its impetus from developments in post-structuralist and psychoanalytical theory, particularly as a means of asserting the breakdown of dualist structures of meaning and the application of homosexual and bi-sexual identifications. Butler's *Gender Trouble* (1990) clearly made a profound contribution to the field, most notably with her idea that gender is masquerade – not that these are roles one can adopt or not at will, but that they are the result of social scripts we actively conform to or reject (always with the possible costs of public censure or worse). She clarifies what is meant by gender performativity by saying that it 'is not a matter of choosing which gender one will be today. Performativity is a matter of reiterating or repeating the norms by which one is constituted; it is not a radical fabrication of a gendered self' (Butler in Phelan 1997: 17). At heart queer theorists, in common with queer political radicals, are out to undermine the naturalness of gender in order to decentre heterosexuality as a privileged identity.

For some the word is still closely linked to the establishment of a personal identity, even as it deflects singular identity: 'I use the word queer to mean more than lesbian. Since I first used it in 1980 I have always meant it to imply that I am not only a lesbian but a transgressive lesbian – femme, masochistic, as sexually aggressive as the women I seek out, and as pornographic in my imagination and sexual activities as the heterosexual hegemony has ever believed' (Allison 1995: 23). Queer theory increasingly becomes associated with theories of individual sexual identity and has been especially popular in film theory and analysis of popular culture. It has introduced terms such as 'genderfuck' which dramatise this sense of the liberatory potential of playing with gender categories through pastiche and exaggeration – and as best embodied by performers such as Madonna in the realms of popular culture. The mass media has also proved itself adept at producing a 'queer' spectacle for a large liberal audience, as the 2002 BBC adaptation of Sarah Waters' novel about lesbian life in 1880s' London, *Tipping the Velvet* (1999) demonstrates. It serves as a reminder that the 'transgressive' can all too readily be appropriated for mainly heterosexual spectacle.

Radical feminists are among those most sceptical of queer theory and for Sue Wilkinson and Celia Kitzinger, 'radical feminist analyses are ignored or marginalised at best, subverted or derided at worst. . . . queer politics is often expressed in terms explicitly oppositional to feminism – especially radical feminism' (Wilkinson and Kitzinger in Bell and Klein 1996: 379). They see it as overly fascinated with SM and sexual violence and valorising gay male culture at the expense of lesbian culture and the feminist critique of heterosexuality as a main site of women's oppression. Sheila Jeffreys is another outspoken critic of queer theory, partly because she feels that queer effaces lesbian identity under a male homosexual norm and partly because of 'the unwillingness of postmodernist theory to wish to talk about vulgar things like oppression' (Jeffreys 1994: 176).

Whether there is any truth in assertions that queer *theory* is irredeemably apolitical, it is clear that organisations such as ACTUP and Queer Nation have been instrumental in a new force in gay and lesbian politics which is witty, ironic and resolutely challenging to a social order which was, for example, slow to rise to the problems of AIDS in the 1980s. It might, however, be reasonable to recognise that some aspects of queer theory work well as a positive assertion of an endlessly multiple and transgressive self against a culture of heterosexism, but not as a means to alleviate the pain and injustice of being punished or abused for one's perceived sexual identity. Lynne Segal quotes American critic Suzanna Walter who remarks, 'wearing a dildo will not stop me from being raped as a woman or being harassed as a lesbian' (Walter quoted by Segal 1999: 68).

**See also:** *heterosexism, lesbian continuum, sexuality*

### FURTHER READING

Phelan (1997) is a useful and wide-ranging collection, whereas Burston and Richardson (1995) is a good collection for looking at the way 'queer' has translated into popular culture. Jeffreys (1994) is one of the more outspoken critics of queer theory and politics; whereas Segal (1999) offers a more balanced account of the meeting of queer and feminism.

# race/ethnicity

The concepts of race and ethnicity are often used interchangeably. However, both this practice and each of the individual concepts themselves are the subjects of extensive debate. The everyday, common-sense meaning of race entails the idea that the human population is made up of a number of biologically different groups. Within this understanding, a person's bodily appearance and especially their skin colour are often regarded as determining their membership of a racial group. The idea of a biologically differentiated human population was promoted by nineteenth-century scientists, and was subsequently used to justify ideologically the hierarchical division of humans into dominant and subjected racial groupings. By the middle of the twentieth century, with increased understanding of genetics, it was widely established that there was, in fact, no scientific basis for the concept of race. Importantly, however, despite 'the evidence that races in the biological sense did not exist . . . large sections of the population, and indeed whole societies, continued to conduct themselves as though they did' (Mason 2000: 7). There is, then, a contradiction between scientific knowledge (which denies the existence of races), and common-sense understandings and practices (which serve to categorise people into different groups on the basis on physical appearance). It is this contradiction that is the source of extensive debates in social science as to the best way to conceptualise relations between groups of people who (may) themselves believe and (may) be believed by others, to be, in some way, 'different'.

Sociologists invariably accept the scientific argument that biological races do not exist. However, there has been debate as to whether the scientific refutation of race means that the concept itself should be wholly abandoned. Miles (for example, 1989) has argued that, since the concept of race has no scientific validity, its continued use merely serves to promulgate racist ideology. Other writers have argued that the concept of race should be retained (for example, Anthias and Yuval-Davis 1992; Gilroy 1987). This is because of the extent to which a 'discourse in which the idea of "race" is present remains a powerful feature of common-sense thinking and of the ordering of social relations' (Fenton 1999: 4). A compromise position, favoured by many writers, is to place the term in inverted commas, thereby indicating its fundamentally problematic character. If sociologists use the concept of race at all, they do so, not to identify biological categories of human beings, but rather to describe *racism* in social relations, whereby people's 'structural positions and social actions are ordered, justified and explained by reference to systems of symbols and beliefs which emphasise the social and cultural relevance of biologically rooted characteristics' (Mason 2000: 8).

Given the contested character of the concept of race, many social scientists seeking to understand and explain 'differences' between groups of human beings have been drawn to the concept of ethnicity. In contrast to the emphasis on biologically determined differences imbued in the concept of race, the emphasis in the concept of ethnicity is on cultural differences; it is therefore a more sociologically appropriate way of conceptualising difference. 'Ethnicity at its most general level involves belonging to a particular group and sharing its conditions of existence. This will include not only being regarded as having the right credentials for membership but also being able to muster ethnic resources which can be used for struggle, negotiation and the pursuit of political projects, both at the level of individuals making their way but also for the group as a whole in relation to other groups' (Anthias and Yuval-Davis 1992: 8). Examples of ethnic credentials or resources held in common might include language, religion, beliefs about common ancestry and nationality, or claims to territory, as well as other aspects of culture which might serve to sustain a sense of distinctive group identity. For Modood et al. (for example, 2002), physical appearance (especially skin colour) can also be a marker of ethnicity, in that it 'clearly contributes to picking out people who in Britain are thought (by themselves, and by others) to be members of ethnic minorities' (2002: 422). However, Modood et al. are careful to emphasise that a focus on skin colour is context-dependent and is not essential to any theory of what makes a group of people an ethnic group; for example, skin colour is largely irrelevant in the ethnically conflictual relations between Catholics and Protestants in Northern Ireland. Modood and colleagues also emphasise the 'interactive' or relational character of ethnicity (2002: 420). In other words, ethnic groups are shaped through social relations with other ethnic groupings. Racist discourses and practices are clearly an important element in this respect, acting to shape the cultures and experiences of both dominant and minority ethnic groups. The ethnic credentials and resources of one group may serve to fuel the racist beliefs and practices of another group.

133

This is one reason why some writers use the terms 'race' and ethnicity interchangeably, while others refer to 'racialised ethnicities' (for example, Madood et al. 2002). Mason (2000) similarly regards ethnicity as 'situational' or context-dependent, so that people might regard themselves and be regarded by others as belonging to one or more ethnic groups in one setting, but to another ethnic group or groups in a different setting. Ethnicity is, then, 'more a matter of the processes by which boundaries are created and maintained between ethnic groups than it is of the internal content of the ethnic categories' (2000: 12).

Writers working within the field of gender studies have noted that the mainstream literature on 'race' and ethnicity has largely ignored gender. As Maynard (1994) explains, the focus has been largely on ethnic minority men and their experiences in the public sphere. If women were studied at all, it was invariably as the wives, mothers or daughters of these men. More recently, feminists have emphasised the interrelations between gender and ethnicity. Black feminist writers in particular have argued that analyses of gender that do not fully examine and theorise ethnicity and racism are fundamentally flawed (for example, hooks 1984). For Amos and Parmer (1997: 58), black women 'cannot simply prioritise one aspect of our oppression to the exclusion of others, as the realities of our day-to-day lives make it imperative for us to consider the simultaneous nature of our oppression and exploitation. Only a synthesis of class, race, gender and sexuality can lead us forward, as these form the matrix of black women's lives.' Similarly, Afshar and Maynard (1994) emphasise that race and gender interrelate dynamically, in highly complex and contradictory ways; therefore 'diversity among women cannot be seen as a static phenomenon' (1994: 6). Ethnic credentials or resources are themselves gendered, as are racist ideologies, making gender a key process in the creation and maintenance of boundaries of ethnic 'differences'. As explained by Anthias and Yuval-Davis, there exist culturally specific practices relating to masculinity, femininity, and sexuality and to roles within households and within paid work (for example Anthias and Yuval-Davis 1992: Chapter 4). Black feminist writers point to the importance of recognising the ways in which the experiences of black women can be very different from those of white women, not least due to racism. For example, Hill Collins (1990) identifies the important role of 'controlling images' through which African-American women are racially stereotyped in terms of their gender (as 'Mammy', 'matriarch', 'welfare recipient' or 'hot mamma'). Carby (1997) cites racism in her critique of white feminist analyses of the family. 'We would not wish to deny that the family can be a source of oppression for us but we also wish to examine how the black family has functioned as a prime source of resistance to oppression. We need to recognise that during slavery, periods of colonialism and under the present authoritarian state, the black family has been a site of political and cultural resistance to racism' (1997: 46). Similarly, Amos and Parmer (1997) describe 'Eurocentric' and 'ethnocentric' tendencies in feminism. In illustration of their argument, Amos and Parmer identify the family, sexuality and the women's peace movement as three critical areas of differences between the experiences of white and black women. Thus, the protests at Greenham Common in the 1980s meant that many white middle-class women experienced 'police brutality' for the first time. However, 'Black women are up against the state every day of our lives, and the terror of a coercive police force, a highly trained military and the multifarious arm of the "welfare" state are very familiar grounds to us' (1997: 57).

Overall, then, 'race' and ethnicity have been central concepts, alongside those of gender and class, in postmodernist-influenced critiques of universalism and essentialism, and in debates about diversity and difference in gender relations.

**See also:** *class, essentialism, post-colonial theory*

### FURTHER READING

Mason (2000) is a good sociological introduction to race and ethnicity in modern Britain, although little specific attention is given to gender. The volume edited by Mirza (1997) draws together key black British feminist writings, while that edited by Afshar and Maynard (1994) presents a range of empirical evidence on the interrelations of 'race' and gender and of the consequences of racism for women of different ethnic groups.

135

# representation

From the outset of the second wave, representation became one of the crucial areas of feminist debate. It was argued that the way women perceived themselves and were perceived was ineluctably shaped by the ways in which images of women were constructed and communicated to the population at large. It was suggested that these images reinforced dominant ideologies of gender difference and the qualities of ideal-type femininity; that they perpetuated such differences and entrenched them in the consciousness of subsequent generations. One of the things that is unique about this period of feminism was its absolute conviction that people were materially affected by the images they saw – that they affected attitudes and behaviour. Emerging at a period where the mass media, advertising, popular fiction and film were becoming more sophisticated, more adept at commercial aspects of making images, feminists were in their own way identifying that the image had taken on a new importance and might be assuming a closer relationship to 'things'.

One of the first publicised demonstrations by the Women's Liberation Movement in the USA was that which took place outside the 1968 Miss America contest in Atlantic City. It is an example of how feminists felt that pageants such as these not only celebrate a very narrow band of acceptable feminine appearance and behaviour, but that they illustrate the stranglehold of the beauty and fashion industries on women, making them regularly unhappy with their own appearance, and simultaneously obsessed by their products. Feminists set up a 'Freedom Trash Can' outside the venue inviting women to discard any objects which speak to the oppression of women through the enforcement of idealised standards of beauty – such as girdles, bras and glossy magazines. For the 1970 Miss World protestors in London, 'Beauty contests epitomise the traditional female road to success' (Wandor 1972: 251), the dream that economic security can be secured by displaying the desired accoutrements of feminine youthfulness, and this became the dominant image of women in every aspect of advertising and consumerism.

The aims of these feminists backfired to some extent; even though they were at pains to show that their argument wasn't against the women themselves, they came to be portrayed by the media as jealous ugly women who were out to spoil the fun of those who willingly conformed to the standards of 'proper' femininity. Feminists learnt an early lesson: that the media could largely control the interpretation of their demonstrations and that they could either choose to avoid such attention or offer critiques that might expose its practices and support some genuinely feminist practitioners with a different story to tell. From this time, it has been asserted, a critique of the media became a central feature of debates within the Women's Movement (Baehr and Gray 1996: xi).

Nonetheless, for some it is difficult to look back at early attempts to represent women in different ways with any degree of seriousness. For instance, one of New York's feminist groups, Cell 16, were famous for their strict regime of celibacy and physical training: 'they pioneered the popular movement look of khaki pants, work shirts, combat boots, and short hair', and demonstrated against the tyranny of female appearance by publicly cutting off the long hair of one of their members (Echols 1989: 162). Their rejection of all things feminine was a tactical refusal to adopt a look which was near compulsory for women in the late 1960s (bra, girdle, stockings, high heels, skirts, make-up, matching accessories), but this is largely forgotten and their attempts to produce a 'neutral' look are now seen as dour and humourless. Fashion is a minefield for feminists because no one can really avoid making a statement about themselves by the clothes they wear – the idea that you can reject the meanings of fashion and clothing is, according to Elizabeth Wilson, absurd since 'even the determinedly *un*fashionable wear clothes that manifestly represent a reaction against what *is* in fashion' (Wilson 1985: 5). This sums up the chief problems feminists experienced when they challenged conventional modes of representing women and femininity in most contexts – that those meanings were constantly in flux and it was difficult to generalise how women felt about the images they encountered in daily life, or how straightforward resistance would change those meanings.

This concern with images is also witnessed in the success of feminist literary criticism, which emerged as an identifiable 'field' following Kate Millett's classic *Sexual Politics* (1971). Initially submitted as a PhD thesis, Millett's was one of the early groundbreaking texts in feminist literary criticism in its work on the sexualised construction of women in novels by some of the key twentieth-century male writers such as D.H. Lawrence, Norman Mailer and Henry Miller. The term 'sexual politics', first coined by Millett, came to be a key concept in feminist writings. As she says, 'sexual politics obtains consent through the "socialization" of both sexes to basic patriarchal polities with regard to temperament, role, and status. As to status, a pervasive assent to the prejudice of male superiority guarantees superior status in the male, inferior in the female' (Millett 1977: 26). Millett extends definitions of politics to embrace all relationships of power, particularly defined along gender and racial lines and particularly those which are enforced through informal means such as through marital relationships.

Perhaps partly because more women studied in the humanities than other academic subject areas during the 1960s and 1970s, and therefore a higher proportion might stay on to take PhDs and become academics, literary studies had a strong feminist presence. Feminist literary criticism became an emerging, if embattled, strand of literary studies, where one of the key activities of early feminist criticism was to evaluate the ways in which women characters had been represented in past fiction by men and

137

women, and how women writers might represent women in the future in order to give more positive role models for women readers. Much of this work identified what were regarded as 'stereotypes' of feminine behaviour and physical appearance and this work was extended to wider cultural criticism to show how women and men might be affected by the way gender is represented to them.

The field of feminist literary criticism gradually expanded to include film theory and studies in popular culture as well as fine art and fashion, and these critical perspectives have informed the creative practices of women across the arts ever since. Representation is still a key issue in all fields, but one which has grown away from the rather simplistic notion of the stereotype, given that many images are more contradictory than this term allows. Early feminist criticism perhaps over-exaggerated the passivity of the spectator and later critics have been keen to show how women as viewers can appropriate images to their own ends; that there are a plurality of meanings to be yielded and which are grasped by women. Nonetheless the range of images of women available are still limited and dominated by those of young, white, thin, hairless, able-bodied women. Even in a period where the portrayal of women of colour and lesbians is more frequent, often the issues addressed around their characters (say, in soaps or dramas) are primarily to do with race/racism or with sexual matters, so that despite the positive effects of having the image made visible, these representations have a 'special' status, often on the margins. When examining representations of women in popular culture, feminists have learned to look at what is absent as well as what is all too present. Even though the heated debates around pornography problematised the issue of whether we are affected by what we see, at a more general level feminists have still agonised over this relationship between the image and social reality.

In the early days of the second wave, feminists were optimistic that having exposed the narrowness of representations of femininity available, there would be some kind of response. But any change that has happened has been slow and not exactly what these critics had in mind – not surprisingly so since the mass media know how much these images sell. Feminist practitioners in the arts are themselves generally operating at the margins of profit or commercial viability and although there have been groundbreaking artists such as Judy Chicago and Mary Kelly, photographers such as Cindy Sherman and Della Grace and filmmakers such as Marleen Gorris, few (such as the director Sally Potter) have done more than nudge their work into the mainstream. Effectively, the feminist study of representation falls into two key areas – the study of negative representations of women and femininity and the study of oppositional work by feminist practitioners – and sadly the former area is by far the most documented, even to this day.

For many feminists, a greater variety of images of women available in the mainstream would be an important step forward, and visibility for black and lesbian women, for example, is a huge leap. Popular representations of men *and* women have changed enormously since the onset of feminism's second wave. Though people might be divided about the motives behind such characterisations, there are now images of men taking a caring parenting role, as the focus of straightforward 'glamour' shots and, as a result of the increasing availability of gay male style in the mainstream, appearing in fashion shoots for heterosexual men. With these seemingly 'progressive' images of men, as with those of the successful businesswoman or the tailored and glamorous working mother, there remains a question mark as to their purpose: 'The question is, whether the token woman, even the token image of woman, functions as a trailblazer, a thin end of the wedge, or as a diversion from issues that affect the generality of women, a co-option of feminist values for commercial ends' (Marshment in Robinson and Richardson 1997: 133).

There is no hard and fast answer to such a question since it is indeed the case that feminist rhetoric has been deployed in popular culture to subvert the political message and encourage women to empower themselves through the 'choices' of consumerism. Further, an idea of puritanical feminism is held up for scrutiny and found to be joyless and irrelevant by a whole cluster of magazines and soaps aimed at the youth market, where instead busty 'babes' make a comeback. Representation is important not least because the images of women reflected back to them may be objectionable, but also because they tell us something about how women's lives are valued and the difficulties in being represented (more literally) in the public sphere.

As Margaret Marshment observes, 'representation is a political issue. Without the power to define our interests and to participate in the decisions that affect us, women – like any other group in society – will be subject to the definitions and decisions of others' (Marshment in Robinson and Richardson 1997: 125).

**See also:** *pornography, second wave feminism*

### FURTHER READING

Kate Millett's *Sexual Politics* (1971) is an interesting read because it grounds so much of modern feminist thought, but also because it is a real

139

combination of literary and political analysis. Marshment's essay on representation (Robinson and Richardson 1997) is a concise and wide-ranging introduction to the area; for more detail on feminist experiments with visual culture, see Carson and Pajaczkowska (2000). For a sample of critical approaches to women and the media, see Baehr and Gray (1996); Wilson (1985) is a beautifully written analysis of fashion. Whelehan's (2000) analysis of 'retrosexism' argues that there still needs to be some consideration of the relationship between images and things regardless of how unfashionable that might appear in a postmodernist arena.

# reproductive technologies

The concept of reproductive technologies refers to a wide range of medico-technological knowledge and practices concerned with human sexual reproduction. The oldest types of reproductive technologies are those which aim to control fertility, either through the prevention of conception (the withdrawal method, condoms), the termination of a pregnancy (through inducing a miscarriage or abortion) or through infanticide. A second type of reproductive technologies is those medical practices used in the management of childbirth, such as caesareans and episiotomies, forceps, labour-inducing drugs, and foetal monitoring. A third grouping are 'technologies of conception' whose purpose is to overcome or bypass infertility, through procedures such as artificial insemination, surrogacy, the freezing of sperm or eggs, and *in vitro* fertilisation (or IVF). A further category of reproductive technologies is designed to 'improve' the health and genetic characteristics of the foetus, and, more generally, the population as a whole. Relevant practices here include ultrasound scans, amniocentesis tests and genetic screening. A fifth grouping of reproductive technologies has the purpose of ameliorating the effects of ageing on the sexual reproductive body. For example, hormone replacement therapy (or HRT) for menopausal women and Viagra for men who have difficulty gaining or sustaining erections.

The availability of and access to technologies of fertility control have

**140**

long been issues of concern for feminists, stemming from a belief that the attainment of egalitarian gender relations is heavily dependent upon women having control over their own reproductive capacities. An important analysis of the liberating potential of reproductive technologies was made by Shulamith Firestone in the early 1970s. For Firestone (1979), inequalities between men and women are biologically based, with their differing reproductive capacities being fundamentally important. Before the advent of reliable forms of fertility control, women's capacity to conceive, carry, give birth to and breast feed a child meant that they were 'at the continual mercy' of their biology. Consequently, women became dependent upon men for survival (1979: 8–9). For Firestone, this natural difference in reproductive capacity between men and women gradually led to the development of other socially based gender differences. The elimination of gender differences therefore requires the replacement of natural reproduction by artificial means, through the use of technology. All aspects of the debilitating processes of natural reproduction must be removed from women's bodies, a strategy which would ultimately require foetuses to grow in 'artificial wombs'. For Firestone, it is through such technological practices that women's ownership of their bodies will be achieved (1979: 11).

Rather than sharing Firestone's optimistic perspective on the liberating potential of reproductive technologies, more recent feminist writers are, at best, ambivalent about such technologies. For example, there is a broad consensus that technologies of fertility control have largely benefited women (for example, through the increased range and reliability of methods of contraception and the wider availability of abortion). Yet, many concerns remain about equality of access, the health risks and unpleasant side effects of some forms of contraception, and the use of sterilisation and contraception by injection on women in underdeveloped countries (for example, Richardson 1993). Some feminist writers are especially critical of particular groupings of the newer reproductive technologies, such as those involved in the management of childbirth (for example, Davis-Floyd 1998), the various technologies of conception (for example, Davis-Floyd and Dumit 1998), the foetal/genetic screening technologies (for example, Steinberg 1997) and technologies such as HRT (for example, Klein and Dumble 1994). Arguably, the most controversial of these reproductive technologies is IVF, not least because of the interconnections between it and foetal screening and genetic engineering. In IVF, eggs from a woman are fertilised by sperm outside rather than inside a woman's body. There are various stages to this procedure, but in general, hormonal drugs are given to stimulate ovulation and, following

141

intensive monitoring and testing, surgery is then performed to 'collect' any eggs. Fertilisation takes place in a 'test tube' and the eggs are then (re)placed inside a woman's body. IVF-related techniques include the freezing of eggs, sperm and embryos, and the donation of sperm, eggs and embryo. One international feminist group who strongly oppose technologies like IVF are the Feminist International Network of Resistance to Reproductive and Genetic Engineering (or FINRRAGE). For this group of writers and campaigners, the science at the basis of technologies of conception could ultimately lead to men removing the 'last woman-centred process' from women's control (Hanmer 1987: 96). It is argued that the new technologies of conception, originally developed to assist the minority of women who are infertile, could be employed as the first-choice methods of all human reproduction. The technological processes are argued to give men as a social grouping a heightened degree of control over human reproduction, offering guarantees of paternity and enabling the birth of boys rather than girls (via sex selection). In the analyses of FINRRAGE, technologies such as IVF amount to the 'taking over' of women's reproductive capacities by men as an expression of 'womb envy'. Far from extending women's rights and choices through liberating them from their biology (as argued by Firestone), the 'technological invasion' of women's bodies by science amounts to a patriarchal strategy to take away from women the one advantage they have over men. The new technologies, in this perspective, are a scientifically-based, medicalised form of violence against women's bodies. As such, they are to be feared and resisted as patriarchal practices which continue the long-standing exploitation of women's bodies for masculine advantage (see for example, Corea et al. 1987; Arditti et al. 1989).

This interpretation of new reproductive technologies offered by FINRRAGE is regarded as overstated by some other writers. It is said to place too much emphasis on the powers and interests of 'patriarchal' medicine and science, while simultaneously minimising the knowledge and agency of women themselves (for example, Stanworth 1987b; Steinberg 1997). Rather than interpreting reproductive technologies as either uniformly liberating (as does Firestone) or uniformly oppressive of women (as do FINRRAGE), these writers analyse reproductive technologies within the broader network of power relations within societies. Wajcman (1991), for example, draws attention to the wider contexts shaping the development, availability and use of reproductive technologies. For example, she points to the commercial interests of pharmaceutical companies who have made large profits from the contraceptive pill. Similarly, Roberts (1981) highlights a 'masculine hegemony' which operates to regulate the availability and use of reproductive technologies, through the medical profession, the law and the state and religious ideology, as well as through women's relationships with men in the context of male-dominated rules of heterosexuality. Such an approach encourages a recognition that technologies of reproduction can have both advantages and disadvantages for gender relations – they are something of 'a double-edged sword' (Stanworth 1987a: 15). In societies where women are constrained by culturally dominant constructions of femininity in which motherhood is central, such technologies can be argued to extend women's 'choices' and, therefore, control over their own bodies and lives. Yet, in the context of masculine domination of science and medicine, techniques like IVF can represent an increase in men's control over women's bodies.

Writers working from a post-structuralist perspective have challenged those feminist analyses which may have made universalistic assumptions about the impact reproductive technologies have on 'women'. For example, Bryld (2001) examines the relationship between discourses on reproductive technologies and discourses about lesbians in Denmark. Bryld argues that 'the lesbian' was not a significant concept within Danish official discourses until the intensification of public and political debate about technologies of conception, which were constructed as enabling 'lesbian motherhood'. Ultimately, the Danish parliament voted in favour of lesbians and single women being denied access to technologies of conception within medical clinics. Steinberg (1997) is critical of many feminist interpretations of reproductive technologies for a common tendency to generalise about all women, having in fact used the experiences of the minority of women who are infertile as the main template for their analysis. As an alternative, Steinberg proposes an 'anti-oppressive feminist standpoint' approach. In the analysis of IVF, such an approach means that women's experiences of these technologies cannot be seen as universal, nor as separate from the complex power relations of social institutions, including science, medicine and technology. Steinberg's own work considers the ways in which discourses about IVF and IVF-based genetic screening operate to (re)produce dominant relations of scientific and medical expertise, along with popular or 'common-sense' understandings about kinship and the family, while also acting to reinscribe (hetero)sexist, racist and ableist social divisions.

**See also:** *body, cyborg*

143

Collections edited by Stanworth (1987b) and by Corea et al.(1987) remain key examples of feminist analyses of reproductive technologies. Steinberg (1997), by virtue of being more recent, is able to pay greater attention to IVF-based genetic technologies and to discourses of the rights and personhood of the embryo. Zawelski (2000) focuses on reproductive technologies in her examination of the similarities and differences between 'modernist' and 'postmodernist' (or post-structuralist) feminisms.

# – second wave feminism –

Second wave feminism is a term used to describe a new period of feminist collective political activism and militancy which emerged in the late 1960s. The concept of 'waves' of feminism was itself only applied in the late 1960s and early 1970s and therefore its application to a previous era of female activism tells us a great deal about the dawning second wave. As Mary Evans reflects, 'if every generation has to re-invent the wheel – or tends to believe that it has just invented the wheel – so feminism in the West in the 1960s and 1970s took some time before it recognized its history and the longevity of the struggle that it represented' (1997: 7). Not only is the wave analogy a way of charting historical movement since feminism's first 'wave', which dated roughly from the mid-nineteenth century to the 1920s, it signals a shift in the key political issues for feminist thought.

Whereas the first wave lobbied for women's enfranchisement via the vote and access to the professions as well as the right to own property, the second wave feminists talked in terms of 'liberation' from the oppressiveness of a patriarchally defined society. Equality had not been achieved by enfranchisement and so it was time to reflect on life beyond the public sphere. While the struggle for the vote remained the symbolic centre of first wave feminism, arguably for second wave feminists the key site of struggle was the female body itself – its representation and the meanings attached to the bald fact of biological difference. In this light, Simone de Beauvoir's famous declaration that 'One is not born, but rather becomes, a woman' (1972: 295) guided new thinking on the way gender differences were perceived as constructed so that women's chief battle was against the ideological positioning of women as much as their material position was of crucial importance to the first wave feminists.

De Beauvoir's *The Second Sex*, first published in 1949 (five years after French women were first enfranchised) was an important document for modern feminists, as was Betty Friedan's *The Feminine Mystique* (1963), and second wave feminists were committed to building a body of knowledge which specifically addressed the ways in which women have historically been marginalised, both culturally and socially. Moreover, second wave feminism problematised what equality might achieve, not least because of the differing social roles women and men were still ideologically required to take, and gradually there was a greater focus on differences between men and women and the meanings attached to them. Second wave feminism often raised the possibility of enormous social change which would make existing social structures untenable, imbued as they were with patriarchal realities. These visions for social change ultimately depended on the broader lens of political allegiances – whether it be liberal, Marxist, radical and so forth. The revolutionary potential of such thought itself underscored the obstacles to realising such change, which would involve questioning the very fabric of people's private lives and emotional investments.

As discussed in the entry on 'feminisms', many of the women who gave feminism its new radical impetus were refugees from New Left and civil rights political movements. These radical feminists' decision to organise in small groups and to engage in consciousness raising, direct action and demonstrations that were more like street theatre, meant that this new brand of feminism, or the 'women's liberation movement' quickly communicated itself to the public consciousness. Though many of the media dismissed these 'women's libbers' as bra-burners and man-haters, the movement did seem to gain a groundswell of support from women in the USA and slightly later in Europe, from the late 1960s, and it did profoundly influence the shape of modern feminist thought much further afield.

Second wave feminism is not just about the emergence of a new radical feminism but it also marks key shifts in the politics of liberal and Marxist feminists. They too came to focus on debates which only emerged during this period and were defined much more by what Kate Millett had termed 'sexual politics' – such as the family, abortion, sexuality, the sexual division of labour, rape and domestic violence. For Marxist feminists in particular this meant a more marked shift from classic Marxist principles to a consideration of how gendered relations could be entered into a class-

145

based analysis of power. The idea fostered by the explosion of second wave radicalism, that anyone could 'join' the women's movement, encouraged a kind of inclusiveness which prompted the emergence of all kinds of sub-groupings, many of which were established to allow critical space for lesbians, women of colour and working-class women. The strengths of the second wave are that it created the conditions within which such heterogeneity was possible; the weakness was that it still came to be marked out by an informal 'mainstream' of white middle-class, heterosexual women who seemed at times reluctant to give anything but token space to dissenting or critical voices.

This notion that 'membership' of feminism is very much a question of political choice rather than a formal matter, is crucial to the identity and shape of second wave feminism. Jo Freeman puts it thus:

> Membership in the movement is purely subjective – the participants are those who consider themselves participants – and not always accompanied by membership in a small group. Some of these groups require dues or, more often, regular attendance at meetings and participation in the common tasks. These requirements are not deter-minant of movement participation, however, as it is easy to quit one group and join another or even start one's own . . . Given its decentralised, segmentary, reticulate nature, the younger branch of the movement can best be described as a social sys-tem rather than a political organization. (1975: 104)

At times when it felt as if certain dominant voices were threatening to 'hijack' feminism for their own ends it is reassuring if also a little frustrating to remember that feminism still has no core orthodoxy and is still reinventing itself.

The view of feminism represented by Freeman is not one agreed by all. Christine Hoff Sommers in her book *Who Stole Feminism?* acts as if it is a movement with one rightful owner, as she tries to demonise much of the work of second wave activism – 'credos and intellectual fashions come and go but feminism itself – the pure and wholesome article first displayed at Seneca Falls in 1848 – is as American as apple pie and it will stay' (Sommers 1994: 275). Sommers implies here that second wave feminism derailed the 'authentic' movement which for her lies somewhere in feminism's first wave with the Seneca Falls Convention and its call for suffrage. But, just as the mutability of feminism itself makes it difficult for Sommers to make the claim that feminism has been 'stolen', so it is difficult to accuse Sommers of anti-feminism for suggesting it.

Although one can date the beginnings of the second wave as emerging around 1968, it is much harder to say whether it has ended or been supplanted by another wave of feminism. As we shall see in the entry on the so-called third wave, there has not been a subsequent groundswell of popular consciousness or an emerging political wing of feminism that has changed the fundamental terms of the second wave. Indeed, most commentators would agree that modern feminism lost its dynamism in the late 1980s and, although there is much evidence of effective grassroots feminist activism and support, much feminist energy has since been concentrated in the academy on women's studies programmes. Nonetheless it is clear that third wave activism has once again moved the debate into a new territory: whereas for the second wave it was into the personal lives and relationships of women, for the third wave it is into the miasma of the mass media, celebrating its contradictions as well as its possibilities.

In the entry on first wave feminism the usefulness of the 'wave' analogy was questioned. When we look back at the history of the second wave it is also beguiling to see the most productive insights being produced at the 'crest' of the activist wave up until the early 1980s. It is important, however, to accept that our 'memories' of those events (whether personal or mediated through historical accounts and documents) are structured and given meaning by the whole raft of feminist theory which succeeded it. What is certain, as Linda Nicholson remarks, is that 'something happened in the 1960s in ways of thinking about gender that continues to shape public and private life' (1997: 1).

**See also:** *consciousness raising, first wave feminism, third wave feminism*

### FURTHER READING

There are a number of different accounts of feminism available including Tong (1989), Whelehan (1995) and Evans (1997). For a selection of key critical essays from feminism's second wave, the collection edited by Nicholson (1997) is essential reading.

# separatism

Separatism is perhaps one of the most misunderstood and emotive practices to emerge from second wave feminism. For many it smacks of angry all-women caucuses promulgating irrational anti-male hatred; and for most it is assumed that all women who choose separatism are lesbians. In actuality there are different degrees of separatism and very different approaches to what separatism is for. For many mainstream feminists in the early second wave, separatism was about acknowledging the ways in which women's struggle for autonomy had in the past been hampered by men and male-dominated institutions and that therefore at the level of debate, at least, it would be preferable for feminists to meet in women-only groups in order to develop the precepts and theories that would form the backbone of modern feminism.

Having emerged in their droves from the New Left and civil rights movements there was a point where many feminists where committed to both feminist and left-wing activism, but recognised the need for women to consider feminist issues separately. Women had experienced sexism with the Movement (the term for the New Left in the USA), but had also developed key political allegiances as well as learning important political lessons (see Echols 1989: 51–101). For many to see a separate women's movement was to regard feminism as retreating into liberalism and losing its radical edge; and for many a long year Marxists in particular dubbed feminism a bourgeois diversion. Separatism was not agreed upon as a strategy and there have always been different levels at which it is employed – anything from banning men from conferences and discussion groups, to organising social events, to arranging one's whole life away from direct contact with men. Many early women liberationists saw the virtue in separatism at the level of discussion and theory making simply because they felt that men tended to hijack discussions and dominate them.

For radical feminists and lesbian groupings long-term separatism was an attractive prospect. Many radicals felt that men would only transform themselves if women were to withdraw all their labour (including emotional sustenance and sexual servicing) and direct their attention to other women and the work of the Women's Liberation Movement. For those who wanted to retain their social and sexual connections with men, workplace women-only collectives were popular during the 1970s and 1980s and encouraged women to boost a female-oriented economy by only employing women builders, printers, etc. (to this day the UK publisher, the Women's Press, only publishes work by women authors). Social separatism was another dimension – the establishment of cultural events, concerts, arts or music festivals allowed for a celebration of women's culture and admiration of their creativity outside of spheres where their work might otherwise have been devalued. For so-called cultural feminists (radical feminists who believe that women have intrinsically different values and virtues from men), such events were a clear political statement in themselves and no longer marked a temporary separation from men, but rather the attempt to concretise separate spheres.

Lesbian, black women, women with disabilities, working-class women are examples of clusters within feminism who might equally want to declare some kind of partial separatism from what became inevitably a feminist 'mainstream' of white, middle-class, heterosexual, able-bodied women who held considerable sway over what were communicated as the key issues for feminism. Caucuses within conferences or separate local groups enabled women who felt themselves for whatever reason to be cast out to the 'margins' of feminism, to find a degree of relief by demanding their own sphere of debate. Such 'discursive separatism' has advanced feminist scholarship and knowledge to address a much wider constituency, and even those who reject, for example, lesbian separatism find separation at the level of debate productive. As the Combahee River Collective observed in 'A Black Feminist Statement', '[a] political contribution which we feel we have already made is the expansion of the feminist principle that the personal is political. In our consciousness-raising sessions, for example, we have in many ways gone beyond white women's revelations because we are dealing with implications of race and class as well as sex. Even our black women's style of talking/testifying in black language about what we have experienced has a resonance that is both cultural and political . . . No one before has ever examined the multilayered texture of black women's lives' (in Nicholson 1997: 66; originally collected in Hull et al. 1982). Black women, for many reasons, might want to maintain strong links with black men and anti-racism movements, and generally see oppression as emerging from multiple and sometimes contradictory sources.

Separatism at the level of debate and policy-making, as a political necessity, is the most widespread use of the practice in feminism, but in the last decade or so it is more common once again to see men participating in feminist conferences and symposia as both participants and audience, just as they did at the earliest conferences (not always to a warm welcome). Those within feminism with more socialist or liberal leanings as well as black feminist groups were perhaps always more likely to look kindly on the inclusion of men since part of their movement's philosophy would be devoted to the active transformation of men as well as the transformation of women's lives, and lesbians were by no means automatically committed to full separatism simply because their sexual orientation didn't invite certain emotional investments from men.

Radical feminists have always been much more fiercely divided about where men should come in and when, which is partly due to there being contestation within this group about whether men and women are simply different because of the cultural impact on our lives or whether they are destined to be different. These arguments often rest on questions of whether men are naturally violent and women naturally nurturing and certainly some of the structuring of women's involvement in the peace movement – particularly, say, the Greenham women in the UK – emphasised women's pacificism and their special social responsibilities as mothers. For some, probably the minority, men are a separate species, as they were for Valerie Solanis, controversial author of the SCUM (Society for Cutting Up Men) Manifesto. As Carol Anne Douglas says, 'All radical feminists are separatists to some degree. We all acknowledge the importance of doing at least some political work independently of men. Most lesbians (depending on how they define their separatism) are separatists in the sense that they do not sleep with or become romantically involved with men. Some separatists, however, reportedly have carried separatism to the point of criticising other lesbians for occasionally seeing their fathers or brothers. I suspect that this degree of separatism is relatively uncommon' (1990: 257).

Many, perhaps most, early second wave feminists felt that separatism was indeed a temporary strategy, and that men could be reintegrated once the consciousness-raising process could be seen to have been successful, and that in material terms women could be said to be on an equal footing with men. There was also the fear of being ghettoised – of feminist politics not being taken as seriously as other debates within the 'malestream' and to some extent this became a self-fulfilling prophecy, something that was never going to be easy to resolve, when men were identified as so much a part of the problem.

'New' feminists such as Naomi Wolf prefer to see women and men healing the rifts between them, and in general terms there is a feeling that a new 'generation' of feminism must invite men within it. Nonetheless she sees a token separatism as an essential part of a 'power' feminist's networking portfolio. The 'power group' for Wolf is a collecting of women's skills, contacts and information which allows the furthering of other women's professional careers in the same way that 'old boys' networks have operated for privileged white men for centuries. She aims to wipe away the stereotype of the women's group as necessarily nurturing and non-competitive for something more practical at a material and individual level, because 'women tend to assume that a group must do some self-sacrificing chore rather than create resources for its own members and open up opportunities for others in a way that feels good' (Wolf 1993: 310). This ambition takes us far beyond the original definitions of the term 'separatism', but serves to remind us that the practice can carry several quite contradictory meanings with less predictable consequences.

**See also:** *consciousness raising, feminisms*

### FURTHER READING

Douglas (1990) is a useful, and rare, introduction to radical feminism and lesbian politics which offers a good range of perspectives on separatism. To get a sense of the political dimensions of separatism, Echols (1989) gives an evocative account of the move from New Left politics to feminism. Collins (1990) makes a good case for analyses which take into account the specificity of black African-American experience and then use them to deal with deficiencies in white feminism.

# sexual contract

**151**

In political theory, drawing on the writings of Hobbes, Locke and Rousseau, the development of government and the state is understood as if they originated in a social contract. In a groundbreaking critique of political contract theory, Pateman developed the concept of the sexual contract to draw attention to the gendered nature of the social contract. 'The original pact is a sexual as well as a social contract; it is sexual in the sense of patriarchal – that is, the contract establishes men's political right over women – and also sexual in the sense of establishing orderly access by men to women's bodies' (1988: 2).

The story of the social contract as told by Hobbes, Locke and Rousseau differs in detail but each suggests that civil society originated when previously free and equal individuals consented to become subjects of the state, thereby exchanging unfettered freedom for regularised social order, to the greater benefit of all. As Pateman reiterates, the social contract does not depict an actual historical event, but is a story, a fiction, developed as a way of understanding the origins of the state and its legitimate authority over its citizens. Classic social contract theory has been fundamentally important in shaping politics as a discipline and in establishing its key areas of concern, including notions of the individual and of citizenship. Pateman claims that political theorists have, though, tended to reconstruct what were necessarily *masculine* citizens of the classic social contract texts into abstract, gender-neutral individuals. In so doing, political theory has failed to recognise men's domination over women as political and has omitted from the subject matter of politics such things as marriage, sexuality, motherhood, domestic labour and sexual violence (1989: 3). In Pateman's analysis of the classic texts of the social contract story, it is only men who are held to possess the necessary capacities for civil citizenship; for they, unlike women, are individuals who can overcome their passions, exercise justice and uphold the law. In the classic stories, the new, contractual, social order drawn up by men is comprised of two spheres: one, the masculine, civil, public, political domain; and the other, feminine, private and removed from politics. Pateman's re-reading of the classic texts shows that women are incorporated into the new social order differently from men, as beings whose sexual embodiment is seen to prevent them from having the same political standing as men (1989: 4).

In her book, *The Sexual Contract*, Pateman aims to detail the consequences in Anglo-American societies of women's exclusion from the category of 'the individual' or 'the citizen' and to show how patriarchal political right is 'continously renewed and reaffirmed through actual contracts in everyday life' (1988: 114). Pateman focuses her analysis on the examples of the employment contract, the marriage contract, and the prostitution contract. In each case, the subject of all these contracts is the kind of property that individuals are held to own in their own persons (via their bodies). Pateman argues that these contractual forms appear to be based on a free agreement between consenting parties of equal standing, but in fact are based on gender relations of domination and subordination. Under the governing terms of the sexual contract, women do not enter these agreements with the same status of citizenship enjoyed by men. Contractual relations in employment, marriage and prostitution enact men's patriarchal privileges, including their right of sexual access to women's bodies. In the marriage contract, for example, men gain rights of access to women's bodies and to their labour as housewives and mothers. Although changes in law mean that wives now have a recognised legal existence independent of their husbands, the wedding custom of a bride being 'given away' by her father to her husband acts to reproduce the sexual contract, as does the tendency for most married women to take on the family name of their husband, rather than retain their own. In employment, Pateman argues, central assumptions of the sexual contract (of men as breadwinners, of women as housewives and mothers) mean that women have not been incorporated into the workforce in the same way as men and do not have the same status as 'workers'. For Pateman, a key part of the story of the sexual contract relates to men's claims over women's bodies and her analysis of marriage, employment and prostitution considers the ways in which these contractual relations uphold the law of 'male sex-right' created in the social-sexual contract. For example, Pateman points to work-place sexual harassment as a way in which men maintain their patriarchal right (1988: 142), while prostitution is identified as a dramatic example of the public aspect of men's 'right of command' over the use of women's bodies (1988: 17). Pateman's argument, then, is that the sexual contract is not only associated with the private sphere of family relations and domesticity, 'The original [social-sexual] contract creates the modern social whole of patriarchal society. Men pass back and forth between the public and the private spheres and the writ of the law of male sex-right runs in both realms' (1988: 12).

The concept of the sexual contract has been influential across a range of academic disciplines, particularly in relation to Pateman's central theme of the discrepant status of women's citizenship. For example, the concept has informed debate on women, the welfare state and citizenship (for example, Lister 1997), including in relation to employment (for example, Crompton 1997). In the study of political institutions, Puwar (2001) has used the sexual contract to analyse the masculine exclusionary mechanisms that make it difficult for women to operate effectively within legislatures and the civil service. The concept has also informed analyses of judicial systems, particularly in relation to the legal processing of cases of rape. For example, McHugh (1995) focuses on a rape case where a lack of physical resistance by the woman was ruled to imply her willingness to engage in sexual relations, despite her repeated verbal resistance. McHugh argues that such an example substantiates the presence of the sexual contract within the masculine-dominated legal system.

Pateman's argument on the sexual contract has been subjected to a range of criticisms. Some writers focus on the sexual contract as an argument about the origins and nature of patriarchy, including its relationship with other forms of inequality, namely class and 'race'. In the view of Johnson (1996), Pateman implies that men's advantageous

153

(relative to women) employment contract within the capitalist system presupposes women's incorporation into the private sphere via the marriage contract. According to Johnson, Pateman therefore provides a gender-reductionist explanation of capitalism, depicting capitalism as but a form of patriarchy (although, see Pateman's (1996) reply). Pateman's treatment of race and ethnicity can also be criticised in that she pays insufficient attention to the ways in which the sexual contract interacts with what Mills (1997) calls 'the racial contract'. Other writers have criticised Pateman's work on the sexual contract for the way it depicts power relations between women and men. For Fraser (1997), Pateman portrays dominance and subordination as dyadic, with women as the subjects of individual masters (men). The need for a more nuanced, relational view of gendered power relations is emphasised by O'Connell Davidson (1998) in her study of prostitution. Prostitute use is shown to be more than a simple matter of patriarchal domination, when account is taken of the context of agreements reached between a prostitute and a client. Other criticisms of the sexual contract arise from its continued applicability, in the light of significant changes in gender relations during the late twentieth century. Changes in women's legal standing, including the recognition in Britain in 1991 of rape within marriage, and their increased participation in paid work and formal politics, are developments which can be argued to reflect the dismantling of the sexual contract in contemporary Western society. Pateman (1997), however, strongly refutes the claim that the sexual contract has been effectively dismantled and points to women's continuing subordination across the societies of the world. Brown (1995, cited in Squires 1999) suggests that, while it may be difficult to identify the legacy of the sexual contract in specific examples of contemporary contractual relations (like the marriage contract), it remains important to recognise that the sexual contract continues to operate at the level of discourse.

**See also:** *citizenship, public/private*

## FURTHER READING

For a summary of debates generated by the concept of the sexual contract, see Squires (1999). A range of views on the 'rewriting' of the sexual contract can be found in Dench (1997), including those of Pateman herself. More recently, in an interview with Puwar (2002), Pateman recounts the origins of her work on the sexual contract, and reviews and refutes some of the criticisms it has attracted.

154

Sexuality is a difficult term to define since, as will be shown, it does not simply relate to 'sex'. Michel Foucault's groundbreaking *The History of Sexuality* has revolutionised the way contemporary theorists perceive sexuality; it was he who suggested that 'homosexuality' as an 'identity' that could be applied to an individual was a fairly recent invention, with the terms homosexuality and heterosexuality only appearing in 1869. Foucault shows that sexual perversions before the latter part of the nineteenth century were dealt with as acts that anyone could perform and be punished for, but a marked shift was effected when the 'homosexual became a personage, a past, a case history, and a childhood, in addition to being a type of life, a life form, and a morphology, with an indiscreet anatomy and possibly a mysterious physiology. Nothing that went into his total composition was unaffected by his sexuality' (Foucault 1979: 43). Foucault is suggesting that sexual practices come to define and delimit a person – a reversal of ancient legal definitions of, for example, sodomy.

During the nineteenth and twentieth centuries, the burgeoning interest in sexology (the scientific study of sexual practices, primarily interested in 'deviance') and psychoanalysis meant that what was known about individuals' sexual appetites and predilections multiplied and was used to police sexuality as well as predict the personality types associated with each act. Gradually as more people were encouraged to consider their anxieties and neuroses and speak their desires, it became more common for people to see sexual desire as saying something profound about their deepest selves – as if their 'sexuality' lay at the heart of the mystery of human life.

Foucault's examination explains this increasing association of sexuality with the real self as an effect of the multiplying discourses of sex, which allow scientists frenetically to gather more and more information about increasingly arcane fetishes and desires. Foucault and other theorists show how normative sexuality, in response to the identification of deviance, becomes bound to reproductive imperatives, the idea that 'sexual difference is essential to sexual desire' (Jackson in Jackson and Jones 1998: 139). These kinds of links self-evidently make all kinds of appeals to nature and have shaped what is considered normal – so that heterosexual penetrative intercourse is regarded as *the* determinant of heterosexual sex because it facilitates procreation, seen as governing 'normal' sexual

155

response (regardless of what sexual practices heterosexuals individually favour). This focus on the natural is part of the 'endeavour to expel from reality the forms of sexuality that were not amenable to the strict economy of reproduction: to say no to unproductive activities, to banish casual pleasures, to reduce or exclude practices whose object was not procreation' (Foucault 1979: 36). This attempt to create irreducible meanings from sexual response is in Foucault's view further evidence that these meanings are actually socially constructed.

John Gagnon and William Simon, in common with Michel Foucault, emphasise the ways the meanings of sexuality are socially created – particularly the way that the body is imbued with all kinds of essential meanings: 'we have allowed the organs, the orifices, and the gender of the actors to personify or embody or exhaust nearly all of the meanings that exist in the sexual situation. Rarely do we turn from a consideration of the organs themselves to the sources of the meanings that are attached to them, the ways in which the physical activities of sex are learned, and the ways in which these activities are integrated into larger social scripts and social arrangements where meanings and sexual behaviour come together to create sexual conduct' (Gagnon and Simon 1974: 5). They believe that Freud and Freudian psychoanalysis over-emphasised the association of the body with the natural – the idea that anatomy is destiny – regardless of the meanings that we attribute to the body and the different taboos on exposure or touch which shift across time and cultures. Similarly they assert that sexologists focus too much on sexual acts with little concern for their shifting social significance, arguing with Foucault that the act is meaningless without the social/cultural setting that makes it illicit or licit, homo or heterosexual.

One of the tensions for modern feminism was that it tried to analyse the way heterosexual sex is informed by patriarchal relations of power at the same time as wanting to focus on sex as a positive life-force for women. These ambitions have to be set in the context of post-1960s' libertarian thinking and the emergence of the so-called 'sexual revolution', where discussions about heterosexuality, homosexuality and desire were becoming more open, and where sexual health and the banishing of sexual ignorance became real aims. Within this framework, early second wave feminists were beginning to demand the right to be sexually active without censure and to find ways to portray women as desiring *subjects* rather than as *objects* of desire. Regrettably, the will to find new ways for women to express desire freed from the language of patriarchy became buried in a gradual reticence about feeling able to talk about heterosexuality at all.

Heterosexuality for women is always going to be linked to fear of conception and how one deals with the possible consequences, and perhaps too often feminist debate focused on contraception and abortion at the expense of imagining a sexual future for women where they had their own language of desire. For all the discussions about sexuality and the important documents that emerged from the early Women's Liberation Movement, such matters were left unresolved. Anne Koedt's momentous 'The Myth of the Vaginal Orgasm' (1968), a pamphlet that was reproduced in thousands and circulated from the USA to Europe and beyond, debunked the precedence of penetrative sex in order to declare once and for all the centrality of the clitoris to female sexual excitement. Contemporary commentators have since claimed that Koedt went too far and was inaccurate in her claim that the vagina had virtually no sensation at all. These critiques are valid, but should not detract from her intention to unseat the centrality of Freudian notions of female sexual response, geared as it was to the notion of the passive receiving woman and the active predatory man.

What emerged as the two key feminist debates on sexuality were pornography and political lesbianism. The 1982 Conference, 'The Scholar and the Feminist: Toward a Politics of Sexuality' held at Barnard College, New York is reported as disintegrating into open conflict around the issue of pornography. This conference was set up in the context of what one of its organisers, Carole Vance, saw as an increasing backlash in the 1980s against abortion reforms (especially in the USA) and excessive 'permissiveness'; with the emergence of the powerful New Right, feminism and radical thinking from the 1960s were seen as directly responsible for moral degeneration. This meant that any 'outlaw' expressions of sexuality – gay and lesbian or active heterosexual female, or adolescent – were treated with renewed censure, and AIDS was tastelessly seen as moral retribution on gays (the group most intensely affected by the virus at first in the USA and Europe). For many feminists the huge feminist anti-pornography movement ironically gave fuel to the backlash so that 'pornography, according to its critics, was now the central engine of women's oppression, the major socialiser of men, and the chief agent of violence against women' (Vance 1992: xix); this could only further problematise the exploration of female sexuality.

Feminists such as Ti-Grace Atkinson had implied that all feminists were lesbians in the political sense, and the notion of 'political lesbianism' developed from this connection, initially intended as a political statement, but later becoming more closely attached to sexual practice. For the Leeds Revolutionary Feminists of 1979, 'Our definition of a political lesbian is a women-identified woman who does not fuck men. It does not mean

157

compulsory sexual activity with women' (quoted by Gonda in Jackson and Jones 1998:117). While this is an emphatic denial that political lesbianism has anything to do with sex, it also dictates to women what is and is not acceptable even if the principle was to unseat the hegemony of heterosexuality. Women who were heterosexual and feminist were being implicitly forbidden to engage in sexual contact by some political lesbian groups, thus condemning all heterosexual practices as intrinsically oppressive without any possibility of change. Lesbians were seemingly expected to accept that their sexual choices were to be freely utilised for 'political' purposes regardless of their own desires, so the new dawn of female desire seems to have disappeared under the weight of some fairly thorny feminist political contradictions. Lynne Segal observes this shift within some quarters of the women's movement as from radicalism to 'bleak sexual conservatism' (Segal 1994: xii) and heterosexual feminists dealt with this by barely talking of sex at all.

What also emerged in the controversy around porn at the Barnard Conference was also a rejection of this desexualised image of the lesbian as the political conscience of feminism, and the emergence of pro-sex or anti-censorship lesbians claiming a full sexual identity in all its varieties. The tensions were clear: where lesbian feminists such as Sheila Jeffreys were clinging to a certain model of lesbian sexuality (often termed 'vanilla' lesbianism by pro-sex lesbians), others were questioning the validity of claims of authentic lesbian sex, especially if the social constructionist view of sexuality were to be endorsed. For Jeffreys this is nothing but a 'heresy', as the title of her 1994 publication *The Lesbian Heresy* suggests, and discussing what she sees as the increasing predominance of SM and penetrative sexual practices among lesbians, she says that 'a new generation of lesbians are cheerfully adopting the values and practices of gay male culture to the extent, as some of them are prepared to admit, of wishing that they were gay men' (Jeffreys 1994: 143).

Carole Vance asked whether the feminist concept of 'the personal is political' meant 'that sexual life was singularly and entirely political? If so, it was perhaps logical to expect that feminists who shared the same politics should have identical or highly similar sexual lives, and that there should be a close conformity between political goals and personal behaviour' (Vance 1992: 21). She is trying to foreground the perils of equating the construction of sexuality so closely with patriarchal interests and oppression; it needlessly removes pleasure from the equation and contributes to the caricature of the radical feminist as puritanical and anti-pleasure (which came to inform the popular view of all feminists by the 1990s).

The problem in the past with analysing heterosexuality is, as Jo Van Every asserts, that '[t]here is relatively little discussion of the fact that heterosexual relationships encompass much more than sex' (Van Every in Richardson 1996: 40). Carol Smart takes the example of sex education which highlights the dangers rather than actually educating children about sexual pleasure: 'It is hard to imagine sex educators today daring to speak openly of pleasure and joy, or of discussing the benefits of young women learning to masturbate, so that they know their own bodies before they experiment with another person' (Smart in Richardson 1996: 175). The definitions of heterosex as yet remain too crude, too focused on its 'institutional' embodiment, and fail to take into account how individual women negotiate, resist and challenge the institutional discourses of heterosex while still being defined by them. Celia Kitzinger and Sue Wilkinson attempted to address some of these questions in their collection about heterosexuality (1993); as lesbian feminists they shifted the margin/centre roles usually assigned to homo/heterosexuality and wrote to heterosexual women asking what their sexuality meant to them. What it underscored is that heterosexuality is not a political identity for women the way lesbianism can be: '[b]ecause "lesbian" is an intrinsically politicised identity, and heterosexuality is not, the two terms are not commensurate, do not belong in the same conceptual space' (Kitzinger and Wilkinson 1993: 8). Their intention, therefore, was to encourage a politicisation of the category heterosexual. One contributor sums up this feeling of role reversal: 'to be invited to write *in the name of heterosexuality* by another is to experience the force of being positioned as Other' (Young in Kitzinger and Wilkinson 1993: 37). This kind of exercise might help feminists emerge from the impasse around how to redefine heterosexuality and, as Segal argues, if we 'really cannot offer a response to much of women's sexual experience, other than to condemn it as part of a repressive social order, we can only dishearten rather than inspire the majority of women' (1994: xii). If one embraces the view that sexuality is socially constructed, then one way beyond the heterosexual impasse is to explode the hetero/homo binary and embrace the playful resistances of queer theory. After all, queer theory shows that 'heterosexuality is "unstable", dependent on ongoing, continuous and repeated performances by individuals "doing heterosexuality", which produce the illusion of stability' (Richardson 2000: 40). What might be emphasised here, as in the rhetoric of earlier feminism, is the radical possibilities of self-determinism – 'when we reclaim our sexuality we will have reclaimed our belief in ourselves as women. When this intense and powerful part of our nature is no longer suppressed we will refuse to do meekly as we are told.

We will refuse to be compliant, submissive and weak' (Hamblin in Allen et al. 1974: 96).

**See also:** *heterosexism, lesbian continuum, queer theory*

### FURTHER READING

For greater insights into sexuality, Foucault (1979) is surprisingly readable, as is Gagnon and Simon (1974); Jeffrey Weeks's books (e.g. 1985) are also a rich source of information and debate. For the key radical feminist texts, see A. Koedt, 'The Myth of the Vaginal Orgasm' (1968) in Koedt et al. (1973), Gunew (1991) or Jackson and Scott (1996). Jeffreys (1994) offers a highly controversial lesbian feminist view on sexuality and Vance's collection (1992) is essential reading on the pro-sex, anti-censorship position. Richardson (2000) re-examines the key concepts in relation to sexuality and its connection to the state and sexual citizenship.

# socialisation

In sociology, the concept of socialisation refers to the process whereby individuals learn the culture (for example, language, formal and informal rules of behaviour and sets of knowledge) of the particular society they live in. The concept of socialisation features in explanations of gender difference, where emphasis is given to the process of how individuals learn to become masculine or feminine in their identities, appearance, values and behaviour. The primary stage of socialisation occurs during infancy and childhood, via interaction between adults (especially parents) and children. Socialisation is, though, a life-long process. As individuals grow up and older, they continually encounter new situations and experiences and so learn new aspects of femininity or masculinity throughout their lives.

There are a number of different theoretical approaches to gender socialisation, including role-learning theory (or sex-role theory) and psychoanalytic theory. According to role-learning theorists (for example, Hartley 1966; Parsons and Bales 1956; Weinreich 1978), girls and boys learn the appropriate behavioural roles for their sex during primary socialisation, through interaction with adults, especially parents. The social practices of adults are important in a number of ways. For example, adults provide infants and children with clothes of 'appropriate' colours and styling, according to whether they are a boy or a girl, and similarly equip them with an 'appropriate' stock of toys. Adults also act as role models, and children imitate their behaviour, playing for example, 'mummies and daddies', or 'Bob the Builder'. Children are encouraged to conform to roles and behaviour appropriate to their sex through a system of rewards and punishments operated by adults. Girls may be praised for wearing a pretty dress, but may be discouraged from playing football or climbing trees, while boys may be praised for being brave and be admonished for playing with dolls. In addition to the positive and negative sanctions operated by adults, children themselves begin to internalise appropriate behavioural norms and characteristics and thereby unconsciously regulate their own behaviour, in line with the masculine or feminine roles into which they are socialised. Role-learning theorists identify families as of paramount importance in gender socialisation, but the education system and the mass media are also regarded as key agencies because of the stereotypical models of masculinity and femininity they encourage or convey.

Although a useful counter to biological theories of inequalities between women and men, role-learning theory has attracted a variety of criticisms. It is said to portray individuals as 'over-socialised' (Wrong 1961), as passively conforming to pre-determined social roles rather than actively amending, recreating or redefining roles in a reflexive and purposeful way. Role-learning theory may emphasise the social acquisition of roles, but Connell (1987) argues that it implicitly relies on a dichotomous biological distinction and so ultimately has a non-social conception of the basis of differences between women and men. For Walby (1990), the most serious weakness of role-learning theory is that it fails to explain where the specific and differentiated content of gender roles come from, and whose interests they represent. Moreover, as Stanley and Wise note, 'the existence of feminists, lesbians, men who oppose sexism and other people who aren't like the stereotype for their sex' is inadequately explained by this theory, other than as 'failed products' of socialisation (1993: 104).

An example of psychoanalytic socialisation theory is provided by Nancy Chodorow (1978). Chodorow's theory emphasises the importance of the mother–child relationship, its role in gender socialisation, and ultimately, in the reproduction of gender inequality throughout society. Like Freud, Chodorow argues that, as part of psychological development, a child becomes less emotionally dependent upon its mother. This is a

161

separation which occurs in contrasting ways for boys and girls. Because girls and their mothers experience each other as 'alike', girls remain more closely attached to their mothers for longer. Psychologically, the consequences are that a girl's developing sense of self is interrelated with those of other people. 'Girls emerge with a stronger basis for experiencing another's needs or feelings as one's own (or of thinking that one is so experiencing another's needs and feelings)' (1978: 167). Boys and their mothers experience each other as 'opposites'. For boys, their sense of self is created through a more abrupt break from their attachment to their mother: their sense of masculine self develops against their mother's femininity. The psychological outcome is that the self-identity of boys (and men) is less bound up with those of others: they are more emotionally independent and autonomous in their personal relationships. 'Women's mothering, then, produces asymmetries in the relational experiences of girls and boys as they grow up, which account for crucial differences in feminine and masculine personality, and the relational capacities and modes which these entail' (1978: 169). For Chodorow, the mother's primary role in the socialisation of children therefore acts to generate a psychology and ideology of masculine dominance and feminine subordination: it is a fundamental feature of the reproduction of gender inequality. Chodorow's thesis of the 'reproduction of mothering' is valuable for its attention to the emotional socialisation processes that produce masculine and feminine psyches. However, Sayers (1986) is critical of Chodorow's thesis, arguing that it neglects the wider social contexts which affect mother–child relations. Sayers also asks, if women do not experience themselves as independent agents, how can the increase in women's assertion of their independence and autonomy be explained?

Socialisation theories usefully suggest ways in which individuals learn their femininity or masculinity within social contexts. One implication of such theories is that gender inequality can be reduced, if not eradicated, if the content of the roles learnt through socialisation were changed through, for example, anti-sexist child rearing or parenting by men. Socialisation as a *concept* is widely used to describe how individuals socially acquire their gender identity, and such usage rarely implies an adherence to the wider tenets of, say, role-learning theory. However, it is a concept that must be used with critical awareness, in order to avoid the pitfalls of socialisation theory proper. These include a tendency to depict individuals as socially programmed, voluntary and passive conformers and the downplaying of structural processes and institutional factors which act to constrain individuals. In Connell's words, 'Socialization theory . . . has been credible only to the extent that social scientists have been willing to ignore both choice and force in social life' (1987: 195). Individuals are not 'cultural dopes', passively accepting pre-written scripts for gender behaviour, but nor are they entirely free to develop and act out their own scripts.

**See also:** *femininities, masculinity/masculinities, stereotype*

### FURTHER READING

Oakley (1972) is a somewhat dated but still useful text on gender socialisation theories. Stanley and Wise (1993) distinguish between feminist and non-feminist socialisation theories, and subject both to critical evaluation.

# standpoint

In everyday life, the notion of a standpoint expresses the idea that our view of something (say, of a painting) is influenced by where we stand in relation to it (for example, close or at a distance). In simple terms, standpoint theorists in gender studies similarly propose that understanding of the world is related to (gendered) social position. This basic idea of the importance of social position or location has been developed by standpoint theorists into complex arguments about the production, status and purpose of research-generated knowledge, and has formed an important critique of 'traditional' scientific epistemologies (or theories of knowledge). A standpoint, then, is an identification of 'a morally and scientifically preferable grounding for [the] interpretation and explanation of nature and social life' (Harding 1986: 26).

Along with Dorothy Smith (1988), Nancy Hartsock is widely cited as a key author of standpoint theory. Hartsock has developed her arguments in several publications over a number of years. Her initial formulation was published in 1983, as 'The Feminist Standpoint: Developing the Ground for a Specifically Feminist Historical Materialism' (Hartsock 1998; see also Hartsock 1983). For Hartsock, feminists have paid insufficient attention to the epistemological consequences of their claim that women's lives are structurally different to men's lives. In addressing this

163

issue, Hartsock draws on Marx's argument that understanding and knowledge are structured by location in material (or economic) life, and Lukàc's development of the 'standpoint of the proletariat'. For Hartsock, the following features of standpoint theory are particularly important: (i) material life structures understanding and knowledge; (ii) those groups occupying different positions in the structure of material life will therefore have differing 'worldviews'; (iii) the power of the dominant group means that their perspective is hegemonic; and (iv) as a consequence, 'the vision of the oppressed' must be struggled for. Key to this process of struggle are systematic analysis, and education (via political activity), and from this, social change and liberation may result (1998: 107). In developing her theory, Hartsock focuses on the sexual division of labour as the basis of the feminist standpoint, arguing that women's dual responsibility for the production of material things and human beings means that they, more so than men, are immersed in 'concrete, many-qualitied, changing material processes' (1998: 114). This is a structural position that (potentially) makes available to women a 'privileged vantage point' from which to 'understand patriarchal institutions and ideologies as perverse inversions of more human social relations' (1998: 107). In labelling her standpoint theory 'feminist', Hartsock not only identifies the feminist perspective on women's shared experiences as her 'preferable grounds' for interpretation of social life, but also emphasises the liberatory potential and the achieved character of knowledge gained through standpoint (1998: 111).

Standpoint epistemologies, of which Hartsock's is one example, represent an important critique of 'traditional' models of scientific enquiry and of knowledge. In Harding's term, standpoint theories represent a 'successor science' in that they aim to reconstruct the practice and purpose of science (1986: 142). For example, in focusing on women as an oppressed group, feminist standpoint theories counter the androcentric focus of research and knowledge claims. Standpoint theories also challenge dominant notions of truth and reality, and of the place of objectivity, values and bias in the production of knowledge. For example, in feminist standpoint theories, contrary to conventional scientific methodology, the social identity of the researcher is regarded as important (women are argued to have a privileged, or less perverse, access to social 'reality') and attention is given to power relations in the research process. Furthermore, standpoint theories posit a relation between research and politics. Feminist standpoint theories (for example) can be characterised as advocating research on or about women, which generates knowledge in opposition to dominant (patriarchal) constructions of women's position and experiences, and so is also research *for* women. In Welton's summary, 'The political significance of standpoint rests on its claims to represent marginalized knowledges, while the epistemological force emerges from the standpoint claim to a privileged view of reality' (1997: 8).

Versions of standpoint theory have been applied in a range of empirical studies across many disciplines (see Hirschmann 1997 for a review; see also Maynard and Purvis 1994). Standpoint theory, though, has arguably had its highest profile in debates *about* feminist research, methodology and epistemology. The writings of standpoint theorists have been criticised, defended and reformulated, with the reformulations themselves attracting critical attention (see references in 'Further Reading', below). The key criticisms stem from the initial tendency of feminist standpoint theorists (like Hartsock) to ground their approach in the 'shared experiences' of women, apparently undifferentiated by class, ethnicity or sexuality. This tendency has attracted charges of essentialism or biological determinism. For example, Fraser and Nicholson (1990) argue that Hartsock's discussion of women's reproductive capacities means that she, at least partly, bases her grounding of standpoint theory in biology. The concept of apparently undifferentiated 'women' of early standpoint theory has also led to accusations by postmodernists that the theory is universalist (for example, Smart 1995). As Harding puts it in her review of postmodernist critiques, 'Can there be *a* feminist standpoint if women's (or feminists') social experience is divided by class, race and culture?' (1986: 26). In her later writing, Hartsock (for example, 1998) concedes that her early focus on 'women' was simplified in that it omitted other important social relations, and she now writes of 'multiple standpoints'. Moreover, other feminists such as Hill Collins (1990) have found value in standpoint theory in the development of black feminist standpoints, or lesbian standpoints. However, the reconstruction of a singular standpoint into multiple standpoints does not satisfy all the critics of the approach. In the view of Hekman (1997), the recognition of multiple standpoints is at odds with the standpointist claim of privileged vantage points on social reality. Smart (1995) also remains critical of the 'refined' versions of standpoint theory. She argues that, although its advocates now embrace 'multiple' standpoints, they simultaneously retain a commitment to the idea that some perspectives are less partial and perverse than others: a position Smart characterises as 'having one's cake and eating it' (1995: 205). In their evaluation of the issue, Stanley and Wise agree with writers like Hartsock and Hill Collins that an 'epistemology of the oppressed' provides a different view on the hegemonic reality. However, rather than engaging in the ethically and politically objectionable exercise of evaluating relative degrees of oppression and suffering in search of the 'truest' perspective, Stanley and Wise propose that the grounds of preference should be what best fits with the proponent's experience of living or being or understanding. In other words, knowledge should be understood as situated, specific and local to the social location of its producers (1993: 228).

The debate on standpoint theory has clearly reflected broader concerns in gender studies, especially the issue of how to research and theorise gender relations in such a way as to integrate difference while simultaneously giving recognition to enduring inequalities of power between 'men' and 'women'. As Hartsock herself concludes, whatever its shortcomings, standpoint theory has successfully produced 'a fertile terrain for feminist debates about power, politics and epistemology' (1998: 230).

**See also:** *difference, essentialism, postmodernism*

### FURTHER READING

A flavour of the debates on the benefits and shortcomings of standpoint theory can be found in *Signs: A Journal of Women in Culture and Society* (Vol. 22, No. 2, 1997), and also in a special issue of *Women and Politics* (Vol. 18, No. 3, 1997). Maynard (1994) discusses standpoint theory in her excellent overview of debates on feminism and research. Ramazanoglu (1989a) considers how her 1960s' study of shift-working women might have been improved if she had taken a feminist standpoint approach. For a discussion of men's standpoint, see Coltrane (1994).

# stereotype

The concept of a stereotype was introduced into social science in 1922, when Lippman used it to describe the 'typical picture' that comes to mind when thinking about a particular social group (Macrae et al. 1996). A stereotype can be thought of as a cognitive method or procedure, used by our mind in order to simplify the complex barrage of information it experiences. From this perspective, a stereotype is a method of understanding, which works through classifying individual people into a group category. This definition of a stereotype, however, omits the important issue of content. As a 'typical picture' about a social group, a stereotype may be negative or positive, accurate or inaccurate, justified or unjustified. It is, though, the negative, the inaccurate, and the unjustified stereotypes that cause us most concern (Schneider 1996). An adequate understanding of a stereotype must also include the idea that stereotypes are not only contained within an individual's mind, but also exist at a collective level. This shared element of the content of stereotypes makes it possible to identify some easily recognised gender stereotypes. For example, that women are emotional and unpredictable, are bad drivers and like chocolate, or that men are rational and instrumental, bad at housework and like sport. With these points in mind, a gender stereotype can be defined as a standardised and often pejorative idea or image held about an individual on the basis of their gender. At a general level, the effects of stereotyping can mean that, rather than treating people as individuals, 'we treat them instead as artificial persons, which means as an extension of the category we have constructed' (Enteman 1996: 10).

Research within the field of gender studies has examined the presence of gender stereotyping in key agencies of socialisation, such as families, the education system and the media. For example, it is through the application of 'sex role' stereotypes by adults, especially parents, that infants and children learn what is deemed appropriate or inappropriate behaviour for their sex (for example, Parsons and Bales 1956). In a study of secondary schools, Riddell (1992) found that teachers stereotyped girls as mature, neat and conscientious, while boys were seen as aggressive and lacking in discipline. As a consequence, teachers devoted more attention to boys as a strategy of maintaining order in the classroom. Riddell also found that many of the teachers she studied subscribed to a gendered ideology in which femininity was equated with actual or potential motherhood. This dominant stereotype also served to marginalise girls and women as actual or potential workers, and so may have compromised the schools' policy of equal opportunities. Studies of reading materials and textbooks used in schools have been shown to contain gender stereotypes. Masculine characters tend to predominate and to be depicted in a wide range of roles, while the few female characters tend to be stereotyped in domestic settings (Lobban 1974; Best 1993).

Research on gender stereotyping in the media also suggests that femininity is routinely associated with domesticity and sexuality. In a classic study, Tuchman (1981) examined media depictions of American women from the 1950s onwards. Her findings were that women were stereotyped either as sexual objects, or as housewives, or in jobs which were reflections of their domestic/caring role. Tuchman described such

167

narrow and constricting representations as amounting to the 'symbolic annihilation of women', in that they failed to accurately reflect the range of women's lives in reality. In its review of research evidence from the 1990s onwards, a report by the European Commission (1999) argued that changes in the portrayal of gender can best be described as 'tentative and ambiguous'. One finding was that women continue to be underrepresented on television. In Britain, for example, only 30 per cent of people on television are women. Moreover, studies also showed that, compared with men, 'women portrayed in the media are younger, more likely to be shown as married, and less likely to be shown in paid employment' (1999: 12).

While it is relatively easy to identify stereotypical attitudes about gender held by, say, teachers, or stereotypical images transmitted through television, it is more difficult to establish a strong and direct link between such stereotypes and systematic discrimination experienced by groups to whom the stereotypes are applied (Pickering 1995). For example, to claim that there is a direct link between media representations and gender inequality involves a whole host of assumptions, not least that audiences are passive and fully accepting of the dominant gender stereotypes the all-powerful media communicate to them. In studies of media representations, the focus has shifted away from whether stereotypes of gender reflect the 'reality' of gendered experiences and identities. Instead, media representations are increasingly regarded as key ways in which understandings of gendered 'reality' are constructed, and attention is given to the processes through which audiences exercise power in actively negotiating meanings of the 'text' (the magazine, advertisement, film or television programme). 'Depending on the socio-economic and cultural placings that media consumers already occupy, the text's preferred interpretation may in certain instances be negotiated or refused altogether' (Moores 1993: 6).

The issue of power in relation to stereotyping is also addressed by Jenkins (2000), whose discussion is framed in terms of social processes of group categorisation. Jenkins points out that some groups have greater power to make categorisations than others, and to generate consequences of their categorisations. If repeated and reinforced across different contexts, such categorisations are 'crucial in setting the limits to possibility' for those so defined. 'The effective categorisation of a group of people by a more powerful Other is thus never "just" a matter of classification . . . As an intervention in that group's social world it will to an extent and in ways that are content-specific, change that world and the experience of those living in it; in other words, it has *consequences*' (2000: 21–2, original emphasis).

See also: *(the) Other, socialisation*

## FURTHER READING

Pickering (2001) provides a critical assessment of the concept of stereotyping from the perspective of sociology and media studies, and links it closely to the concept of the Other. A classic review of gender stereotyping in education is provided by Delamont (1990), although see Paechter (1998) for more recent evidence.

A report by the European Commission (1999) provides an analytical overview of European media research on gender portrayal, and includes many references to British evidence.

# third wave feminism

Third wave feminism has numerous definitions, but perhaps is best described in the most general terms as the feminism of a younger generation of women who acknowledge the legacy of second wave feminism, but also identify what they see as its limitations. These perceived limitations would include their sense that it remained too exclusively white and middle class, that it became a prescriptive movement which alienated ordinary women by making them feel guilty about enjoying aspects of individual self-expression such as cosmetics and fashion, but also sexuality – especially heterosexuality and its trappings, such as pornography. Moreover, most third wavers would assert that the historical and political conditions in which second wave feminism emerged no longer exist and therefore it does not chime with the experiences of today's women. Third wave feminists seem to largely be women who have grown up massively influenced by feminism, possibly with feminist mothers and relations, and accustomed to the existence of women's studies courses as the norm as well as academic interrogations of 'race' and class. These young, mainly university-educated women may well also have encountered post-structuralist and postmodernist theories, so that their approach to staple feminist concepts such as identity and sisterhood will be sceptical and challenging.

According to the conservative critic Rene Denfeld, the third wave was conceived by Rebecca Walker (daughter of the writer Alice Walker) and

169

Shannon Liss in the early 1990s (Denfeld 1995: 263), but it seems likely that the term was applied across a number of sources synchronically and, like the second wave, its history is dispersed and caught up with the political tendencies of the age. It is interesting to point out, though, that much of its impetus derives from the writings of women of colour. Most third wave feminists seem to separate their perspectives from so-called 'post-feminism'; as Lesley Heywood and Jennifer Drake assert, 'Let us be clear: "post-feminist" characterizes a group of young, conservative feminists who explicitly define themselves against and criticize feminists of the second wave' (1997: 1). They, conversely, seem very conscious of the second wave's recent history and may well see their work as part of a continuum of feminist radical thought and theorising. This is in opposition to some contemporary commentators on feminism such as Katie Roiphe, whose *The Morning After* (1994) portrayed US campuses as overrun with misguided feminist radicals exaggerating the dangers of date rape and sexual harassment to the detriment of relationships between men and women – clearly part of the conservative tendency rejected by third wavers.

Naomi Wolf, however, gets a more mixed reception, but her *Fire with Fire* (1993) in many ways fits the third wave mould, particularly in her dismissal of what she calls 'victim feminism' – where women are supposedly encouraged to see themselves rendered passive by oppression within a second wave formulation. Wolf articulates her perspective as part of a generational shift in common with practically all third wave feminism whose genesis is based on a resistance to the 'old guard' or framed in terms of the need for the 'daughter' to break away from her feminist 'mother' in order to define her own agenda.

Third wave feminism seems to have emerged from the academy in the loosest sense – that its key spokespeople developed these ideas as a response to their own feminist education – but is equally present in popular cultural forms, as these feminists see their lives as just as powerfully shaped by popular culture, particularly music, television, film and literature. Media figures such as the rock star Courtney Love represent third wave icons in their tendency to refuse to adhere to a feminist party line, but also in their resistance to comply with the types of 'feminine' behaviour deemed compatible with media and mainstream success. The Riot Grrrl movement which began around 1991, has close links with the emergence of third wave feminism and illustrates their claim that popular culture can be the site of activism, and that media such as music can be used to communicate political messages. The musical style of Riot Grrrls was heavily influenced by 1970s' punk and it embraced punk's inclusivity – the idea that anyone with a passion for music, but perhaps without formal training, could be involved in performance. Their influence soon went beyond the music scene to a broader-based movement – the 1992 Riot Grrrl convention in Washington, DC, for example, had workshops on sexuality, rape, racism and domestic violence (Klein in Heywood and Drake 1997: 214). Examples of Riot Grrl and subsequent third wave activism include making music (not an inconsiderable ambition in an industry famously dominated by men), running record labels, publishing fanzines and setting up cultural events. As all this suggests, being part of feminism's third wave means realising one's own politics through the mass media and popular culture – this is diametrically opposed to the ambitions of second wave feminism to keep its 'authenticity' by generally shunning the blandishments of the media for fear of being absorbed by patriarchal power structures. Despite the marginal and maverick status of Riot Grrrl performers, there is more generally an investment in women who have made success in a man's world, using all the usual 'patriarchal' indicators of success, such as money, fame, media savvy. The sources for third wave inspiration reflect this cultural multi-lingualism, so that a third wave feminist is as likely to read Mary Wollstonecraft as she is to pick up Elizabeth Wurtzel's *Bitch* (1999) or settle down to watch the latest episode of *Buffy*.

Beyond their cultural tastes, third wavers pride themselves on their global perspective and there is a commitment to look at the material conditions of people's lives while embracing some of the key tenets of second wave feminism. Men and heterosexuality have a less problematic place in third wave feminism – and their analysis tends to take into account the dispossession of young males as well as females. In the USA in particular, its focus on a certain generation acts as a counterpoise to the characterisation of American generation-Xers as whining and idle.

It is certain that third wave activism is still in its relative infancy and that more academic commentaries will gradually emerge, which will themselves broaden its scope at the same time that they attempt to account for its particular philosophy. Very much at the heart of feminism's third wave is the sense of generational conflict – one generation claiming its own space and fashioning the movement in its own image – in fact 'generation X feminism' is defined by age more than anything else. This marks a very different transition from the first to second waves of feminism, where the shape of political action and feminist purpose was transformed from a discourse of rights to that of liberation. There are hints of good old second wave collective activity in the websites, the zines and the concerts such as Ladyfest (which began in

2000 and are happening across the USA and Europe), but it has a more individualist edge, reflecting among other things a radical suspicion of the politics of identity, and a marked shift to 'lifestyle' politics (the idea that your politics said something about your individual taste in the same way that your clothes, furniture and car did – and was in fact part of the 'package') evident since the mid-1980s. Of course second wave feminism was itself largely a 'young' movement, comprised mainly of women who were in their twenties and thirties during its height, but they have grown old with it and presumably never imagined that its essential message couldn't be conveyed to a new generation. Catherine Redfern, editor of the web-based *The F-Word* declares that 'Second wavers often misunderstand young women's enthusiasm for the term "third wave". They think it's because we don't respect their achievements or want to disassociate ourselves from them. In actual fact I think it simply demonstrates a desire to feel part of a movement with relevance to our own lives and to claim it for ourselves, to stress that feminism is active today, right now . . . a lot has changed between Gen X and the baby boomers, partly because of the achievements of 70s feminism. Having said that, feminism still has unfinished business' (Redfern 2002).

**See also:** *second wave feminism*

### FURTHER READING

Lesley Haywood and Jennifer Drake (1997) offer a lively account of the meanings of third wave feminism to date; Naomi Wolf (1993) is one of the most influential books for this generation of feminists. Because this is a movement that generates intense debate on the web, it is worth looking at some of the sites available, such as 'The third wave – Feminism for the new millennium' (http://www.io.com/~wwwave/) or the UK's 'The F-Word' (http://www.thefword.org.uk).

# violence

The issue of what types of behaviour are defined as violent is both a complex and politically significant one. The validity of definitions of violence, in both cultural and legal terms, reflects the power some social groupings have to make their perspective count as to what is, or is not, 'violence'. Violence may be narrowly defined, as in the legal sense of it being the unlawful use of physical force by an individual against others. A broader approach defines violence as behaviour which harms others, either physically or emotionally. One example of this broader conceptualisation is the idea of a 'continuum of violence' (Kelly and Radford 1998) within which a range of harmful behaviour is included, from physical acts of murder and rape to verbal acts of sexualised and racialised abuse. The political consequences of following a narrower or a more broader definition of violence are several. It affects perceptions of the prevalence and frequency of violent behaviour and of the connections between different forms of behaviour. It also shapes the process of recognising who the perpetrators and victims are, and what the causes and consequences of violence are, as well as the development of appropriate policy responses to counter violence.

Whether a narrow or more broader concept of violence prevails, however, it remains the case that violence is gendered. In other words, it exhibits patterns of difference between men and women, being especially associated with the behaviour of men. Connell identifies a range of ways in which men 'predominate across the spectrum of violence' (2000: 22), whether as members of the armed forces, as violent criminals under the law, as abusers of family members, or as participants in and audiences of the various contact sports which centre around the use of physical force. Official criminal statistics for Europe, Australia and the United States suggest that men are held to be responsible for around 85 per cent of all violent crimes (Breines et al. 2000). Such evidence is suggestive of the important role played by violent behaviour in contemporary constructions of masculinities.

It is men's violence against women that has especially been the concern of feminist researchers. Conceptualised as a broad range of men's harmful behaviour toward women, including rape, domestic violence and sexual harassment, violence has been identified as a key mechanism in the subordination of women by men (for example, Brownmiller 1976; Radford and Stanko 1996; Walby 1990). One manifestation of the subordinating effect of violence against women is indicated by survey evidence which shows that women are more fearful about violent crime than men, and that this fear impacts upon their freedom of movement when outside the home. The British Crime Surveys have consistently shown that more women are 'very worried' about rape than any other crime (Simmons 2002).

For many writers, the full extent of men's violent behaviour toward women is not officially recognised in legal terms, and nor does it appear in the official crime statistics. Walklate (1995), for example, points to the routine and 'everyday' nature of women's experiences of the intimidating, often sexualised and sometimes violent behaviour of some men, much of which is not categorised or penalised as 'criminal'. Kelly and Radford (1996) interviewed women and uncovered a range of experiences of men's sexually abusive behaviour, often from strangers in public places. This behaviour ranged from sexually abusive comments to threats, to unwanted physical contact and even attempted and actual sexual assault. These experiences invoked feelings of intense fear, sickness, intimidation and/or anger in those who were subjected to them. Yet, Kelly and Radford found that, often, the significance of the experience was minimised by the women through their use of the phrase 'but nothing actually happened' or 'nothing really happened'. Kelly and Radford argue that the use of this phrase in the face of the obvious distress such experiences of abuse had caused illustrates the extent to which women are encouraged to downplay the violence they routinely experience. Men have also been shown to minimise the significance of their own abusive, threatening and violent behaviour. Cavanagh, Dobash, Dobash and Lewis (2001) studied men who had used violence against their women partners, with a view to examining the men's understandings of their own behaviour. It was found that the men used a range of rhetorical devices to minimise the significance of their violent behaviour and thereby define it as 'not violent' at all. For Cavanagh and her colleagues, men's power to define their behaviour as 'not violent' is a reflection of the advantageous position they hold in the structure of gender relations.

Other researchers have studied the difficulties faced by women who have experienced men's violence and who then use the criminal justice system in an attempt to get their attacker/abuser convicted of a crime. Studies of the way the police and the courts handle cases of rape and domestic violence reveal how 'masculine' definitions of violence often predominate over 'feminine' ones (Lees 1997; Wright 1995). Edwards argues that, whether in cases of sexual harassment, domestic violence or rape, the woman is 'frequently monitored for the extent to which she provoked her own demise' (1987: 141). In cases of domestic violence, this often means that the woman herself is blamed – for arousing anger in her aggressor, or in cases of repeated violence, for not leaving him. In cases of rape, this may mean that women are held to be somehow responsible for their own experience. For example, through 'leading' the man on to a point where his 'sexual urge' for intercourse 'had to be satisfied', or for dressing 'provocatively'. Evidence that the significance of violence by men against women is minimised – by women, by men and within the criminal justice system – is suggestive of the extent to which it is a 'normalised' feature of contemporary gender relations within which masculinities predominate over femininities. It is this 'normalisation' of men's violent behaviour that is increasingly challenged and resisted, whether by individual women and men in their everyday experiences or by academic researchers, campaign groups and support organisations, and professionals working within the criminal justice system.

The close links between masculinities and violence means that, for men, violence is 'embedded in a network of physicality, experience and male culture such that it is more easily used and more readily available as a resource' (Dobash and Dobash 1998). A number of studies have looked at the relationship between masculine identity and different forms of violent behaviour. For example, Owen (1996) examines the way in which violence between boys/men is regarded as 'normal' and as important in the attainment of a masculine identity. Participation in violence between boys/men, whatever the outcome, therefore has the effect of bolstering masculinity. Similarly, Tomsen and Mason (2001) argue that the attainment and protection of masculine identities are of key importance in understanding the behaviour of those who harass and who are physically violent towards gay people. Behaving violently towards women partners is also important for masculine identity, but, as Dobash and Dobash (1998) argue, its significance lies in reasserting women's subordination (that is, the outcome of the violence) rather than in the process of participating in the violence itself. Within the field of gender studies, then, violence is understood through the problematising of masculinities, a perspective which, in the context of wars, civil wars and terrorism, has influenced the development of international policies aiming to secure peace on a global scale (Breines etal. 2000).

**See also:** *masculinity/masculinities*

### FURTHER READING

Hearn (1998) looks at men's responses to violence against women, while Hatty (2000) analyses masculinities and violence and their representations in media forms, including the cinema. Boddy (1998) addresses the important question of cultural variations in definitions of violence towards women, through a study of female circumcision.

# women's studies

Women's studies, as an area of academic study, came into being during the emergence of feminism's second wave and a new dawn of political activism. The first courses were developed in the late 1960s in the USA, and although some courses were present in adult and higher education in the UK, it wasn't until 1980 that the first MA in women's studies was offered at the University of Kent, followed by other master's and undergraduate degrees elsewhere (see Robinson in Robinson and Richardson 1997: 4). Women's studies programmes, courses or modules have also developed across Europe, Australia, Asia and the Middle East, until it has become in Mary Maynard's words, 'something of a global educational phenomenon' (Maynard in Jackson and Jones 1998: 247), even though the scope of the framework of such courses will depend on cultural context and social and institutional attitudes to the field. Because second wave feminism focused much more on the way ideas and knowledge itself exclude women's interests and identity, the establishment of women's studies – which in its title alone announces that women are worthy of study in their own right – was a logical step in the development of a feminist epistemology (theory of knowledge). As Adrienne Rich observed '[w]omen in colleges where a women's studies program already exists, or where feminist courses are beginning to be taught, still are often made to feel that the "real" curriculum is the male-centred one; that women's studies are . . . a "fad"; that feminist teachers are "unscholarly," "unprofessional," or "dykes"' (Rich 1980: 136), and this belittling of the women's studies curriculum or the validity of women's studies research is still in evidence, although generally covertly.

As Victoria Robinson argues, 'this connection of the academic world to a social movement meant that the setting-up and teaching of such courses was a profoundly political act; theoretical analysis was seen as being intimately connected to social change' (Robinson in Robinson and Richardson 1997: 2). Women's studies has both a 'formal' presence in the academy where it is a recognised discipline (though one subject to the vicissitudes of funding and institutional support) and an 'informal' one, where existing subject areas offer courses or aspects of courses that specifically deal with women and/or gender difference. Women's studies' formal presence is constantly under threat because its status as a subject is still contested at institutional or governmental level or dependent on

176

more material concerns. As Mary Evans notes, 'one of the ironies of the history of women's studies in Britain in the 1980s was the increased toleration for it precisely because of market factors, and the income potential for women's studies' (1997: 115). Moreover, much as students still flock to women's studies classrooms, it is also true that many seek the security of the established disciplines when it comes to naming their degrees, suspecting, perhaps rightly that future employers may be more willing to take on graduates with qualifications in disciplines that they recognise and whose value they understand.

Women's studies, in its questioning of Western epistemology and the means by which knowledge is gained and who has the right to possess it, is necessarily transformative and cannot rest easily within the boundaries of education as it is traditionally perceived. Women's studies is resolutely interdisciplinary or multidisciplinary and often it is taught by academics coming in from their own fields, whereas others might be gathered into a centre where their disciplinary differences are contained under the umbrella of 'women's studies'. Not only does it operate as a critique of existing knowledges, but it also expresses a commitment to provide further analyses of women's lives. As women's studies has become more and more established, students graduating with qualifications in the field again strengthen its position as an autonomous area of study with a rich and diverse research culture. Yet in common with other areas of enquiry such as postmodernism and post-structuralism, which also seek to interrogate the basis of knowledge acquisition, students are required to write standard essays, or sit exams in order to demonstrate that they have understood the key debates in that area in such a way that returns them to the very discursive norms that are being challenged in the classroom. This is one of the paradoxes of teaching feminism in the academy; another is that implicitly one must address the personal lives and circumstances of the student, to get them to think at least about the means by which they are inscribed as women or men, masculine or feminine. This sometimes means that a classroom setting can shift into a 'consciousness raising session' which students may find either illuminating or unsettling, given the existing relations of power between the student and tutor, but which they may also find lacks the intellectual 'rigour' they are accustomed to find in other areas. Many feminist practitioners in a women's studies setting call into question the relationship of power between teacher and taught, between knowledge and experience and therefore this requires women's studies academics to be analytical about their own practices and the ways in which they themselves use knowledge. Ultimately, women's studies is delivered

177

within a system which is geared towards qualifications and, in many areas, a notion that there are 'key' ideas which must be digested and regurgitated: feminist pedagogy can only fit into such demands if it attempts to be transparent about the contradictory impulses in delivering such courses. It is also the case that many of the students studying women's studies may be happy enough to engage with it as a topic, but without connecting this to any feminist sympathies of their own

Given that learning about feminist politics in women's studies may politicise individuals, what is the relationship of 'academic' feminism to activism? For some, the radical impetus of feminism has been swept away by its entry into academic circles; for others, there is a clear dividing line between 'political' feminism and 'academic' feminism which casts the latter as increasingly navel-gazing and obfuscatory in its use of 'high' theory 'jargon'. As early as 1971 Lillian Robinson warned of the dangers of institutional acceptance in her essay 'Dwelling in Decencies' (in Robinson 1978); Adrienne Rich's essay 'Toward a Woman-Centered University' written in 1973 (in Rich 1980b) sees women's studies adapting itself to the production of knowledges that might directly help with women's real lives – for example, research projects on health or birth control. Within this utopian image of the university as a place that furthers the interests of all women, including those who service the education needs of others as caterers, administrators and so forth, she also acknowledges the ways in which women can exploit the resources of the institution in order to produce books and articles whose influence may be felt far beyond the academy. Feminist tutors and their published work have a consciousness raising role for students and what they may do with the ideas they learn and debate is incalculable – so that even now it is hoped that not only does women's studies have a legitimate disciplinary position within the academy, but that its location there helps sustain feminist work outside.

Since the late 1980s it became more common to find the term 'women's studies' contested and at times replaced in favour of 'gender studies', the rationale being that feminist theories had opened up the wider possibility of the analysis of gender difference and its maintenance, so that masculinity and male social roles might be of legitimate concern. Although the term gender studies in an academic arena may seem to be inclusive, more attractive to male students and academics, for many feminists the term women's studies makes a far more important political point to remind us that women and their contributions to knowledge were largely neglected in the academic institution for so many years, and its presence goes some way to remind us that in the past traditional

178

disciplinary divisions in academia might be referred to from a feminist viewpoint as 'men's studies'. Even if one holds the view that women's studies lasts only as long as it takes for feminist perspectives to be sufficiently absorbed into existing disciplines, the debate hasn't reach the critical point at which such a decision is made, and is unlikely to do so for a number of years. This fact in itself offers compelling reasons for retaining women's studies as a separatist area of study.

As both women's and gender studies, feminist work continues to be undertaken within the academic institution and the publications produced, conferences organised and opportunities for communication between feminists are valued as part of the maintenance of a thriving feminist scholarship. The system, as Rich cynically suspected, does provide individuals with access to resources and even when the position of women's studies seems embattled (as it does in the UK currently), the work from feminist academics continues to push forward the boundaries of feminist thinking. Just as some of the advocates of third wave feminism are the product of a 'feminist' education, so the other individuals who carry feminist ideas into education, social work, policy-making and mainstream politics help to continue to bring feminist ideas to a wider audience.

**See also:** *men's movement/men's studies*

### FURTHER READING

Adrienne Rich's classic essay, 'Toward a Woman-Centered University' (in Rich 1980b) gives a radical feminist position on women's studies and also imagines some of its utopian possibilities; for a general introduction to the field of study, Robinson and Richardson (1997) is thorough with an interesting range of contributions. hooks (1989) provides a useful commentary on how feminist knowledge can lose its critical fervour or return to a mainstreaming of certain perspectives.

179

# bibliography

Adkins, L. (1995) *Gendered Work*, Buckingham: Open University Press.

Afshar, H. and Maynard, M. (eds) (1994) *The Dynamics of 'Race' and Gender: Some Feminist Interventions*, London: Taylor and Francis.

Alberti, J. (1989) *Beyond Suffrage. Feminists in War and Peace 1914–1928*, London: Macmillan.

Allen, S., Sanders, L. and Wallis, J. (eds) (1974) *Conditions of Illusion: Papers from the Women's Movement*, Leeds: Feminist Books Ltd.

Allison, D. (1995) *Skin: Talking about Sex, Class and Literature*, London: Pandora.

Althusser, L. (1984) *Essays on Ideology*, London: Verso.

Amos, V. and Parmar, P. (1997) 'Challenging Imperial Feminism', in Mirza, H. (ed.) *Black British Feminism*, London: Routledge.

Anon. (1971) 'Ourselves', *Shrew*, Vol. 3, No. 3.

Anon (1974) 'Where Do We Go From Here?...', *Brothers*, Spring.

Anthias, F. (2001) 'The Concept of "Social Division" and Theorising Social Stratification: Looking at Ethnicity and Class', *Sociology* 35 (4): 835–54.

Anthias, F. and Yuval-Davis, N. (1992) *Racialised Boundaries*, London: Routledge.

Arber, S. and Ginn, J. (1995) *Connecting Gender and Ageing*, Buckingham: Open University Press.

Arditti, R., Klein, R. and Minden, S. (eds) (1989) *Test-tube Women*, 2nd edition, London: Pandora Press.

Ashby, M. (1999) 'Beyond the New Feminism?', *Sybil*, Issue 8, May–June.

Ashcroft, B., Griffiths, G. and Tiffin, H. (eds) (1995) *The Post-Colonial Studies Reader*, London: Routledge.

Assiter, A. (1996) *Enlightened Women: Modernist Feminist in a Postmodern Age*, London: Routledge.

Assiter, A. and Carol, A. (1993) *Bad Girls and Dirty Pictures: The Challenge to Reclaim Feminism*, London: Pluto Press.

Baehr, H. and Gray, A. (eds) (1996) *Turning it On: A Reader in Women and Media*, London: Arnold.

Balsamo, A. (1996) *Technologies of the Gendered Body: Reading Cyborg Women*, Durham: Duke University Press.

Banks, O. (1981) *Faces of Feminism*, Oxford: Martin Robertson.

Barrett, M. (1988) *Women's Oppression Today: Problems in Marxist Feminist Analysis* (Revised Edition), London: Verso.

Barrett, M. (1991) *The Politics of Truth: From Marx to Foucault*, Cambridge: Polity.

Barrett, M. and McIntosh, M. (1982) *The Anti-social Family*, London: Verso.

Barrett, M. and Phillips, A. (eds) (1992) *Destabilising Theory: Contemporary Feminist Debates*, Cambridge: Polity Press.

Baudrillard, J. (1990) *Revenge of the Crystal: A Baudrillard Reader*, London: Pluto.

Baxter, J. (2000) 'The Joys and Justice of Housework', *Sociology* 34 (4): 609–31.

Beechey, V. (1979) 'On Patriarchy', *Feminist Review* 3: 66–82.

Bell, D. and Klein, R. (eds) (1996) *Radically Speaking: Feminism Reclaimed*, London: Zed Books.

Benn, M. (1998) *Madonna and Child: Towards a New Politics of Motherhood*, London: Jonathan Cape.

Best, L. (1993) "'Dragons, Dinner Ladies and Ferrets": Sex Roles in Children's Books', *Sociology Review* 2(3): 6–8.

Beynon, J. (2002) *Masculinities and Culture*, Buckingham: Open University Press.

Bhopal, K. (1997) *Gender, 'Race' and Patriarchy*, Aldershot: Ashgate.

Bly, R. (1991) *Iron John: A Book About Men*, Dorset: Element Books.

Bock, G. and James, S. (eds) (1992) *Beyond Equality and Difference*, London: Routledge.

Boddy, J. (1998) 'Violence Embodied? Circumcision, Gender Politics and Cultural Aesthetics', in Dobash, Emerson R. and Dobash, R. (eds) *Rethinking Violence Against Women*, London: Sage.

Bolt, C. (1995) *Feminist Ferment: The 'Woman Question' in the USA and England, 1870–1940*, London: UCL Press.

Bottero, W. (1998) 'Clinging to the Wreckage? Gender and the Legacy of Class', *Sociology* 32 (3): 469–90.

Bowles, G. and Duelli Klein, R. (eds) (1983) *Theories of Women's Studies*, London: RKP.

Bradley, H. (1996) *Fractured Identities: Changing Patterns of Inequality*, Cambridge: Polity.

Brannen, J. and Moss, P. (1991) *Managing Mothers: Dual Earner Households After Maternity Leave*, London: Unwin Hyman.

Brennan, T. (ed.) (1989) *Between Feminism and Psychoanalysis*, London: Routledge.

Breines, I., Connell, R. and Eide, I. (2000) *Male Roles, Masculinities and Violence*, Paris: UNESCO.

Brook, B. (1999) *Feminist Perspectives on the Body*, London: Longman.

Brooks, A. (1997) *Postfeminisms: Feminism, Cultural Theory and Cultural Forms*, London: Routledge.

Brownmiller, S. (1976) *Against Our Will: Men, Women and Rape*, London: Secker and Warburg.

Brownmiller, S. (2000) *In Our Time: Memoir of a Revolution*, London: Aurum Press.

Bryld, M. (2001) 'The Infertility Clinic and the Birth of the Lesbian: The Political Debate on Assisted Reproduction in Denmark', *European Journal of Women's Studies* 8 (3): 299–312.

Bryson, V. (1999) *Feminist Debates: Issues of Theory and Political Practice*, Basingstoke: Macmillan.

Burchill,

Burston, P. and Richardson, C. (eds) (1995) *A Queer Romance: Lesbians, Gay Men and Popular Culture*, London: Routledge.

Butler, J. (1990) *Gender Trouble: Feminism and the Subversion of Identity*, London: Routledge.

Butler, J. (1999) *Gender Trouble*, London: Routledge, 2nd edition.

Butler, J. (1993) *Bodies that Matter: On the Discursive Limits of 'Sex'*, London: Routledge.

Cabinet Office (2001) *Civil Service Statistics 2000*, London: HMSO.

Caine, B. (1997) *English Feminism, 1780–1980*, Oxford: Oxford University Press.

Caine, B. and Sluga, G. (eds) (2000) *Gendering European History, 1780–1920*, London: Leicester University Press.

Carby, H. (1997) 'White Woman Listen! Black Feminism and the Boundaries of Sisterhood', in Mirza, H. (ed.) *Black British Feminism*, London: Routledge.

Carson, F. and Pajaczkowska, C. (eds) (2000) *Feminist Visual Culture*, Edinburgh: Edinburgh University Press.

Cavanagh, K., Dobash, Emerson, R., Dobash, R. and Lewis, R. (2001) '"Remedial Work": Men's Strategic Responses to Their Violence Against Intimate Female Partners', *Sociology* 35 (3): 695–714.

181

Central Office of Information (1996) *Women in Britain*, Aspects of Britain series, second edition, London: HMSO.

Chodorow, N. (1978) *The Reproduction of Mothering*, Berkeley: University of California Press.

Christian, H. (1994), *The Making of Anti-Sexist Men*, London: Routledge.

Code, L. (ed.) (2000) *Encyclopaedia of Feminist Theory*, London: Routledge.

Cohen, J. (2000) 'Is Privacy a Legal Duty? Reconsidering Private Right and Public Virtue in the Domain of Intimacy', in D'Entreves, M. and Vogel, U. (eds) *Public and Private: Legal, Political and Philosophical Perspectives*, London: Routledge.

Cole, M. (1998) 'Gender and Power. A Comparative Analysis of Sex Segregation in Polish and American Higher Education, 1965–1985', *Sociology*, 32 (2): 277–98.

Collins, P. H. (1990) *Black Feminist Thought: Knowledge, Consciousness and the Politics of Empowerment*, London: Routledge.

Coltrane, S. (1994) 'Theorising Masculinities in Contemporary Social Science', in Brod, H. and Kaufman, M. (eds) *Theorising Masculinities*, London: Sage.

Connell, R. (2000) 'Arms and the Man', in Breines, I., Connell, R. and Eide, I. (eds) *Male Roles, Masculinities and Violence*, Paris: UNESCO.

Connell, R.W. (1987) *Gender and Power*, Cambridge: Polity.

Connell, R.W. (1995) *Masculinities*, Cambridge: Polity Press.

Connell, R.W. (2000) *The Men and the Boys*, Cambridge: Polity Press.

Connell, R.W. (2001) 'Introduction and Overview', *Feminism and Psychology* 11 (1): 5–9.

Corea, G. et al. (1987) *Man-made Women*, Bloomington: Indiana University Press.

Cott, N. (1987) *The Grounding of Modern Feminism*, New Haven, CT: Yale University Press.

Coward, R. (1999) *Sacred Cows: Is Feminism Relevant to the New Millennium?*, London: HarperCollins.

Crompton, R. (1996) 'Gender and Class Analysis', in Lee, D. and Turner, B. (eds) *Conflicts About Class*, London: Longman.

Crompton, R. (1997) *Women and Paid Work in Modern Britain*, Oxford: Oxford University Press.

Crompton, R. (2000) 'The Gendered Restructuring of the Middle Class: Employment and Caring Work', in Crompton, R., Devine, F., Savage, M. and Scott, J. (eds) *Renewing Class Analysis*, Oxford: Blackwell.

Crompton, R. and Scott, J. (2000) 'Introduction: The State of Class Analysis', in Crompton, R., Devine, F., Savage, M. and Scott, J. (eds) *Renewing Class Analysis*, Oxford: Blackwell.

Crowley, H. and Himmelweit, S. (1992) *Knowing Women: Feminism and Knowledge*, Cambridge: Polity Press.

Culler, J. (1983) *Deconstruction: Theory and Criticism after Structuralism*, London: Routledge & Kegan Paul.

Daley, C. and Nolan, M. (eds) (1994) *Suffrage and Beyond: International Feminist Perspectives*, Auckland: Auckland University Press.

Davidoff, L. (1998) 'Regarding Some "Old Husbands'" Tales: Public and Private in Feminist History', in Landes, J. (ed.) *Feminism, the Public and the Private*, Oxford: Oxford University Press.

Davies, C. (1996) 'The Sociology of Professions and the Profession of Gender', *Sociology* 30 (4): 661–78.

Davis-Floyd, R. (1998) 'From Technobirth to Cyborg Babies', in Davis-Floyd, R. and Dumit, J. (eds) *Cyborg Babies: From Techno-Sex to Techno-Tots*, London: Routledge.

Davis-Floyd, R. and Dumit, J. (eds) (1998) *Cyborg Babies: From Techno-Sex to Techno-Tots*, London: Routledge.

De Beauvoir, S. (1972) *The Second Sex*, Harmondsworth: Penguin Books.

De Beauvoir, S. (1997) *The Second Sex*, London: Virago (first published 1953).

de Groot, J. and Maynard, M. (eds) (1993) *Women's Studies in the 1990s: Doing Things Differently*, Basingstoke: Macmillan.

Delamont, S. (1990) *Sex Roles and the School*, second edition, London: Routledge.

Delamont, S. (2001) *Changing Women, Unchanged Men?*, Buckingham: Open University Press.

Delphy, C. and Leonard, D. (1992) *Familiar Exploitation*, Cambridge: Polity.

Dench, G. (ed.) (1997) *Rewriting the Sexual Contract*, London: Institute of Community Studies.

Denfeld, R. (1995) *The New Victorians: A Young Woman's Challenge to the New Feminist Order*, New York: Warner Books.

D'Entreves, M. and Vogel, U. (eds) (2000) *Public and Private: Legal, Political and Philosophical Perspectives*, London: Routledge.

Dietz, M. (1998) 'Citizenship with a Feminist Face: The Problem with Maternal Thinking', in Landes, J. (ed.) *Feminism, the Public and the Private*, Oxford: Oxford University Press.

Dobash, Emerson, R. and Dobash, R. (1992) *Women, Violence and Social Change*, London: Routledge.

Dobash, Emerson, R. and Dobash, R. (1998) 'Violent Men and Violent Contexts', in Dobash Emerson, R. and Dobash, R. (eds) *Rethinking Violence Against Women*, London: Sage.

Donovan, J. (1992) *Feminist Theory: The Intellectual Traditions of American Feminism* (expanded edn.) New York: Continuum.

Douglas, C.A. (1990) *Love and Politics: Radical Feminist and Lesbian Theories*, San Francisco: ism press.

Downey, G. and Dumit, J. (eds) (1997) *Cyborgs and Citadels*, Sante Fe, New Mexico: School of American Research Press.

Dworkin, A. (1988) *Letters from a War Zone: Writings 1976–1987*, London: Martin Secker and Warburg.

Dyhouse, C. (1989) *Feminism and the Family in England, 1880–1939*, Oxford: Blackwell.

Echols, A. (1989) *Daring to Be Bad: Radical Feminism in America 1967–1975*, Minneapolis: University of Minnesota Press.

Edgell, S. (1980) *Middle Class Couples*, London: George Allen and Unwin.

Edley, N. and Wetherall, M. (1995) *Men in Perspective*, London: Prentice Hall/Harvester Wheatsheaf.

Edwards, S. (1987) '"Provoking Her Own Demise": From Common Assault to Homicide', in Hanmer, J. and Maynard, M. (eds) *Women, Violence and Social Control*, London: Macmillan.

Elam, D. (1994) *Feminism and Deconstruction: Ms. En Abyme*, London: Routledge.

Elshtain, J. (1993) *Public Man, Private Woman: Women in Social and Political Thought*, 2nd edition, New Jersey: Princeton University Press.

Enteman, W. (1996) 'Stereotyping, Prejudice and Discrimination', in Lester, P. (ed.) *Images that Injure: Pictorial Stereotypes in the Media*, London: Praeger.

Equal Opportunities Commission, www.eoc.org.uk

European Commission (1999) *Images of Women in the Media*, Luxembourg: Office for the Official Publication of the European Communities.

Evans, M. (1985) *Simone de Beauvoir*, London: Tavistock.

183

Evans, M. (1997) *Introducing Contemporary Feminist Thought*, London: Polity Press.

Evans, S. (1979) *Personal Politics: The Roots of Women's Liberation in the Civil Rights Movement and the New Left*, New York: Alfred A. Knopf.

Fallaize, E. (ed.) (1998) *Simone de Beauvoir: A Critical Reader*, London: Routledge.

Faludi, S. (1992) *Backlash: The Undeclared War Against Women*, London: Chatto & Windus.

Faludi, S. (1999) *Stiffed: The Betrayal of the Modern Man*, London: Chatto & Windus.

Faust, B. (1981) *Women, Sex and Pornography*, Harmondsworth: Penguin.

Felski, R. (1997) 'The Doxa of Difference', *Signs:* 23 (1) 1–21.

Felski, R. (2000) *Doing Time: Feminist Theory and Postmodern Culture*, New York: New York University Press.

Feminist Anthology Collective (1981) *No Turning Back: Writings from the Women's Liberation Movement 1975–1980*, London: The Women's Press.

Fenton, S. (1999) *Ethnicity*, Basingstoke: Macmillan.

Firestone, S. (1979) *The Dialectic of Sex: The Case for Feminist Revolution* (first pub. 1970), London: The Women's Press.

Foucault, M. (1979) *The History of Sexuality – Volume 1: An Introduction*, trans. R. Hurley, Harmondsworth: Allen Lane.

Fraser, N. (1997) *Justice Interruptus: Critical Reflections on the 'Postsocialist' Condition*, London: Routledge.

Fraser, N. and Nicolson, L. (1989) 'Social Criticism without Philosophy: An Encounter between Feminism and Postmodernism', in Ross, A. (ed.) *Universal Abandon: The Politics of Postmodernism*, Edinburgh: Edinburgh University Press.

Fraser, N. and Nicholson, L. (1990) 'Social Criticism without Philosophy: An Encounter Between Feminism and Postmodernism', in Nicholson, L. (ed.) *Feminism/Postmodernism*, London: Routledge.

Freeman, J. (1975) *The Politics of Women's Liberation: A Case Study of an Emerging Social Movement and its Relation to the Policy Process*, New York: Longman.

Freud, S. (1977) *On Sexuality: Three Essays on the Theory of Sexuality*, trans. A. Richards, Harmondsworth: Pelican Books.

Friedan, B. (1965) *The Feminine Mystique* (first pub. 1963), Harmondsworth: Penguin Books.

Fuss, D. (1989). *Essentially Speaking: Feminism, Nature and Difference*, London: Routledge.

Fuss, D. (ed.) (1991) *Inside/Out: Lesbian Theories, Gay Theories*, London: Routledge.

Gagnon. J.H. and Simon, W. (1974) *Sexual Conduct: The Social Sources of Human Sexuality*, London: Hutchinson.

Gatens, M. (1996) *Imaginary Bodies: Ethics, Power and Corporeality*, London: Routledge.

Gavron, H. (1983) *The Captive Wife*, London: RKP, first published 1966.

Geldalof, I. (2000) 'Identity in Transit. Nomads, Cyborgs and Women', *The European Journal of Women's Studies* 7 (3): 337–54.

Gelsthorpe, L. and Loucks, N. (1997) 'Magistrates' Explanations of Sentencing Decisions', in Hedderburn, C. and Gelsthorpe, L. (eds) *Understanding the Sentencing of Women*, Home Office Research Study 170, London: Home Office.

Gershuny, J. (1997) 'The Changing Nature of Work', Paper presented at the British Association Conference, Leeds, 8 September.

Gershuny, J., Godwin, M. and Jones, S. (1994) 'The Domestic Labour Revolution: A Process of Lagged Adaptation', in Anderson, M., Bechofer, F. and Gershuny, J. (eds) *The Social and Political Economy of the Household*, Oxford: Oxford University Press.

Gilligan, C. (1982) *In a Different Voice: Psychological Theory and Women's Development*, London: Harvard University Press.

Gilroy, P. (1987) 'There Ain't No Black in the Union Jack': The Cultural Politics of Race and Nation, London: Hutchinson.

Goldberg, S. (1979) Male Dominance: The Inevitability of Patriarchy, London: Abacus Sphere.

Goldthorpe, J. (1983) 'Women and Class Analysis: A Defence of the Traditional View', Sociology 17: 465–88.

Goldthorpe, J., Lockwood, D., Bechhofer, F. and Platt, J. (1969) The Affluent Worker in the Class Structure, Cambridge: Cambridge University Press.

Gottfried, H. (1998) 'Beyond Patriarchy? Theorising Gender and Class', Sociology 32 (3): 451–68.

Grace, S. (1995) Policing Domestic Violence in the 1990s, Home Office Research Study 139, London: HMSO.

Greer, G. (1971) The Female Eunuch, London: Paladin.

Gregson, N. and Lowe, M. (1994) Servicing the Middle Classes: Waged Domestic Labour in Britain in the 1980s and 1990s, London: Routledge.

Griffin, S. (1981) Pornography and Silence: Culture's Revenge Against Nature, London: The Women's Press.

Grosz, E. (1994) Volatile Bodies: Towards a Corporeal Feminism, Bloomington: Indiana University Press.

Gunew, S. (ed.) (1991) A Reader in Feminist Knowledge, London: Routledge.

Hables Gray, C. (1995) The Cyborg Handbook, New York: Routledge.

Hakim, C. (1979) Occupational Segregation, Department of Employment Research Paper No. 9, London: HMSO.

Halliday F. (1994) Rethinking International Relations, Basingstoke: Macmillan.

Hanmer, J. (1987) 'Transforming Consciousness: Women and the New Reproductive Technologies', in Corea, G. et al., Man-made Women, Bloomington: Indiana University Press.

Haraway, D. (1991) Simians, Cyborgs and Women: The Reinvention of Nature, London: Free Association Press.

Haraway, D. (1992) Primate Visions: Gender, Race and Nature in the World of Modern Science, London: Verso.

Haraway, D. (1997) Modest_Witness@Second_Millennium. FemaleMan_Meet_OncoMouse: Feminism and Technoscience, London: Routledge.

Harding, S. (1986) The Science Question in Feminism, Milton Keynes: Open University Press.

Hartley, R. (1966) 'A Developmental View of Female Sex-Role Identification', in Biddle, J. and Thomas, E. (eds) Role Theory, London: John Wiley.

Hartmann, H. (1979) 'Capitalism, Patriarchy and Job Segregation by Sex', in Eisenstein, Z. (ed.) Capitalist Patriarchy and the Case for Socialist Feminism, London: Monthly Press.

Hartmann, H. (1982) 'Capitalism, Patriarchy and Job Segregation by Sex' in Giddens, A. and Held, D. (eds) Classes, Power and Conflict, London: Macmillan.

Hartsock, N. (1983) Money, Sex and Power: Toward a Feminist Historical Materialism, Boston: Northeastern University Press.

Hartsock, N. (1998) The Feminist Standpoint Revisited and Other Essays, Oxford: Westview Press.

Hatty, S. (2000) Masculinities, Violence and Culture, London: Sage.

Hawkes, G. (1996) A Sociology of Sex and Sexuality, Buckingham: Open University Press.

Hearn, J. (1998) The Violences of Men, London: Sage.

Hearn, J. and Morgan D. (eds) (1990) Men, Masculinities and Social Theory, London: Unwin Hyman.

185

Hekman, S. (1990) *Gender and Knowledge: Elements of a Postmodern Feminism*, Cambridge: Polity.

Hekman, S. (1995) *Moral Voices, Moral Selves: Carol Gilligan and Feminist Moral Theory*, Cambridge: Polity.

Hekman, S. (1997) 'Truth and Method: Feminist Standpoint Theory Revisited', *Signs: A Journal of Women in Culture and Society* 22 (2): 341–65.

Heywood, L. and Drake, J. (eds) (1997) *Third Wave Agenda: Being Feminist, Doing Feminism*, Minneapolis: University of Minnesota Press.

Hirschmann, N. (1997) 'Feminist Standpoint as Postmodern Strategy', *Women and Politics* 18 (3): 73–92.

Holland, J., Ramazanoglu, C., Sharpe, S. and Thomson, R. (1996) 'Reputations: Journeying into Gendered Power Cultures', in Weeks, J. and Holland, J. (eds) *Sexual Cultures*, London: Macmillan.

hooks, b. (1982) *Ain't I a Woman: Black Women and Feminism*, London: Pluto Press.

hooks, b. (1986) 'Sisterhood: Political Solidarity Between Women', *Feminist Review*, No. 23, Summer.

hooks, b. (1989) *Talking Back: Thinking Feminist, Thinking Black*, London: Sheba.

Hull, G.T., Bell Scott, P. and Smith, B. (eds) (1982) *All the Feminists are White, All the Men are Black, But Some of Us Are Brave: Black Women's Studies*, New York: The Feminist Press.

Humphries, J. (1984) 'Class Struggle and the Persistence of the Working Class Family', in Giddens, A. and Held, D. (eds) *Classes, Power and Conflict*, London: Macmillan.

Jackson, S. (1998) 'Feminist Social Theory', in Jackson, S. and Jones, J. (eds) *Contemporary Feminist Theories*, Edinburgh: Edinburgh University Press.

Jackson, S. and Jones, J. (1998) *Contemporary Feminist Theories*, Edinburgh: Edinburgh University Press.

Jackson, S. and Scott, S. (1996), *Feminism and Sexuality: A Reader*, Edinburgh: Edinburgh University Press.

Jaggar, A. M. (1983) *Feminist Politics and Human Nature*, Brighton: Harvester Press.

Jameson, F. (1991) *Postmodernism or the Cultural Logic of Late Capitalism*, London: Verso.

Jardine, A. and Smith, P. (eds) (1987) *Men in Feminism*, London: Methuen.

Jeffreys, S. (1990) *Anticlimax: A Feminist Perspective on the Sexual Revolution*, London: The Women's Press.

Jeffreys, S. (1994) *The Lesbian Heresy: A Feminist Perspective on the Lesbian Sexual Revolution*, London: The Women's Press.

Jenkins, R. (2000) 'Categorisation: Identity, Social Process and Epistemology', *Current Sociology* 48 (3): 7–25.

Jenks, C. (ed.) (1998) *Core Sociological Dichotomies*, London: Sage.

Johnson, C. (1996) 'Does Capitalism Really Need Patriarchy?', *Women's Studies International Forum* 19 (3): 193–202.

Johnston, J. (1973) *Lesbian Nation: The Feminist Solution*, New York: Touchstone Books.

Jordan, G. and Weedon, C. (1995) *Cultural Politics. Class, Gender, Race and the Postmodern World*, Oxford: Blackwell.

Kauffman, L.S. (ed.) (1993) *American Feminist Thought at Century's End: A Reader*, Oxford: Blackwell.

Kelly, L. and Radford, J. (1996) '"Nothing Really Happened": The Invalidation of Women's Experiences of Sexual Violence', in Hester, M., Kelly, L. and Radford, J. (eds) *Women, Violence and Male Power*, Buckingham: Open University Press.

Kelly, L. and Radford, J. (1998) 'Sexual Violence Against Women and Girls', in Dobash, Emerson R. and Dobash, R. (eds) *Rethinking Violence Against Women*, London: Sage.

Kent, S. (1988) 'The Politics of Sexual Difference. World War One and the Demise of British Feminism', *Journal of British Studies* 27 (3) 232–53.

Kershaw, C., Chivite-Matthews, N., Thomas, C. and Aust, R. (2001) *The 2001 British Crime Survey*, Home Office Statistical Bulletin 18/01, London: Home Office.

Kiernan, K. (1992) 'Men and Women at Work and at Home', in Jowell, R, Brook, L., Prior, G. and Taylor, B. (eds) *British Social Attitudes: The 9th Report*, Aldershot: Dartmouth.

Kirkham, P. (ed.) (1996) *The Gendered Object*, Manchester: Manchester University Press.

Kitzinger, C. and Wilkinson, S. (eds) (1993) *Heterosexuality: A Feminism and Psychology Reader*, London: Sage.

Klein, R. and Dumble, L. (1994) 'Disempowering Mid-Life Women: The Science and Politics of Hormone Replacement Therapy', *Women's Studies International Forum* 17 (4): 327–43.

Koedt, A. (1968) 'The Myth of the Vaginal Orgasm', reprinted in S. Gunew (ed.) (1991) *A Reader in Feminist Knowledge*, London: Routledge.

Koedt, A., Levine, E. and Rapone, A. (eds) (1973) *Radical Feminism*, New York: Quadrangle Books.

Landes, J. (ed.) (1998) *Feminism, the Public and the Private*, Oxford: Oxford University Press.

Lash, S. and Urry, J. (1987) *The End of Organised Capitalism*, Cambridge: Polity.

Laurie, H. and Gershuny, J. (2000) 'Couples, Work and Money', in Berthoud, R. and Gershuny, J. (eds) *Seven Years in the Lives of British Families*, Bristol: Policy Press.

Lees, S. (1989) 'Learning to Love: Sexual Reputation, Morality and the Social Control of Girls', in Cain, M. (ed.) *Growing Up Good*, London: Sage.

Lees, S. (1997) *Ruling Passions. Sexual Violence, Sexual Reputation and the Law*, Buckingham: Open University Press.

Lewis, J. (1980) 'In Search of a Real Equality: Women Between the Wars', in Gloversmith, F. (ed.) *Class, Culture and Social Change: A New View of the 1930s*, Brighton: Harvester.

Lewis, R. (1995) *Gendering Orientalism*, London: Routledge.

Liddington, J. and Norris, J. (1978) *One Hand Tied Behind Us: The Rise of the Women's Suffrage Movement*, London: Virago.

Lister, R. (1997) *Citizenship: Feminist Perspectives*, London: Macmillan.

Lobban, G. (1974) 'Presentation of Sex Roles in British Reading Schemes', *Forum* 16 (2): 57–60.

Lurie, S. (1997) *Unsettled Subjects: Restoring Feminist Politics to Poststructuralist Critique*, Durham, NC: Duke University Press.

Lyotard, J. (1984) *The Postmodern Condition: A Report on Knowledge*, Manchester: Manchester University Press.

Maccoby, E. and Jacklin, C. (1975) *The Psychology of Sex Differences*, Stanford, CA: Stanford University Press.

Macdonald, M. (1995) *Representing Women: Myths of Femininity in the Popular Media*, London: Edward Arnold.

MacEwen Scott, A. (1994) 'Gender Segregation and the SCELI Research', in MacEwen Scott, A. (ed.) *Gender Segregation and Social Change*, Oxford: Oxford University Press.

MacInnes, J. (1998) *The End of Masculinity*, Buckingham: Open University Press

Mackinnon, C. (1982) 'Feminism, Marxism, Method and the State: An Agenda for Theory', *Signs: A Journal of Women in Culture and Society* 7 (3): 515–44.

Macrae, C. , Stangor, C. and Hewstone, M. (eds) (1996) *Stereotypes and Stereotyping*, London: The Guildford Press.

187

Maharaj, Z. (1995) 'A Social Theory of Gender: Connell's Gender and Power', *Feminist Review* 49: 50–65.

Mansfield, P. and Collard, J. (1988) *The Beginning of the Rest of Your Life? A Portrait of Newly-wed Marriage*, London: Macmillan.

Marshall, B. (1994) *Engendering Modernity: Feminism, Social Theory and Social Change*, Cambridge: Polity.

Marshall, T. H. (1950) *Citizenship and Social Class*, Cambridge: Cambridge University Press.

Mason, D. (2000) *Race and Ethnicity in Modern Britain*, 2nd edition,Oxford: Oxford University Press.

Matthews, J. (1984) *Good and Mad Women: The Historical Construction of Femininity in Twentieth Century Australia*, Sydney: George Allen and Unwin.

Maynard, M. (1988) 'Women's Studies', in Jackson, S. and Jones, J. (eds) *Contemporary Feminist Theories*, Edinburgh: Edinburgh University Press.

Maynard, M. (1994) 'Methods, Practice and Epistemology: The Debate about Feminism and Research', in Maynard, M. and Purvis, J. (eds) *Researching Women's Lives from a Feminist Perspective*, London: Taylor and Francis.

Maynard, M. (1995) 'Beyond the Big Three: The Development of Feminist Theory into the 1990s', *Women's History Review* 4 (3): 259–81.

Maynard, M. (2001) 'Feminism and Postmodernism in Social Theory', in Burgess, R.G. and Murcott, A. (eds) *Developments in Sociology*, London: Prentice Hall.

Maynard, M. and Purvis, J. (eds) (1994) *Researching Women's Lives from a Feminist Perspective*, London: Taylor and Francis.

Maynard, M. and Purvis, J. (eds) (1996) *New Frontiers in Women's Studies*, London: Taylor and Francis.

McClintock, A. (1995) *Imperial Leather: Race, Gender and Sexuality in the Colonial Context*, New York: Routledge.

McHugh, J. (1995) 'Traumatic Development: Contractual Theory of Rape in America', *Feminist Legal Studies* 3 (2): 237–47.

McNair, B. (1996) *Mediated Sex: Pornography and Postmodern Culture*, London: Arnold.

Messner, M. and Sabo, D. (1990) *Sport, Men and the Gender Order*, Illinois: Human Kinetics Books.

Meyers, D. (ed.) (1997) *Feminist Social Thought: A Reader*, New York: Routledge.

Miles, R. (1989) *Racism*, London: Routledge.

Millett, K. (1977) *Sexual Politics* (first published 1971), London: Virago.

Mills, C. (1997) *The Racial Contract*, London: Cornell University Press.

Minsky, R. (ed.) (1996) *Psychoanalysis and Gender: An Introductory Reader*, London: Routledge.

Mirza, H. (ed.) (1997) *Black British Feminism*, London: Routledge.

Mitchell, J. and Oakley, A. (eds) (1986) *What is Feminism?*, Oxford: Blackwell.

Modleski, T. (1991) *Feminism Without Women: Culture and Criticism in a 'Postfeminist' Age*, New York: Routledge.

Modood, T., Berthoud, R. and Nazroo, J. (2002) '"Race", Racism and Ethnicity: A Response to Ken Smith', *Sociology*, 36 (2): 419–17.

Moi, T. (1994) *Simone de Beauvoir*, Oxford: Basil Blackwell.

'The Monday Group' (1974) 'Our Attempts at Consciousness Raising', *Birmingham Women's Liberation Newsletter*, May, p. 24.

Moore-Gilbert, B. (1997) *Postcolonial Theory: Contexts, Practices, Politics*, London: Verso.

Moores, S. (1993) *Interpreting Audiences: The Ethnography of Media Consumption*, London: Sage.

Morgan, D. (1992) *Discovering Men*, London: Routledge.

Morgan, R. (ed.) (1970) *Sisterhood is Powerful: An Anthology of Writings from the Women's Liberation Movement*, New York: Vintage Books.

Morris, A. (1987) *Women, Crime and Criminal Justice*, Oxford: Basil Blackwell.

Morris, L. (1985) 'Renegotiation of the Domestic Division of Labour in the Context of Male Redundancy', in Newby, H., Bujra, J., Littlewood, P., Rees, G. and Rees, T.L. (eds) *Restructuring Capital: Recession and Reorganisation in Industrial Society*, London: Macmillan.

Nestle, J. (1987) *A Restricted Country: Essays and Short Stories*, London: Sheba Feminist Publishers.

Nicholson, L. (ed.) (1990) *Feminism/Postmodernism*, London: Routledge.

Nicholson, L. (ed.) (1997) *The Second Wave: A Reader in Feminist Theory*, London: Routledge.

Oakley, A. (1972) *Sex, Gender and Society*, London: Temple Smith.

Oakley, A. (1974) *The Sociology of Housework*, London: Martin Robertson.

Oakley, A. (1992) *Social Support and Motherhood*, Oxford: Blackwell.

Oakley, A. and Mitchell, J. (1997) *Who's Afraid of Feminism? Seeing Through the Backlash*, London: Hamish Hamilton.

Oakley, A. (1998) 'Science, Gender and Women's Liberation: An Argument Against Postmodernism', *Women's Studies International Forum* 21 (2): 133–46.

O'Connell Davidson, J. (1998) *Prostitution, Power and Freedom*, Cambridge: Polity.

OED (Oxford English Dictionary) online http://www.oed.com/public/publications/online.htm

Okely, J. (1986) *Simone de Beauvoir*, London: Virago.

Ortner, S. (1974) 'Is Female to Male as Nature is to Culture?', in Rosaldo, M. and Lamphere, L. (eds) *Woman, Culture and Society*, Stanford, CA: Stanford University Press.

Owen, J. (1996) 'Childish Things: Men, Ageing and Violence', in Pilcher, J. and Coffey, A. (eds) *Gender and Qualitative Research*, Aldershot: Avebury.

Paechter, C. (1998) *Educating the Other: Gender, Power and Schooling*, London: Falmer.

Pahl, R. (1984) *Divisions of Labour*, Oxford: Basil Blackwell.

Paluski, J. and Waters, M. (1996) 'The Reshaping and Dissolution of Social Class in Advanced Society', *Theory and Society* 25: 667–91.

Parsons, T. and Bales, R. (1956) *Family Socialization and Interaction*, London: Routledge.

Pateman, C. (1988) *The Sexual Contract*, Cambridge: Polity.

Pateman, C. (1989) *The Disorder of Women*, Cambridge: Polity.

Pateman, C. (1996) 'A Comment on Johnson's "Does Capitalism Really Need Patriarchy?"', *Women's Studies International Forum* 19 (3): 203–5.

Pateman, C. (1997) 'Beyond the Sexual Contract', in Dench, G. (ed.) *Rewriting the Sexual Contract*, London: Institute of Community Studies.

Pease, B. (2000) *Recreating Men: Postmodern Masculinity Politics*, London: Sage.

Phelan, S. (ed.) (1997) *Playing with Fire: Queer Politics, Queer Theories*, New York: Routledge.

Phillips, A. (1991) *Engendering Democracy*, Cambridge: Polity Press.

Phillips, A. (1993) *Democracy and Difference*, Cambridge: Polity Press.

Phillips, A. (1997) 'What Has Socialism to Do with Sexual Equality?', in Franklin, J. (ed.) *Equality*, London: Institute for Public Policy Research.

Phoca, S. and Wright, R. (1999) *Introducing Postfeminism*, Cambridge: Icon Books.

Pickering, M. (1995) 'The Politics and Psychology of Stereotyping', *Media, Culture and Society* 17: 691–700.

Pickering, M. (2001) *Stereotyping: The Politics of Representation*, Basingstoke: Palgrave.

189

Pilcher, J. (1998) 'Hormones or Hegemonic Masculinity? Explaining Gender Inequalities', *Sociology Review* 7 (3): 5–9.

Pilcher, J. (1999) *Women in Contemporary Britain: An Introduction*, London: Routledge.

Pilcher, J. (2000) 'Domestic Divisions of Labour in the Twentieth Century: "Change Slow A-Coming"', *Work, Employment and Society* 14 (4): 771–80.

Pollert, A. (1996) 'Gender and Class Revisited, or the Poverty of Patriarchy', *Sociology* 30 (4): 639–59.

Pollock, G. (1988) *Vision and Difference: Femininity, Feminism and the Histories of Art*, London: Routledge.

Preves, S. (2000) 'Negotiating the Constraints of Gender Binarism: Intersexuals' Challenge to Gender Categorization', *Current Sociology* 48 (3): 27–50.

Price, J. and Shildrick, M. (1999) *Feminist Theory and the Body: A Reader*, Edinburgh: Edinburgh University Press.

Prokhovnik, R. (1998) 'Public and Private Citizenship: From Gender Invisibility to Feminist Inclusiveness', *Feminist Review* 60: 84–104.

Prokhovnik, R. (1999) *Rational Woman: A Feminist Critique of Dichotomy*, London: Routledge.

Puwar, N. (2001) 'The Racialised Somatic Norm and the Senior Civil Service', *Sociology* 35 (3): 651–70.

Puwar, N. (2002) 'Interview with Carole Pateman', *Feminist Review* 70 (1): 123–33.

Radford, J. and Stanko, E. (1996) 'Violence Against Women and Children', in Hester, M., Kelly, L. and Radford, J. (eds) *Women, Violence and Male Power*, Buckingham: Open University Press.

Ramazanoglu, C. (1989a) 'Improving on Sociology: Problems in Taking a Feminist Standpoint', *Sociology* 23 (3): 427–42.

Ramazanoglu, C. (1989b) *Feminism and the Contradictions of Oppression*, London: Routledge.

Randall, V. (1982) *Women and Politics*, London: Macmillan.

Redfern, C. (2002) 'I love the 70s', *The F Word*, October (http://www.thefword.org.uk/features/the70s.live).

Reskin, B. and Padavic, I. (1994) *Women and Men at Work*, Thousand Oaks, CA: Pine Forge Press.

Rich, A. (1980a) 'Compulsory Heterosexuality and Lesbian Existence', *Signs* 5 (4): 631–60.

Rich, A. (1980b) *On Lies, Secrets and Silence: Selected Prose 1966–1978*, London: Virago.

Rich, A. (1986) 'Compulsory Heterosexuality and Lesbian Existence', in *Blood, Bread and Poetry: Selected Prose 1979–1985*, London: Virago.

Richardson, D. (1993) *Women, Motherhood and Childrearing*, London: Macmillan.

Richardson, D. (ed.) (1996) *Theorising Heterosexuality: Telling it Straight*, Buckingham: Open University Press.

Richardson, D. (1998) 'Sexuality and Citizenship', *Sociology* 32 (1): 83–100.

Richardson, D. (2000) *Rethinking Sexuality*, London: Sage.

Riddell, S. (1992) *Gender and the Politics of the Curriculum*, London: Routledge.

Roberts, H. (1981) 'Male Hegemony in Family Planning', in Roberts, H. (ed.) *Women, Health and Reproduction*, London: Routledge.

Robins, K. (1995) 'Cyberspace and the World We Live In', in Featherstone, M. and Burrow, R. (eds) *Cyberspace, Cyberbodies, Cyberpunk*, London: Sage.

Robinson, L.S. (1978), *Sex, Class and Culture*, London: Methuen.

Robinson, V. and Richardson, D. (eds) (1997) *Introducing Women's Studies*, second edition, Basingstoke: Macmillan.

190

Rosser, C. and Harris, C. (1965) *The Family and Social Change*, London: Routledge and Kegan Paul.

Ruddick, S. (1997) 'Maternal Thinking', in Meyers, D. (ed.) *Feminist Social Thought: A Reader*, New York: Routledge.

Ryan, P. (1978) 'The Ideology of Feminism 1900–1920. An Analysis of Feminist Ideas on Motherhood, Birth Control and Sexuality', unpublished MSc Econ, University of Wales.

Said, E. (1978) *Orientalism*, New York: Vintage Books.

Sarah, E. (ed.) (1982) *Reassessments of 'First Wave' Feminism*, Oxford: Pergamon Press.

Sawicki, J. (1991) *Disciplining Foucault: Feminism, Power and the Body*, London: Routledge.

Sayers, J. (1982) *Biological Politics*, London: Tavistock.

Sayers, J. (1986) *Sexual Contradiction: Psychology, Psychoanalysis and Feminism*, London: Tavistock.

Schneider, D. (1996) 'Modern Stereotype Research: Unfinished Business', in Macrae, C., Stangor, C. and Hewstone, M. (eds) *Stereotypes and Stereotyping*, London: The Guildford Press.

Scott, J. (1997) 'Deconstructing Equality-versus-Difference; Or, the Uses of Post-Structuralist Theory for Feminism', in Meyers, D. (ed.) *Feminist Social Thought: A Reader*, New York: Routledge.

Segal, L. (1987) *Is the Future Female? Troubled Thoughts on Contemporary Feminism*, London: Virago.

Segal, L. (1994) *Straight Sex: The Politics of Pleasure*, London: Virago.

Segal, L. (1999) *Why Feminism? Gender, Psychology, Politics*, Oxford: Polity.

Segal, L. and McIntosh, M. (1992) *Sex Exposed: Sexuality and the Pornography Debate*, London: Virago.

Seidler, V. J. (1989) *Rediscovering Masculinity: Reason, Language and Sexuality*, London: Routledge.

Siim, B. (2000) *Gender and Citizenship*, Cambridge: Cambridge University Press.

Simmons, J. (2002) *Crime in England and Wales 2001/2002*, Home Office Statistical Bulletin 07/02, London: Home Office.

Skeggs, B. (1997) *Formations of Class and Gender*, London: Sage.

Smart, C. (1995) *Law, Crime and Sexuality*, London: Sage.

Smith, D. (1988) *The Everyday World as Problematic*, Milton Keynes: Open University Press.

Sommers C.H. (1994), *Who Stole Feminism?*, New York: Touchstone Books.

Sontag, S. (1979) 'The Double Standard of Ageing', in Carver, V. and Liddiard, P. (eds) *An Ageing Population*, New York: Holmes and Meier.

Speer, S. (2001) 'Reconsidering the Concept of Hegemonic Masculinity: Discursive Psychology, Conversation Analysis and Participants' Orientations', *Feminism and Psychology* 11 (1): 107–35.

Spender, D. (1983) *There Has Always Been a Women's Movement This Century*, London: Pandora.

Spivak, G. C. (1988) *In Other Worlds: Essays in Cultural Politics*, New York: Routledge.

Squires, J. (1999) *Gender in Political Theory*, Cambridge: Polity.

Stanley, L. and Wise, S. (1993) *Breaking Out Again*, 2nd edition, London: Routledge.

Stanworth, M. (1987a) 'Reproductive Technologies and the Deconstruction of Motherhood', in Stanworth, M. (ed.) *Reproductive Technologies*, Cambridge: Polity Press.

Stanworth, M. (ed.) (1987b) *Reproductive Technologies*, Cambridge: Polity Press.

Steinberg, D. (1997) *Bodies in Glass: Genetics, Eugenics and Embryo Ethics*, Manchester: Manchester University Press.

191

*bibliography*

Strachey, R. (1978) *The Cause: A Short History of the Women's Movement in Great Britain*, (first published 1928), London: Virago.

Sullivan, O. (2000) 'The Division of Domestic Labour: Twenty Years of Change?', *Sociology* 34 (3): 437–56.

Sypnowich, C. (2000) 'The Civility of Law: Between Public and Private', in D'Entreves, M. and Vogel, U. (eds) *Public and Private: Legal, Political and Philosophical Perspectives*, London: Routledge.

Tobias, S. (1978) 'Women's Studies: Its Origins, its Organisation and its Prospects', *Women's Studies International Quarterly* 1, 84–93.

Tolson, A. (1987) *The Limits of Masculinity*, London: Routledge.

Tomsen, S. and Mason, G. (2001) 'Engendering Homophobia: Violence, Sexuality and Gender Conformity', *Journal of Sociology* 37 (3): 257–73.

Tong, R. (1998) *Feminist Thought*, 2nd edition, Oxford: Westview Press.

True, J. (2001) 'Feminism', in Burchill, S., Devetak, R., Linklater, A., Paterson, M., Reus-Smit, C. and True, J. (eds) *Theories of International Relations*, second edition, Basingstoke: Palgrave.

Tuchman, J. (1981) 'The Symbolic Annihilation of Women in the Mass Media', in Cohen, S. and Young, J. (eds) *The Manufacture of News*, London: Constable.

Turner, B. (2001) 'The Erosion of Citizenship', *British Journal of Sociology* 52 (2): 189–209.

Twomey, B. (2002) 'Women in the Labour Market', *Labour Market Trends* 110 (3): 109–27.

Vance, C.S. (1992) *Pleasure and Danger: Exploring Female Sexuality*, London: Pandora.

Wajcman, J. (1991) *Feminism Confronts Technology*, Cambridge: Polity Press.

Walby, S. (1990) *Theorising Patriarchy*, Oxford: Blackwell.

Walby, S. (1994a) 'Is Citizenship Gendered?', *Sociology* 28 (2): 379–95.

Walby, S. (1994b) 'Post-postmodernism? Theorising Gender', in *The Polity Reader in Social Theory*, Cambridge: Polity.

Walby, S. (1997) *Gender Transformations*, London: Routledge.

Walklate, S. (1995) *Gender and Crime*, London: Prentice Hall/Harvester Wheatsheaf.

Walter, N. (1998) *The New Feminism*, London: Little, Brown.

Walter, N. (ed.) (1999) *On the Move: Feminism for a New Generation*, London: Virago.

Wandor, M. (ed.) (1972) *The Body Politic: Writings from the Women's Liberation Movement in Britain 1969–1972*, London: Stage 1.

Warde, A. and Hetherington, K. (1993) 'A Changing Domestic Division of Labour?', *Work, Employment and Society* 7 (1): 23–45.

Watson, S. and Doyal, L. (eds) (1999) *Engendering Social Policy*, Buckingham: Open University Press.

Waugh, P. (1998) 'Postmodernism and Feminism', in Jackson, S. and Jones, J. (eds) *Contemporary Feminist Theories*, Edinburgh: Edinburgh University Press.

Weedon, C. (1987) *Feminist Practice and Poststructuralist Theory*, Oxford: Blackwell.

Weeks, J. (1985) *Sexuality and its Discontents: Meanings, Myths and Modern Sexualities*, London: Routledge.

Weeks, J. and Holland, J. (eds) (1996) *Sexual Cultures*, London: Macmillan.

Weinreich, R. (1978) 'Sex Role Socialization', in Chetwynd, J. and Hartnett, O. (eds) *The Sex Role System*, London: Routledge.

Wellings, K., Field, J., Johnson, A. and Wadsworth, J. (1994) *Sexual Behaviour in Britain*, London: Penguin.

Welton, K. (1997) 'Nancy Hartsock's Standpoint Theory: From Content to "Concrete Multiplicities"', *Women and Politics* 18 (3): 7–24.

192

Werbner, P. and Yuval-Davis, N. (1999) 'Women and the New Discourse of Citizenship', in Yuval-Davis, N. and Werbner, P. (eds) *Women, Citizenship and Difference*, London: Zed Press.

West, C. (1989) 'Review of Gender and Power', *American Journal of Sociology* 94: 1487–9.

Wheelock, J. (1990) *Husbands at Home*, London: Routledge.

Whelehan, I. (1995) *Modern Feminist Thought: From the Second Wave to 'Post-feminism'*, Edinburgh: Edinburgh University Press.

Whelehan, I. (2000) *Overloaded: Popular Culture and the Future of Feminism*, London: The Women's Press.

Whitehead, S. (2002) *Men and Masculinities*, Cambridge: Polity.

Whitford, M. (1991) *The Irigaray Reader*, Oxford: Basil Blackwell.

Wilkinson, S. and Kitzinger, C. (1996) 'The Queer Backlash', in Bell, D. and Klein, R. *Radically Speaking: Feminism Reclaimed*, London: Zed Books.

Williams, W. (1997) 'The Equality Crisis: Some Reflections on Culture, Courts and Feminism', in Meyers, D. (ed.) *Feminist Social Thought: A Reader*, New York: Routledge.

Wilson, E. (1985) *Adorned in Dreams: Fashion and Modernity*, London: Virago.

Witherspoon, S. and Prior, G. (1991) 'Working Mothers: Free to Choose?', in Jowell, R., Brook, L. and Taylor, B. (eds) *British Social Attitudes: The 8th Report*, Aldershot: Dartmouth.

Wittig, M. (1992) *The Straight Mind and Other Essays*, Hemel Hempstead: Harvester Wheatsheaf.

Wolf, N. (1993) *Fire with Fire: The New Female Power and How it Will Change the 21st Century*, London: Chatto & Windus.

Woods, T. (1999) *Beginning Postmodernism*, Manchester: Manchester University Press.

Wright, S. (1995) 'The Role of the Police in Combating Domestic Violence', in Dobash, R., Dobash, R. and Noaks, L. (eds) *Gender and Crime*, Cardiff: University of Wales Press.

Wrong, D. (1961) 'The Oversocialized Concept of Man in Modern Sociology', *American Sociological Review*, 26, 183–93.

Young, I. (1990) *Justice and the Politics of Difference*, Princeton, NJ: Princeton: University Press.

Young, M. and Willmott, P. (1975) *The Symmetrical Family*, Harmondsworth: Penguin (first published 1973).

Yuval-Davis, N. (1997) *Gender and Nation*, London: Sage.

Yuval-Davis, N. and Werbner, P. (eds) (1999) *Women, Citizenship and Difference*, London: Zed Press.

Zawelski, M. (2000) *Feminism After Postmodernism*, London: Routledge.